Praise for *The Power of Enterprise-Wide Project Management*

"If a single book can penetrate the complexities of the modern corporation and describe the essential ingredients in establishing enterprise-wide project management, this is it. After presenting the compelling case for institutionalizing project management as a core business management competency, yet acknowledging it requires dedication and commitment over an extended period of time, Dennis Bolles and Darrel Hubbard provide, in a straightforward step-by-step approach, the critical information the corporate leader needs to achieve world-class project management."

—Hugh Woodward, PMP, PMI Fellow
Managing Editor, pmforum.org
Past Chairman, Project Management Institute

"The Power of Enterprise-Wide Project Management is a 'must read' for leaders as well as project/program/portfolio managers in organizations who are serious about getting the most out of their limited project resources. This book is the best I've seen to date in providing practical tools and methods for establishing a successful Enterprise Project Management Office. Dennis Bolles and Darrel Hubbard are two of the most experienced and knowledgeable experts in the industry. They've seen it all, and they've done it all. The proof leaps out on every page of the book. If your goal is to initiate the right projects at the right time and deliver the right results for your organization, this book is for you!"

—Dottie Nichols, USAF ret, PMP
Former PMI Standards Manager
Senior Manager, TNC Management Group

"A new challenge! Project Management that was begun with the proposition to make a single project a success has finally developed to the core competency that plays a critical business function targeting the entire organization. The author now tackles head-on the new proposition as an initiative that top management should approach. A concept of 'Project Business Management' and 'Enterprise-Wide Project Management Office (EPMO)' was created to address Project, Program, Portfolio, and related general management altogether. EPMO is the major topic, mainly talking about establishment and management of EPMO, including specific how-to information. Though this is the book to read for top management, those who are planning to introduce Project Management, as well as aiming at further improvement of business functions, should never fail to read this book establishing its goals. Now's the time to make the difference!"

—Kazuo Shimizu
Director (Permanent), PMI Tokyo Chapter
one of the pioneering practitioners for
Project Management in Japan

"[Provides] excellent guidance and best practices in detail to guide the reader directly to the keys for success in any level of his organization. As Program Manager in a large company, I had the opportunity to implement and test all the aspects addressed in this very comprehensive book. Through my experience, I can confirm that when properly implemented, these recommendations are giving outstanding business results."

—Jean-Claude Dravet, PMP
Founding President of PMI France-Sud Chapter
JCD Conseil-President

"This book provides a wealth of information for the readers to functionally establish enterprise-wide project management processes and best practices in their organizations. The presentation, which reflects the extensive experience of the authors, is comprehensive, practical, and lucid. Speaking for myself and not for NASA, JPL, or Caltech, I would rate this book as excellent and invaluable to forward-looking organizations."

> —Dr. Peter T. Poon
> Telecommunications and Mission Systems Manager,
> Jet Propulsion Laboratory
> California Institute of Technology

"This book clearly and succinctly lays out an approach to move from simple one-off project management to enterprise-wide project optimization as a core business function. The Power of Enterprise-Wide Project Management needs to be in every PMP's library, as well as required reading for anyone in the enterprise project management office."

> —Douglas Clark
> CEO and founder, Métier, Ltd.
> holder of five patents in portfolio management

"This is a demonstration from someone who has done it more than once, a black belt in building Project Management Centers of Excellence. With this [book even] large and complex organizations can save a considerable amount of time and dollars. The guidelines speak for themselves, but the built-in experience of mastering the difficulties and pitfalls is the real asset. If you have read the first book and got inspired, this is a must-read book before takeoff."

> —Eric Stein, PMP
> Nordic TPS PMO leader, Global Technology Services,
> Delivery, Nordic IMT Certified Executive Project Manager

"Read this book and take adventure of the practical takeaways that can be utilized today. It is must reading for everyone interested in PMOs and successfully implementing project management within their organization."

> —Tom Mochal, PMP
> President, TenStep, Inc.
> winner of the 2005 PMI Distinguished Contribution Award

"When my PMP® alumni ask about books for rolling out project management at their companies, The Power of Enterprise-Wide Project Management is my first choice. It should be yours as well."

> —Tony Johnson, MBA, PMP
> CEO and founder, Crosswind Project Management, Inc.
> author of the PMP® Exam Success Series products

"If you wish to buy just ONE book on Project Management, buy THIS book!"

> —Dr. Om P. Kharbanda, Mumbai, India,
> "the Peter Drucker of India" (Irnop, Sweden)

"Here it is! Finally, one powerful book where you can learn everything you need to know about implementing enterprise-wide project management in your organization. It describes how to set up the structure, including the often-missed links between internationally recognized standards and business management as we practice it today. Exploit this book to discover usable solutions and practical applications. With the guidelines from these experienced authors, you can't go wrong!"

—Dorothy Kangas, PMP, SCPM

"Darrel and Dennis have done a great job of not only describing the value proposition behind enterprise project management, but have provided a guide that can be used either in its entirety for those wanting a complete integrated solution as well as used in smaller increments for those who are testing the water of EPM. This book has a series of wonderful templates that are straightforward and easy to understand and implement. Good job!"

—Cynthia Berg, MBA, PMP
Medtronic Microelectronic Center
Keller Graduate School of Management

THE POWER OF ENTERPRISE-WIDE

PROJECT MANAGEMENT

Dennis L. Bolles and Darrel G. Hubbard

⁴AMACOM

American Management Association
New York • Atlanta • Brussels • Chicago • Mexico City
San Francisco • Shanghai • Tokyo • Washington, D.C.

This publication is designed to provide accurate and authoritative information in regard to the subject matter covered. It is sold with the understanding that the publisher is not engaged in rendering legal, accounting, or other professional service. If legal advice or other expert assistance is required, the services of a competent professional person should be sought.

Library of Congress Cataloging-in-Publication Data

Bolles, Dennis.
    The power of enterprise-wide project management / Dennis Bolles
    and Darrel Hubbard.
        p.   cm.
    Includes bibliographical references and index.
    ISBN-13: 978-0-8144-7404-4
    ISBN-10: 0-8144-7404-7
    1. Project management.   I. Hubbard, Darrel.   II. Title.
    HD69.P75.B655 2007
    658.4'04—dc22

                                                    2006019307

Please see pg. iv for additional information regarding the PMI logo and service marks.

Printing number

10 9 8 7 6 5 4 3 2 1

This book is a collaboration of friends and is based on our mutual trust and respect. We dedicate this book to our wives who have supported us in our work throughout our careers that have required us to take time away from them and our families.

Contents

PDF files of the materials listed in the appendixes are available at
www.amacombooks.org/go/EnterpriseWidePM

Foreword

L ooking for a quick fix – skip this book. Looking for a new edge and a competitive advantage to position your company for success in the long run – then read on!

The Power of Enterprise Project Management is a straightforward guide to establishing project business management (PBM) as an *integrative* business function for forward-thinking companies. The PBM methodology model developed in the book provides you with a simple, easy-to-follow top-down hierarchically integrated blend of strategic, tactical, portfolio, program, and project planning and execution processes.

The premise that an *executive level*, enterprise-wide project management office (EPMO) should be created to implement the PBM methodology and direct, often diverse, and resource intensive portfolios, programs, and projects across the enterprise is simple, yet brilliant. How many programs and projects fail because of poor coordination, limited resources, faulty assumptions, not being the right project at the right time, and mid-management in-fighting? Where does that generally get resolved – at the executive level, where direction, priorities, and resources are determined and the final decisions are made. So start there first to achieve success, rather than ending there trying to minimize failure.

This book is structured to provide the key elements needed to understand and implement the concepts of PBM and the EPMO, which are graphically captured in what the authors call the Enterprise-Wide Project Management House of Excellence. The sections of the book are written to expand your understanding of each of these business areas. The Appendices also contain valuable tools, forms, templates, and surveys to support you in developing a PBM methodology and establishing an EPMO. Numerous graphics and visuals throughout the book help the reader (and implementer) understand critical concepts, roles and responsibilities, and business linkages.

Because no two companies are alike, customization is a given – but the basics are here for you to use.

If you have read this far, turn the page and get started!

Richard (Ric) Byham
Director, Continuing Education
University of South Florida

Preface: Project Management Is a Business Function

There is a growing recognition in business management circles that project management is an emerging business function that enables enterprises to become world-class leaders in their markets. There is also a growing pressure on large enterprises in the marketplace to more formally apply the business management of projects to their programs and portfolios. Meeting and exceeding customer expectations by consistently completing projects successfully is also a goal of every enterprise and is the basis for receiving excellence awards from most customers. These are just some of the driving forces influencing enterprises to establish project business management and an enterprise-wide project management office.

If projects are an integral part of the business, it stands to reason that there should be a clear understanding of what is and is not a project, what is required to complete projects to the customer's satisfaction, and how projects are combined into programs and portfolios to meet the enterprise's strategies and business objectives. Properly implemented project management principles, processes, and practices can have a significant impact on an enterprise's time to market, cost to market, and quality to market and on customers' recognition of the enterprise as a world-class leader. If executives and business unit heads can recognize that managing projects has a significant impact on an enterprise's bottom line and that their ability to successfully manage projects depends on the proper application of specific project management processes, knowledge, skills, tools, and techniques, then it makes sense to establish such an important business function at the executive management level of the enterprise. How else can executive management ensure that limited funds and resources are effectively applied across the enterprise to only those projects that support business strategies and objectives and that those selected projects are given the best opportunity to succeed from the very start?

Enterprise-wide adoption of project management processes and best practices also calls for single ownership of an enterprise project management office (EPMO) function. Establishing common processes and practices across an enterprise is very difficult, if not impossible, without establishing exclusive ownership of the EPMO. The EPMO must be recognized as an independent business unit function at the highest level of the enterprise. This recognition provides the EPMO's executive management with the authority, acceptance, adoption, and autonomy required to establish, monitor, and control the distribution of the resources required to successfully apply project business management best practices enterprise wide.

Establishing project management within an enterprise is a significant undertaking and may meet with resistance at various levels for many reasons. One major reason behind some resistance is the most obvious, but it is seldom given sufficient consideration. People generally resist changes because they do not understand why the changes are necessary or what impact the changes will have on them. Most prefer the status quo to something new, especially when it involves how they perform their work. So, communicating the benefits of establishing project management as a functioning business unit enterprise-wide at all levels is a critical step in making project management an integral capability within the enterprise.

Relevance to Management

Most books on project management discuss the concepts and problems that affect the development of enterprise project management and project management offices. Several other good books and articles discuss the importance of establishing project management as a business function, but they primarily address only issues and problems associated with the effort. Most of the books on project management are written primarily for *project and program managers.*

This book is written primarily for *executives and senior managers* who recognize project management is a business function and want to establish project management as a core competency enterprise-wide within their organization. It is a sequel to the Bolles' book *Building Project Management Centers of Excellence,* which describes the value of implementing project management best practices as a core competency.

Throughout this book, the authors strive to answer the following questions regarding project management as a business function that are frequently asked by executives and senior managers:

- What does project management have to do with the overall management of the enterprise?
- How can project management be related to the enterprise's business operations?

- How can project management processes be incorporated or integrated into the business management processes?
- How can project business management benefit the enterprise?
- How can a project management functional organization be incorporated into the enterprise's organizational structure?
- How can mature project business management practices and processes add value to the enterprise's operations?

Unlike other publications, this book provides practical *how-to* information that enterprises of all sizes can use immediately to establish an EPMO and implement project business management enterprise-wide. Knowing what specific actions are required and how to proceed after executive management gives the go-ahead is the basis for this book. The success of an EPMO as a project management center of excellence and the institutionalization of project business management processes enterprise-wide is the end goal.

This book also helps the reader understand that acquiring executive recognition of project management as a business function is the critical first step in establishing project management as a core business management competency. The authors have developed basic models that are useful in helping the reader successfully establish an EPMO as the vehicle to integrate project and business processes, thereby creating and establishing project business management. Project business management is a new approach to managing the project-related business of an enterprise.

Terminology

This book blends terminology from the vocabularies of both general business management and project management, which allows the discussions to be easily understood by business executives, business unit mangers, and portfolio, program, and project managers.

In keeping with that purpose, the authors have defined and developed the term *project business management* (PBM) that is used throughout this book. The use of PBM is meant to eliminate any confusion and suppress the reader's assumptions as to just what the term *project management* means when used in a business context. The principles and concepts of project-related portfolio, program, and project management is complex, and the management processes involved are many. The blending of these principles and concepts with the principles, concepts, and varied processes of general business management motivated the authors to develop the concept of Project Business Management. In addition to the term PBM, the authors extensively employ the following additional conceptual terms throughout this book.

Project Business Management (PBM): The utilization of general business management and project management knowledge, skills, tools, and techniques in applying portfolio, program, and project processes to meet or exceed stakeholder needs, and to derive benefits from and capture value through any project-related actions and activities used to accomplish the enterprise's business objectives and related strategies.

Enterprise Project Management Office (EPMO): The organizational structure within the enterprise that will institute and manage the project business management processes for portfolios, programs, and projects. To be effective in managing the initiating, authorizing, planning, controlling, and executing processes of project business management, the EPMO is located at the executive level of the enterprise.

Enterprise-Wide Project Management (EWPM): The application of project business management practices and processes on an enterprise-wide basis, using an enterprise-wide project management office as the business unit to support management of the enterprise's portfolios, programs, and projects.

Business Unit: Any sized functional organization within the enterprise that is chartered to perform a relatively well-defined business support operation, such as accounting, a service center, product production, sales, human resources, marketing, or a project management office.

Project Business Management Maturity: The maturity of an enterprise's policies, plans, procedures, organizational governance, management personnel, and project business management methodology and processes that identify, plan, implement, control, accomplish, and communicate the enterprise's business strategic initiatives and related business objectives and supporting portfolios, programs, and projects.

Enterprise Project Business Management Governance: The organizational governance used in performing project business management that is a blend of several governance methods, especially those of executive, operations, portfolio, program, and project management. It is employed at different decision-making levels of the enterprise and at different stages within the PBM methodology to support implementation of specific business objectives and their related business strategic initiatives.

There are four additional significant terms (enterprise, organization, enterprise environmental factors, and organizational process assets) used throughout the book, which have been defined by the Project Management Institute (PMI®). These will help the reader better understand the project business management processes developed within the book:

An *Enterprise* is defined as:

> *An enterprise is a company, business, firm, partnership, corporation, or governmental agency.*

This includes associations, societies, for-profit entities, and not-for-profit entities.

The PMI® defines *Organization* as:

> *An organization is a group of persons organized for some purpose or to perform some type of work within an enterprise.*

This includes business unit, functional group, department, division, or subagency.

The PMI® defines *Enterprise Environmental Factors* as:

> *Enterprise environmental factors are any or all external environmental factors and internal organizational environmental factors that surround or influence the project's success. These factors are from any or all of the enterprises involved in the project and include organizational culture and structure, infrastructure, existing resources, commercial databases, market conditions, and project management software.*

The PMI® defines *Organizational Process Assets* as:

> *Organizational process assets are any or all process-related assets from any or all of the organizations involved in the project that are or can be used to influence the project's success. These process assets include formal and informal plans, policies, procedures, and guidelines. The process assets also include the organizations' knowledge bases, such as lessons learned and historical information.*

The meaning of other project management related terms used in the book are as defined in the *PMI® Combined Standards Glossary*, Second Edition (ISBN: 1-930699-49-2).

Organization

This book is organized into six sections that describe the Enterprise-Wide Project Management House of Excellence. The house of excellence has the four major elements, or pillars, and the related foundation that forms the framework of this book. This integrated framework and foundation is required to build a structurally sound enterprise-wide project management capability and is requisite to building and sustaining a successful EPMO, as represented by the roof of the house of excellence.

Enterprise-Wide Project Management House of Excellence

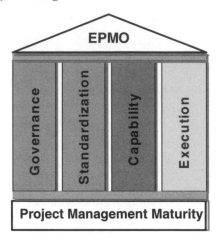

The various components of the house of excellence, which are used to organize the contents of this book, are as follows:

Roof - Section One - Overview: Is a view of project business management from an executive's perspective. It addresses enterprise-wide project management as a business concept, project management as a business function, and the EPMO as a business organization.

Pillar One - Section Two - Governance: Presents the EPMO as a management method and addresses setting policy, establishing charters, and providing an organizational model for the business management of projects, programs, and portfolios.

Pillar Two - Section Three - Standardization: Examines identification and integration of processes and practices, development of standardized project business management processes, and documentation of enterprise-wide portfolio, program, and project management process methodology models, including their associated policies, practices, and procedures.

Pillar Three - Section Four – Capability: Describes assessing the enterprise's abilities, develops a project management competency model, lays out an education and training program, establishes a career path progression plan, and outlines various key enterprise environmental factors.

Pillar Four - Section Five - Execution: Discusses strategic business planning, tactical business planning, business objective (project) prioritization, selection, and initiation, stage-gate reviews, and portfolio, program and project execution planning.

Foundation – Section Six –Maturity: Talks about project business management process and practice maturity, how to evaluate mature institutionalized project business management best practices enterprise-wide; and summarizes a best practice benchmark study survey that developed the four pillars supporting the Enterprise-Wide Project Management House of Excellence.

Initiation and Authorization Theme

Emphasis is placed on the start-up processes for portfolios, programs, and projects. Executives and senior management need to be aware of the impact these processes have on their business practices. The importance of initiation and authorization is evidenced by their positioning in the first two of the five common "process groups" in portfolio, program and project management. It is during those initiating and supporting planning processes, starting with identifying a single strategic initiative down through planning a project, that will accomplish the initiatives where up to 80 percent of the value and benefit of the desired outcome can be created. It is also during these initiating and authorizing processes that executive and senior management's involvement and decision making will have its maximum impact.

Appendices

This book has three appendices that provide links to relevant documents. Appendix A lists the forms, tools, and templates introduced throughout the book; Appendix B introduces the Project Business Management Maturity Model question set; and Appendix C explains the PMO Case Study Survey form that was used to compile a benchmark Case Study Report. The Appendices provide directions on how to obtain copies of these files from either the authors' or the publisher's website. Note that files are provided in Acrobat PDF file format; the publisher's url is listed at the bottom of page xiv and on the back flap of this book. If you would prefer a Microsoft Office 2003 version of the files, which are editable, please contact the authors.

Acknowledgments

W e want to acknowledge those individuals who have graciously provided comments and endorsements for our book, as well as those individuals who have given permission to reprint published material. We want to remember our mentors and peers and those who have supported us in developing a business view of project management. We also want to thank those anonymous participants of the PMO Case Study Survey that is described in Appendix C.

SECTION 1

Overview

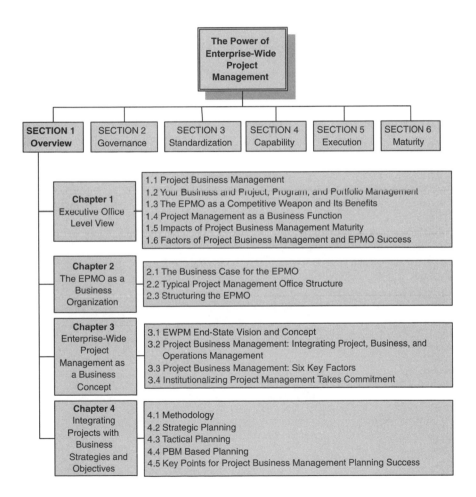

CHAPTER 1

Executive Office Level View

1.1 Project Business Management

Project Management is currently employed in only a few enterprises as a successful business function at the executive level. However, we believe this practice will become a standard practice in future enterprise organizational models. Executives and business unit managers in today's most forward-thinking enterprises are already taking project management disciplines beyond handling specific projects in manufacturing, product development, services, and information technology. They are adopting its powerful methods enterprise wide. The practices of project, program, and portfolio management are applicable to any type of enterprise, whether it is a for-profit company, a not-for-profit company, or a governmental agency. Therefore, the principles, processes, methods, and techniques recommended in this book are aimed at existing enterprises with established business operations and defined functional organizations. This book will guide those enterprises in applying project business management practices, beginning with enterprise level strategic planning and progressing through project execution. We define the term project business management as the utilization of general business management and project management knowledge, skills, tools, and techniques in applying portfolio, program, and project processes to meet or exceed stakeholder needs, to derive benefits, and to capture value through any project-related actions and activities used to accomplish the enterprise's business objectives and related strategies.

Competition, corporate downsizing, and business process re-engineering have influenced many enterprises to investigate the concept of enterprise-wide project management. Project management is recognized as a professional discipline that contributes significant competitive advantages to any enterprise. In addition, project management is now understood as something more than just a set of processes for controlling a project's cost and schedule.

Enterprises in the aerospace, construction, and engineering sectors have routinely employed project management as part of their business operations for decades. However, most other industries have only recently become more aware of the effectiveness of project business management practices and processes and the extent of the body of knowledge pertaining to these practices.

Project management is renowned for streamlining selected operational processes and keeping specific enterprise initiatives on track. This book provides executives and managers with recommendations for employing project management enterprise wide through the use of specific project-oriented business management processes. The enterprise project management office (EPMO) is the vehicle that enables executives to successfully implement project business management practices. The EPMO provides executives with a management oversight capability that keeps all project teams, business units, departments, and divisions aligned with the enterprise's business objectives. The EPMO facilitates the integration of the project, program, and portfolio management processes with the business management operational processes employed by other business unit organizations. Establishing an EPMO at the executive level is the only way to successfully achieve the benefits derived from instituting project management as a business function across the enterprise.

Once the executive management team adopts project business management practices as a way to do business, specific changes in some operational business processes and the addition of supportive business policies supporting the decision are necessary. Applying project business management processes to manage daily business operations requires the application of specific knowledge, skills, tools, and techniques that are often new concepts within an organization's cultural environment.

Executives and business unit managers want the answers to key questions before they agree to implement project business management on an enterprise-wide basis. These questions fall into several categories that we will answer in the following sections of the book.

Section 2: Governance
- How can I tell if my enterprise is already doing some project management?
- What is an enterprise project management office (EPMO)?
- What factors affect the structure of the EPMO and its positioning within the organization?
- What are the business benefits of creating an EPMO?
- How difficult is it to implement an EPMO?
- How can project management be seen as a business function?
- Why is project management seen as a competitive business weapon?

- What are the factors leading to enterprise-wide project management and EPMO success?
- Where do I position the EPMO within my enterprise?
- What actions do I take to establish our EPMO?

Section 3: Standardization
- How do I streamline some of the project related business operational processes?
- How do I successfully integrate project management processes with operations management processes?
- What does an enterprise-wide project methodology include?
- What kind of policies, plans, processes, and procedures are needed to support enterprise-wide project management?

Section 4: Capability
- How can I define the knowledge and skills required by portfolio, program, and project managers?
- How can I assess the organization's capabilities in managing portfolios, programs, and projects?
- How can I establish a career path program that will help train and retain skilled portfolio, program, and project managers?
- What are the elements of an effective education and training program that will develop program and project manager skills, knowledge, and practice capabilities?

Section 5: Execution
- How do I fold project management business-oriented processes into the business management operational processes in planning business objectives?
- How do I oversee management of portfolios, programs, and projects from the executive level?
- What roles do the EPMO and project business management play in strategic, tactical, and operational planning and management?
- What process are used to authorize, initiate, plan, execute, monitor and control, and close portfolios, programs, and projects?

Section 6 Maturity
- How is enterprise-wide project management maturity measured, evaluated, and improved?
- How do I control enterprise operational cost levels (and profits if applicable) while implementing the EPMO?
- What are the issues common to most organizations that implement a PMO or EPMO?

An analogy, which can also be drawn from the *enterprise-wide project management house of excellence* is that the management concepts presented in the governance, standardization, capability, and execution sections of the book and represented by the four major pillars are not stove-pipe in construct, because each concept relies on the other three to carry their load for the enterprise, and they all rest on mature project business management practices. Therefore, they are conceptually and must in reality be interrelated and integrated because they are part of the same project business management support structure.

A cookie-cutter solution for implementing enterprise-wide project management does not exist, because each enterprise is different. However, there are processes, methodologies, techniques, and tools that can be customized and implemented by an EPMO. These are common to organizations that have successfully established enterprise-wide project management operations. We will present what has been shown to work, what needs to be implemented, and what actions need to be taken by executive management teams to become successful.

Although some readers may agree that the concept and principles of project management might be of benefit to their enterprises, it may be difficult for them to understand how it is relevant to their business operations. The information in the following pages will help them understand how it can be made relevant by being successfully integrated long-term into their current day-to-day business operations and existing organizational functions.

1.2 Your Business and Project, Program, and Portfolio Management

To understand how businesses can benefit from enterprise-wide project management, let us analyze if an enterprise has projects and if those projects are managed as either programs or portfolios. A number of the following executive or senior manager positions are typical in most enterprises and are responsible for the operation of the enterprise:

- Board of Directors Member
- Chief Executive Officer (CEO)
- President
- Chief Operating Officer (COO)
- Chief Financial Officer (CFO)
- Chief Information Officer (CIO)
- Chief Technical Officer (CTO)

- Chief Engineer
- Vice President
- Business Unit Head
- Division Head
- Department Head
- Portfolio Manager

Does your enterprise do more than just simple manufacturing production?

If the answer is yes, then the executive management team is also responsible for the business of managing projects, whether the members recognize it or not.

Managing and operating a business involves initiatives to develop new products, transform current products or business operations, implement business reorganization, and perform continuous improvement on products or processes, all of which maintain the growth and health of the enterprise. If the enterprise has these types of initiatives, then projects are part of the business operations. The Project Management Institute (PMI®) defines a project as:

> *A temporary endeavor undertaken to create a unique product, service, or result.*

A project is usually performed with limited resources, including time and funds. From the perspective of the management team, a project is either all of, or a specific component of, a business objective. If projects are occurring, then by implication some form of project management is being performed. PMI® defines project management as:

> *The application of knowledge, skills, tools, and techniques to planned project activities to meet the project requirements to produce desired results that will meet the project's business objective.*

Project management is an approach in which a single individual has the authority and responsibility for overseeing the planning, organizing, directing, and controlling of all the activities. The actual act of managing a project usually involves balancing the competing demands of scope, time, budget, quality, and special requirements. The relationships among these factors mean that if any one factor changes, at least one other must also change.

Does your enterprise have two or more related projects underway simultaneously?

If the answer is yes, then enterprise operations are also dealing with programs. A program is defined by PMI® as:

A group of related projects (defined and selected business objectives) managed in a coordinated way to obtain benefits and control not available from managing them individually. Programs may include elements of related work outside of the scope of the discrete projects in the program.

If there are programs, then by implication some form of program management is being performed, which is defined by PMI® as:

The centralized coordinated management of a program to achieve the program's strategic objectives and benefits.

Does your enterprise have one or more projects or programs underway simultaneously?

If the answer is yes, then business operations are also dealing with portfolios. In an enterprise, a portfolio is a group of projects selected on the basis of business criteria, such as strategic business alignment, organizational impact, and cost/benefit results. A portfolio is defined by PMI® as:

A collection of projects or projects and other work that are grouped together to facilitate effective management of that work to meet strategic business objectives. The projects or programs of the portfolio may not necessarily be interdependent or directly related.

If you have one or more portfolios, then by implication you are performing some form of portfolio management, which is defined by PMI® as:

The centralized management of one or more portfolios which includes identifying, prioritizing, authorizing, managing, and controlling projects, programs, and other related work to achieve specific strategic business objectives.

Portfolio, program, and project management can be viewed as subsets of enterprise-wide project business management, which is both an ongoing business function and management process. Project business management involves coordinated management of multiple projects, programs, and portfolios to optimize the enterprise's return on investment or minimize the funds needed to achieve a broader set of defined strategic objectives or results than could be attained by managing each project separately. It involves the use of common ongoing business functions, such as cost accounting and contracting.

1.3 The EPMO as a Competitive Weapon and Its Benefits

Competing globally, increasing market share, reducing costs, and improving profits in the pursuit of producing better products and services faster through the use of high-technology solutions are just a few of the reasons why most organizations seek better ways to improve time to market, cost to market, and quality to market. The effective use of project management techniques is becoming more widely recognized as an effective approach for improving these areas. Some enterprises even view project management as a key weapon in their arsenals to increase customer satisfaction and outdistance the competition.

To effectively employ project business management, the organization as a whole must recognize and adopt new attitudes that embrace project business management best practices. This enables them to bring the full power of this new competitive weapon to bear in the battle for continuing business growth and, in many cases, ensuring the enterprise's survival in today's highly competitive global market.

Establishing executive ownership and responsibility for project business management within the organization is equated with authority in organizational structures; the closer something is to the top, the higher its level of authority, acceptance, adoption, and autonomy is perceived to be by the organization.

Positioning the project business management function at the top in a hierarchical organizational structure establishes its autonomy and thus "ownership" of the responsibility for setting up, distributing, supporting, and managing the application of project business management best practices. Enterprise-wide adoption of project business management best practices calls for single ownership of the function. Establishing common practices across an organization at all levels is difficult, if not impossible, without a clearly established sole ownership. We do believe, however, that establishing an enterprise project management office is the right thing to do, because global competition in the marketplace will continue to increase. Therefore, project management as a business function is one of the best answers for surviving global competition.

"Enterprise project management is an idea whose time has come. Applying project management on a broader basis within the organization adds speed and productivity to ongoing processes," states Paul C. Dinsmore, an international author and speaker on the subject of enterprise project management.

There are three common questions asked about an Enterprise Project Management Office (EPMO).

What is an Enterprise Project Management Office (EPMO)?

An EPMO is a centralized business function that provides project management business practices, processes, and support services. This functional group is staffed with experts skilled in providing those services, and:

- Reports to an executive management level position independent of other functional groups.
- Provides support directly to portfolio, program, and project managers and their staffs or provides the managers from within the EPMO staff.
- Is responsible for developing, implementing, and monitoring the consistent application of a project business management methodology across the organization.
- Integrates the application of portfolio, program, and project management business practices with the operational business practices throughout the enterprise by coaching, mentoring and training.

What factors affect the structuring of the EPMO and its positioning in the organization?

The size of the organization, type of business, number of physical business locations, quantity and complexity of projects, programs, and portfolios, and functional positioning within the organization all affect how the EPMO is configured and the degree of political autonomy it has within the enterprise. Very few enterprises are organized and operated in the same fashion, unless they have the same ownership. Even then, the management styles of executives can affect how each individual organization is operated. There is no generally recognized standard model used to structure or position an EPMO within an organization; however, we believe the EPMO should be located at the executive level of the enterprise and be operated as an independent functional organization.

Why should an EPMO be created?

We believe there are three primary objectives for implementing an EPMO that also are the reasons to create an EPMO:

- *Institutionalization of Project Management Principles and Practices:* The EPMO becomes the functional owner of project business management development, implementation, and monitoring. It also directs continuous improvement of the PBM policies, processes, and procedures across the organization.

- *Provides a Global View of the Enterprise's Initiatives and Projects:* An EPMO provides an environment in which all planned project-related enterprise initiatives can easily be summarized and rolled up across the enterprise to provide a single global view. Having available, to all management, a global view of the status of planned initiatives and portfolios, programs, and projects in-progress is critical to the strategic and tactical planning processes.
- *Optimization of Resources:* Having a global view that also provides an in-depth familiarity with all projects and programs is necessary before efficient enterprise-wide resource leveling and optimization can occur. An EPMO has this capability, because it is the focal point that gathers, analyzes, monitors, and reports the current state of all projects, programs, and portfolios on a regular basis.

In addition to meeting these three objectives, an EPMO can also provide a multitude of benefits for the entire organization. These benefits include:

- Improved product or service delivery time (time to market).
- Incorporation of a systematic project-based product development approach.
- Providing a results versus task focus to project-based initiatives.
- Reinforcement of continuous improvement through consistent repeatable processes.
- Facilitative proactive project business management.
- Improved communications throughout the enterprise.
- Clearly identified and minimized or mitigated risks.
- Simplified resource planning across multiple projects and programs.
- Managers enabled to anticipate problems rather than react to them.
- Enhanced "what-if" analysis and corrective action planning.
- Defined resource and timing requirements on an enterprise-wide basis to support strategic business plan initiatives.
- Improved project business management skills throughout the organization.

It is difficult to quantify many of the benefits associated with the implementation of project business management principles and processes, especially in the short term. Metrics can be developed to measure improvements once the processes have been established, but initially it will be difficult to categorically predict the specific value or worth of improvements that will be gained by incorporating the EPMO structure into the organization.

1.4 Project Management as a Business Function

For any organizational function to be established, sustained, retained, and operated effectively within an enterprise, it must have a defined purpose and visible support from the senior management. This includes business functions as common as finance, accounting, or marketing; the more esoteric functions such as quality assurance or safety; and the operations support function of information technologies.

Why then do enterprises establish and maintain these functions?

The need for accounting and finance functions, usually managed by a chief financial officer (CFO), is governed first by laws and regulations. It also fulfills the basic need to know if the enterprise is operating within its funding and to manage the enterprise's ability to acquire or reduce the cost of operating funds. In contrast, marketing, usually managed at a vice-presidential level, is driven by the need to inform outsiders of the value and utility of an enterprise's products or services. Accounting, finance, and marketing have long been recognized as business functions, with marketing sometimes reduced in staff but not eliminated during periods of declining business.

What quality assurance and safety have in common is that they have been defined as administrative overhead functions and created within the last fifty years to sustain good product quality or eliminate worker injury.

Quality assurance (QA) is now recognized as benefiting the enterprises' production operations by reducing waste and increasing or maintaining customer satisfaction. Therefore, quality assurance is now seen by most enterprises as a necessary function. During periods of declining business, QA may be reduced in staff, but it is not eliminated. If an enterprise works with the U.S. Government under the Federal Acquisition Regulations, then that business must issue a quality assurance policy statement signed by the chief executive officer (CEO). That policy establishes a quality assurance function and the ability to report quality issues all the way up through the senior executive level regardless of the organizational level where the quality assurance function is positioned within the enterprise or where a person reporting quality issues resides within the enterprise. Because of the close ties between quality assurance and operations, it is usually set up as an organizational business function within the production operations of the enterprise.

Safety in economically developed countries is beneficial to the enterprise because it reduces worker injury, time off the job, and related worker compensation costs. Within the United States, the Occupational Health and Safety Administration (OHSA), as well as many state governments, has promulgated regulations covering safety and health issues for various industries, which make the enterprise economically and sometimes criminally liable for a worker's injury or death. Therefore, enterprises now establish safety policies and see safety as a necessary business function. Depending on the industry, the Safety Officer and the organizational safety function may be located within a high-level administrative function or may report to an operational level person, such as the chief operating officer (COO).

In the last thirty years, information technologies (IT) has grown from a support function within accounting to a business support service function for the total enterprise. It is now usually managed by a chief information officer (CIO). As IT moved from mainframe computer support to the accounting function to being integrated into every administrative and operational aspect of the business, the organizational role of IT moved from a support service within accounting to an executive level function independent of other organizational functions.

The characteristic these functions share with project management is that they are primarily indirect administrative functions that add to the overall cost of the products or services. However, each of these functions also provides a competitive advantage in controlling the cost of or adding value to each product or service, and they are therefore demonstrably beneficial to the enterprise. All of these business support functions also share a common need for executive support, sponsorship, and enterprise-wide policies and procedures. The executives managing these business unit functions that coordinate or support operations within the organization also provide input to the enterprise's strategic planning process.

Why are those supporting services routinely recognized as business functions and what needs to happen to have project management be equally accepted as a business function?

These support services have been incorporated into the operations of most enterprises as the responsibility of an executive, who is expected to manage these services to enable the enterprise to maintain control of its operations, gain economic and operational advantage over the competition, and remain competitive in the marketplace.

To provide some historical perspective, note that accounting has been used since the time of the Phoenician traders and project management on single projects began at least with the construction of the great pyramids of Egypt and continued in certain industries through the mass production era that followed World War II. Now, however, project management is needed as a core business management discipline within the enterprise. It became a business requirement when enterprises began routinely creating initiatives to develop new products, transform products, modify business operations, acquire other enterprises, implement reorganizations, or perform continuous product or process improvements. By definition and practice, project management (as discussed in Chapter 4) is an identifiable specific management discipline within the broad category of general management, as are quality, safety, IT, accounting, and marketing.

In addition to the growing use of project management by public, private, and government enterprises, various professional societies have produced standards for project management, program project management, and portfolio project management. Some of these have become nationally recognized standards. Specific examples produced by the Project Management Institute (PMI®), with its global operations center in Newtown Square, Pennsylvania, include the third edition of *A Guide to the Project Management Body of Knowledge* (PMBOK® Guide, 2004), which was issued as *American National Standards Institute (ANSI)* standard ANSI/PMI99-001-2004, and *A Standard for Program Management* and *A Standard for Portfolio Management*, both of which were issued in May 2006. Many government and nongovernment entities now require an enterprise to show compliance with these standards and associated accreditations when being considered for contracts. As has been done with accounting, quality assurance and safety, all organizations should now establish project management as a business function on an enterprise-wide basis.

Effectively instituting project business management as a needed core competency across the organization requires executive management sponsorship, its long-term commitment, creation of an EPMO at the executive level of the enterprise, and maturation of project business management practices.

1.5 Impact of Project Business Management Maturity

The literature dealing with project management maturity indicates that successful enterprises are becoming increasingly dependent on the use of projects. This supports the argument that project management should be a "core capability" requirement. To achieve this, however, project success cannot be an occasional outcome. Performance that is only good, on average, is not sufficient. Repeatable successful performance on projects, programs, and portfolios needs to be the norm, with continuous improvements of project business management processes being sought and implemented.

The literature published in recent years on project management has reported anecdotal experiences regarding the value of project management as a means to control and affect the maturity of an enterprise's performance and costs. However, most of this information has been qualitative, with a minimal amount of quantitative data.

In the mid 1990s, the Project Management Institute (PMI®) began supporting research on the value of project management. In the first phase of this research, one study evaluated the qualitative values of project management; the results were reported in *The Benefits of Project Management: Financial and Organizational Rewards to Corporations*, by C.W. IBBS, Ph. D. and Young-Hoon Kwak of the University of California, Berkeley, and published by PMI® in 1997. The second phase of this Berkeley research looked at the quantitative values of the return on investment in project management processes versus the maturity of the project management processes capabilities on information technology projects; the results were reported in *Quantifying the Value of Project Management*, by C.W. IBBS, Ph.D. and Justin Reginato of the University of California, Berkeley, and published by PMI® in 2002 (referred to herein as the "Berkeley Study").

The quantitative Berkeley Study, along with data from other project management literature, indicates that the cost of project management ranges between 6% and 12% of the total cost of the project. The Berkeley Study corroborates qualitative analyses showing that the amount of project management costs and the associated results of the project management processes depend on the maturity level of the enterprise's project business management capabilities.

The literature written for today's business leaders also indicates that organizations with low project management maturity jeopardize their likelihood of delivering successful projects and can also incur increased project direct costs. In those enterprises, the cost of project management can reach 20% of total project costs and can directly depend on the maturity of the enterprise's project management capabilities.

Project business management enables the timely communication of accurate, routine, consistent, and visible progress. This information allows executive management to take effective corrective actions when a program or project performance deviates from the approved work plans. However, project management, as with other management functions, can be performed at various levels of effectiveness. One aspect of applying the project business management processes is to work toward improving the usefulness and effectiveness of those processes, as they are used in the selection, planning, execution, and control of projects, programs, and portfolios. To ensure that project business management is effectively used enterprise wide, the EPMO should consistently and incrementally work on improving its capabilities and project business management operations.

Current literature suggests that best-in-class project management organizations with highly mature, well-developed, and effective project business management competency, practices, and capabilities derive the following benefits:

- Routinely achieve on-budget and on-schedule performance with lower total project management cost. By contrast, less mature PM organizations may spend as much, or more, but commonly experience project cost overruns.
- Increase the return on an enterprise's investment in project business management as the project business management processes become more mature and less costly.
- Perform better in delivering projects, programs, and portfolios.
- Produce more predictable project technical, schedule, and cost performance.
- Have lower direct costs in completing a project or program.

The more uniformly and consistently a mature project business management process is applied, the greater will be the results and benefits obtained. The benefits of effective mature project business management increase with the complexity, size, and number of projects, programs, and portfolios, and the EPMO function commonly becomes critical to the success of large capital projects, programs, and portfolios. The purpose of mature project business management processes is to create significant benefits at low cost through documented and implemented structured project business management methodologies.

1.6 Factors of Project Business Management and EPMO Success

The ability to successfully establish enterprise-wide project management using enterprise project management offices is based on many factors and related actions. The following are some of the typical management support actions that can make your efforts succeed:

- Have executive management view project management as a business function.
- Have senior management provide visible support for the project business management effort.
- Ensure the executive sponsor is not removed through reorganization or downsizing until implementation is complete.
- Require middle managers to use the EPMO and not resist implementing enterprise-wide project management to protect their "turf."

- Assure functional organizations provide project resources (staff and equipment) as planned.
- Provide funding as planned.
- Recognize project management as an independent business function, with authority to distribute and control the enterprise-wide project business management best practices.

The following are business process actions that can make your efforts succeed:

- Identify those project management processes that will be employed by the enterprise.
- Have a strong knowledge of project business management practices within the EPMO and generally a good knowledge within the directly related functional organizations.

The following are typical organizational development actions that can make your efforts succeed:

- Establish a corporate goal to institutionalize project management as a core competency.
- Identify and define a project management function that supports the other functions within the organization, which we call the Enterprise Project Management Office (EPMO).
- Establish the application of project management through a formally issued policy statement.
- Prepare and issue a charter that establishes the position of the EPMO at the executive level and defines the roles and responsibilities of the EPMO.
- Prepare and issue enterprise-wide project business management procedures.

To help ensure success, it is necessary to determine current conditions within your enterprise before implementing your enterprise-wide project management business function. This type of analysis is required on any initiative (project) that involves introducing a change that will have an impact on people across the organization, particularly if it affects the way they do their work (see the maturity evaluation methodology in Section 6).

CHAPTER 2

The EPMO as a Business Organization

2.1 The Business Case for the EPMO

Harvey Levine in his September 1996 article, "Teamocracy and Project Management: A Conundrum (A Case for the Project Office)," captured the essence behind the argument for the creation of an EPMO.

> *Where do we get off expecting that all engineers, or programmers, or marketing specialists will possess skills in project management, or in operating a project management software program? Would we likewise put accounting software on each employee's desk, ask them to perform accounting for their area, and then eliminate the corporate accounting function? We don't ask engineers to do marketing. We don't ask programmers to pour cement. Why do we ask them to fill a role for which they are not trained (and which probably isn't in their job description)? This is truly absurd. And it will produce regrettable consequences.*

He further states:

> *. . . the role of the project office to successful project management is more important than ever.*

Creation of project management offices (PMO) has become a hot topic in the marketplace, as evidenced by the numerous articles published in the PMI® publication, *PM Network,* since 1997, and by the number of project management professionals who have attended PMO seminars sponsored by PMI® over the past years. Many industry and government organizations have also created or are in the process of developing their own project management offices, each different in its structure and position.

Today's global market enterprises, regardless of industry or size, are looking to improve their systems and processes to become more competitive. One approach is to establish project management as a core competency throughout the organization. By setting up standardized project business management policies, plans, processes, and procedures within the enterprise, they plan to learn from past mistakes, make processes more efficient, and develop people's skills and talents to work more effectively. The list of organizations attempting to integrate project management disciplines and best practices into the way they manage their businesses is expanding daily; however, those who have succeeded in doing so is significantly smaller.

Typically, the individual who owns project management for the enterprise leads a group responsible for implementing the project business management processes and systems. The name of the group is not nearly as important as its position within the enterprise. Therefore, to indicate the level needed for this function, we call this group the Enterprise Project Management Office (EPMO).

The number of companies that are creating an EPMO grows daily. The numerous articles written about EPMOs and the number of companies sending representatives to seminars and classes to learn about EPMOs attest to the expanding popularity of this business concept. The one caution we offer is that establishing an EPMO is not a trivial pursuit. It requires real dedication and commitment to see the process through to the end. The current reported failure rate of PMOs is greater than two thirds. Although the reasons for these failures are somewhat different for each organization, the shutdowns or failures share a number of common elements discussed below. In the 1960s, the concept of the project management office was developed and practiced successfully in aviation and aerospace companies. The PMO has become more visible today because they are being developed in many more industries. With that visibility comes an increase in failures. Some of those failures are attributed to the lack of PMO knowledge and experience among its initiators or a failure to apply best practices or a lack of sponsor support.

For an EPMO to be successful, it must first be regarded and treated as a key business functional organization throughout the enterprise. Therefore, executives must establish and implement an enterprise strategic objective to institutionalize project business management practices using an EPMO. It is critical that workers at all levels, including line managers, recognize the executive support of the EPMO as a business organization.

The ability of an EPMO to be successful is often directly related to the proper positioning of the EPMO within the organization. By positioning, we mean that the individual manager who owns the responsibility for implementing project business management best practices is a member of the highest level of management. Without support from the executive level, the effort to inculcate project business management within the enterprise will not get off the ground.

The EPMO can only succeed if it has the requisite authority and autonomy required to get the job done. Therefore, positioning is a critical aspect of establishing project business management as an enterprise-wide core competency.

2.2 Typical Project Management Office Structure

The functional organization used to provide and implement project management is referred to by many different names, such as Project Office (PO), Project Management Center of Excellence (PMCoE), or Corporate Project Management Office (CPMO), but it is most often identified simply as a Project Management Office (PMO). Figure 2-1 llustrates how a project management office may fit into an enterprise's organizational structure.

This high-level positioning of the project management office in a hierarchical organizational structure establishes its autonomy.

The project management office is operated using two primary tools: (1) a Project Business Management Methodology (PBMM), which is documented by a series of project business management policies, plans, and procedures that are contained within a Project Business Management Man-

Figure 2-1.   Typical PMO structure. Shaded boxes represent functional staff engaged as project team members. In this scenario, the project managers report directly to a business unit manager and indirectly (see dotted line) to the PMO manager, who controls the processes and methods used to manage projects.

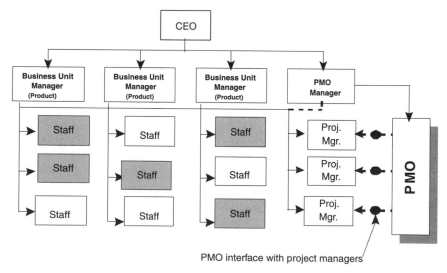

ual. They implement the project business management processes selected for use by the enterprise and which are standardized across the enterprise's business units, and (2) a related Project Business Management System (PBMS), with a supporting project business management information system (PBMIS).

2.3 Structuring the EPMO

The position of an EPMO within a hierarchical organization establishes its degree of authority, acceptance, adoption, and autonomy—and, thus, its "ownership" of the responsibility for establishing, distributing, and supporting project management best practices within the enterprise. Figure 2-2 shows an example of such a structure and illustrates how the EPMO might be implemented in a large organization with multiple divisions, business units, or regional operations. The number of layers and project

Figure 2-2. EPMO Functional Organization Reporting Overview. EPMO = executive level; DPMO = divisional level, BUPMO = business unit level, and PMO = mission critical project level.

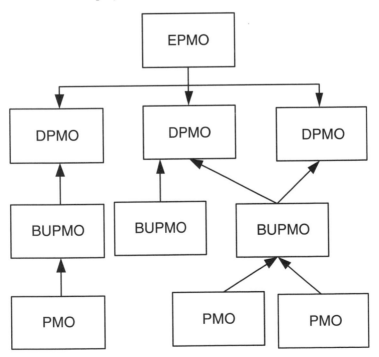

management units within each layer depends on the size of the unit, the number of annual projects in a portfolio, and the complexity of the projects within the various levels of the organization. For small to midsized organizations, the number of layers and functional units may be adjusted to fit the amount of control required by the project activity at each level.

Assigning a name to an organizational function gives it significance and differentiates it from other functions within the organization. The six most common names or titles given to the project management function are:

- Enterprise Project Management Office (EPMO)
- Project Management Office (PMO)
- Program Management Office (PMO)
- Portfolio Management Office (PMO)
- Project Support Office (PSO)
- Project Office (PO)

These titles are often used interchangeably, and it is usually a matter of personal preference and the purpose of the PMO, rather than applica-

Table 2-1.   Project Management Functional Organizational Titles

Title (Focus)	Definition of Responsibility
EPMO (Strategic)	The Enterprise PMO is accountable for enterprise-wide distribution of project business management best practices. Provides leadership with the primary focus of strategic planning and the establishment of enterprise policies governing the effective use of project business management methodology, practices, tools, templates, education, training, and project management competency.
DPMO (Tactical)	The Division PMO is responsible for tactical master planning within major divisions or regions, etc., overseeing the effective application of the project business management standards established by the EPMO within their respective spheres of responsibility or having the responsibility to manage a portfolio.
BUPMO (Operational)	The Business Unit PMO is responsible for operational master planning, which oversees the effective application of the project business management standards established by the EPMO in direct support of all projects within a functional department or having the responsibility to manage a program.
PMO (Operational)	The PMO is responsible for the direct support of a single, mission-critical or major project, which is typically large and complex, and whose success affects multiple areas of the enterprise.

Table 2-2. Project Management Functional Organization RRAA Matrix

Roles	Responsibility	Accountability	Requisite Authority
EPMO	Strategic master planning. Maintain enterprise purpose, vision, mission, and strategic business plan	Reports directly to the CEO/President (highest level corporate officer)	Review and approve master project portfolio and budget plans. Oversee portfolios and programs.
DPMO One for each division, region, or portfolio	Tactical master planning, project portfolio management, and general resource management	Division, region, or portfolio – reports directly to EPMO	Establish project portfolio operational and budget plans and authorize adjustments. Manage portfolios and oversee programs.
BUPMO	Operations master planning and project program management	Functional business unit or program – reports directly to DPMO	Develop project program operational and budget plans and authorize adjustments. Manage programs and oversee projects.
PMO One for each major or mission critical project	Project initiation, planning, execution, monitoring, control, and closing	Specific project – reports directly to BUPMO	Develop project operational and budget plans and authorize adjustments. Manage, control, and report project progress.

tion of any particular standard, that determines which is selected. For definitions of these titles and business focus, see Table 2-1.

Two key issues affect the assigning of titles. The first is defining where the function will reside within the organizational structure (the direct line of report), and the second is what purpose it will serve in that position. Titles often add significance to the roles, responsibility, accountability, and requisite authority (RRAA) of the position. Table 2-2 provides brief RRAA descriptions for each of the roles listed in Table 2-1.

The need to accommodate different management styles, work environments, and product life cycle issues means there is no one-size-fits-all project management organizational structure and that no generally recognized standard model defines how an EPMO should be structured or positioned in an organization.

The main concern in developing an organizational structure is establishing the functional ownership and leadership of the project management discipline at the highest level within the enterprise. Further decomposition of the project management structure depends on the amount of support and control required at each level.

As mentioned earlier, titles can also make a difference. Different titles eliminate confusion when communicating the distinctions among the various project management "offices" within the organization. It is important to note, however, that positioning of the project management function in the organization's management structure has far more importance and has a greater impact on institutionalizing project management best practices than the title assigned.

CHAPTER 3

Enterprise-Wide Project Management
as a Business Concept

3.1 EWPM End-State Vision and Concept

The enterprise-wide project management (EWPM) concept cannot be successful without successful application of the concept, institutionalization of the practices and principles, and execution of the related process. The phrase *enterprise wide* implies that project management will be instituted throughout the enterprise. In addition, classifying it as a business function means that an organizational function, such as the EPMO, will manage the related project business management processes. Enterprise-wide project management is a project business management concept that encompasses the integrated application of:

- Multiple functional organizational structures.
- Portfolio project-related management practices and processes.
- Program project-related management practices and processes.
- Project management practices and processes.
- Business operations management practices and processes.

Business operations are the day-to-day, on-going business processes and activities within an enterprise. The operational functional organizations are the business units that manage and perform the business operations. The authors have defined the term Enterprise-Wide Project Management as "the application of project business management practices and processes on an enterprise-wide basis, using an enterprise-wide project management office as the business unit to support management of the enterprise's portfolios, programs, and projects."

Current research in the project management field shows that best-in-class organizations usually have highly effective project management cultures with advanced project management maturity. The business operations of successful world-class companies are embracing and implementing mature project business management processes. By applying project management and control as core management disciplines, they are not only obtaining beneficial results from their project business management processes but they are also achieving a significantly positive return on their investment in project business management.

All but the smallest business enterprises are involved in some form of project management. Enterprises with more complex operations are also involved in some form of program or portfolio project management. Establishing project management enterprise wide is the key to achieving enterprise business objectives and obtaining the benefits that are expected from accomplishing those projects, programs, and portfolios.

To be successful, project management must first be viewed and treated as a key business function throughout the organization. It is critical that all levels of workers in the organization, including line managers, see that the executive level supports project management as a business function, publicly, completely, and without hesitation. As a first step toward achieving these objectives, executive managers must establish a business strategy and objective to institutionalize project business management practices as core competencies.

Because every enterprise is different, there are no cookie-cutter solutions to implementing enterprise-wide project management. However, by using an Enterprise Project Management Office (EPMO), the portfolio, program, and project management processes, methodologies, techniques, and tools, provided in Sections 2 through 6 of this book can be customized and implemented. Such customization is common with successful enterprise-wide project management operations.

Enterprise-wide adoption of project management best practices calls for single ownership of the EPMO function, locating the EPMO at the executive level of the enterprise's organizational structure, and operating it as an independent functional organization. Unfortunately, establishing a project office has most often been done at a business unit level rather than at the executive level. Positioning the project office at the highest level in the enterprise is especially important when the long-term objective is to instill project management best practices in all areas of the enterprise as a core competency.

Project management as an independent business function and the ownership of project management by the EPMO must be recognized at every level of the organization to establish the level of authority that is required to provide, monitor, and control the distribution of enterprise-wide project management best practices.

Rapidly implementing project management enterprise wide or establishing an EPMO as a project management center of excellence should not be viewed as quick-fix solutions to current problems with planning, managing, and executing projects. The implementation process will require a longer term, foundation-building effort to attain the objective and maturity required to infuse project business management practices as the new way business will be managed.

The end-state vision for enterprise-wide project management is establishing the EPMO as a business functional organization overseeing mature project business management processes. The EPMO helps the enterprise to use mature project business management processes leading to the successful planning and completion of programs and projects on schedule and within budget. The end-state vision includes providing a high return on the enterprise's investment in project business management, assures that the areas of planned cost avoidance are attained, and supports generation of cost reduction for ongoing project work. The timely implementation of enterprise-wide project management can provide a business and economic benefit to the enterprise by reducing project management costs and improving project management effectiveness, while obtaining the business benefits of lower-cost project delivery. This vision requires integration of modern project business management practices throughout all operational areas of the enterprise.

3.2 Project Business Management: Integrating Project, Business, and Operations Management

Enterprise-wide project management combines the following:

- Use of an enterprise project management office.
- Application of project business management practices and processes.

What is modern project business management (PBM)?

The term *project business management* can be interpreted many different ways. If ten executives and senior managers from ten different enterprises are asked what PBM means, there will be as many different answers. To eliminate this confusion, we provided a definition of project business management in the foreword. In addition, the discipline of project business management can be best described in terms of the blended component management practices and integrated processes listed in subchapter 3.1.

The principles and concepts of portfolio management, program management, and project management are complex, and many management processes are involved. All together, when blended with the principles, concepts, and varied processes of general business management and business operations management leads to the concept of project business management. Project business management is the application of those practices and processes on an enterprise-wide basis.

The general operational and business processes for an enterprise are well described in many business books, and the generally accepted project management processes are well documented in standards such as the Project Management Institute's (PMI®) standards: *A Guide to the Project Management Body of Knowledge* (PMBOK® Guide, 3rd ed), *A Standard for Program Management,* and *A Standard for Portfolio Management.*

General management includes all the common management disciplines, such as accounting, marketing, human resources, operations, production, legal, and personnel supervision. The practice of project management is also an identifiable and specific discipline within the broad category of general management. To practice each of these disciplines requires that you know general business practices and also have the specific knowledge and skill associated with a specific business discipline. Project business management requires an understanding of the general project management body of knowledge and how to apply the various project, program, and portfolio processes defined in the project management standards.

Project business management blends the terminology from the vocabularies of both general business management and project management. It integrates the related business and project processes, which allows the project business management processes to be easily understood by business executives, functional mangers, and project managers. The authors use the term project business management to eliminate any confusion and suppress the reader's assumptions as to just what the term *project management* could mean in a business context.

3.3 Project Business Management: Six Key Factors

Six critical factors influence the successful application and implementation of project business management. Less than complete support for any of these will create or foster adverse conditions and attitudes that will affect the degree of success in achieving a total integration of project business management (PBM) into an organization's corporate culture. Those factors are:

1. *Total commitment and support from top executive management down through the organization.* If corporate leaders are not totally convinced that integrating PBM into the enterprise's business manage-

ment processes is the right thing, then how can the staffs reporting to them, which are the people who will be most affected by the change, be convinced it is? Lukewarm support will not get the job done either. Nothing less than enthusiastic support will be needed to convince workers to accept the proposed changes. In many cases, even this level of support is met with skepticism. Acceptance by edict is one way to make sure everyone gets the message to cooperate. Issuing decrees and proclamations may not be the most democratic way, but it usually has the best short-term results. Possibly the most successful way to show commitment is using a combination of cheerleading and a clear message that 100 percent cooperation and participation is needed to make the transition work to everyone's benefit.

Why is it important to gain top executive management support?

PBM implementation can be identified as a key company initiative that supports strategic objectives.

- Financial and human resource commitments can be made by top management at the start.
- PBM can be presented for the value it can add to improving business processes.

How can this level of support be obtained?

- Clearly establish the need by identifying the current problems that can be solved by PBM.
- Find a PBM sponsor who can help sell and continually support the initiative.
- Sell the value of PBM from the top (CEO) down to the functional managers.
- Prepare an implementation plan with the requirements, a budget, and a schedule.

2. *The selection of an executive-level PBM Sponsor is critical.* The following points define why this is such an important step.

   - A PBM sponsor is an executive-level manager who is usually not a direct stakeholder in the implementation of the initiative, but at the same time is a very strong proponent.
   - The PBM sponsor is critical because he/she serves as the primary liaison between the person(s) who is responsible for

the implementation of PBM and the other enterprise policy makers.

- The best PBM sponsor is someone who is well respected and has political clout in the organization. A sponsor can get things done when the normal channels of protocol become clogged or break down.
- The sponsor plays a key role in supporting the progress of a smooth PBM implementation process.

3. *Recognition that PBM requires the full-time dedication of experienced resources.* PBM is a professional discipline that employs specific knowledge, skills, tools, techniques, and principles required in the planning, organizing, implementing, managing, and controlling of portfolios, programs, and projects of various sizes and complexities. Managing portfolios, programs, and projects and providing related supporting services is a full-time job requiring specialized capabilities and experience.

4. *Strict adherence to documented PBM processes and procedures.* Documented enterprise policies, which support project business management processes and procedures, are critical to the successful application of PBM practices throughout an organization. Adherence to a standardized set of PBM processes and procedures provides a consistent approach to managing all portfolios, programs, and projects across the organization and facilitates education and training of PBM skills.

5. *Development and conformity of use of standardized tools.* Designating specific standard project management tools (purchased or developed) will facilitate the creation of common reporting formats and also improve user skills. Uniformity of output allows easier comparisons among portfolios, programs, and projects and improves communications between project teams and management. Routine and targeted communication is a key for maintaining stakeholder confidence.

6. *Absolute commitment to ongoing project management skills development and training.* Project management education and training is a key element in the initial and ongoing PBM integration process. Project management education and training will improve the general management skills of the organization as an added benefit. They can also be utilized as a means to select and advance staff members along a career path.

Fully integrating the principles of PBM throughout an organization takes time and a commitment to providing the means and methods to develop the skills and knowledge required to become proficient in their application. Failure to meet the six critical success factors outlined above directly encumbers the degree of acceptance and hinders the successful implementation of PBM practices within the organization. Conversely, if these resolutions are carefully met, a multitude of benefits will be realized by those enterprises willing to make such long-term commitments to ensure future growth and prosperity.

3.4 Institutionalizing Project Management Takes Commitment

Some senior managers and many mid-level managers have set about implementing project management practices and processes and creating a project management office for their business units, but they have met with varying degrees of success. The most successful are the managers of a business unit within an enterprise that is operated almost as a standalone business. Those project management processes and PMO implementations that were set up within lower level business units and those not set up as operational functions were completely eliminated during periods of lowered business activity. This occurred because the associated practices and processes were neither institutionalized nor matured to a point where they could be viewed as a low-cost, high-return operational business function.

The following two case studies are for-profit project-based enterprises that have attempted to institutionalize project management as a core competency wide. The first one failed; the second is in the process of succeeding.

Company A is a multinational, tier-one automotive supplier that began the process by establishing a Project Management Center of Excellence (PMCoE) in the Information Technology (IT) department. Its objective was to institutionalize project management as a core competency globally within IT. The CIO/VP was the project sponsor and champion who provided the funding and management support to establish the PMCoE internationally across his organization. When the effort began, the management of projects was done on an ad hoc basis, with no project process methodology. Within sixteen months, the PMCoE established a standard project management process methodology and distributed it, along with basic training in project scope and schedule development, in its U.S. and European operations. The IT organization was just beginning to understand the value of project management best practices when the terrorist attack occurred on September 11, 2001, and the change in the U.S. economy caused budget cuts and downsizing. As a result, the PMCoE was eliminated. The IT organization lost sight of the goal of institutionalizing project management and the desire to achieve the goal vanished. This example was repeated in many organizations during the economic downturn that occurred from 2000 through 2003. The CIO/VP's vision of establishing project management as a core competency was not shared and embraced by the overall executive corporate management and not enough time was allowed to quantitatively demonstrate the value that project management could add to the overall enterprise.

Company B is a multinational, tier-one supplier of aerospace electronic systems to the commercial and government aviation industries. Project management had been an integral function within the engineering department of the organization for the past ten years, and the roles and responsibilities of the participants were fairly well defined. The organization had been using a documented methodology for managing projects for 3 to 4 years. A formal project management office (PMO) had not yet been established, but many of the functions typically found in a PMO were being performed by a number of separate groups of individuals who report to the manager of project managers. All of the project managers also reported to a director of project management who had overall control in the engineering department of divisions of the global organization. Management had taken steps to develop project management education and training programs for the organization's general population, project managers, team members, and line managers. The director of project management had begun the process of institutionalizing project management best practices by making arrangements for all of the project managers to become PMP® certified by the Project Management Institute. He also provided membership to PMI® national, the local chapter, and a Special Interest Group. The corporate officers established a committee that developed a common project management methodology, which is to be used to manage all projects enterprise wide. The next logical step is to establish an enterprise-wide project management office at the corporate and divisional levels of the global organization to enable the organization to fully embrace project management as a core competency enterprise wide.

These case study examples and many others show that establishing and institutionalizing project management enterprise wide should not be viewed as either a quick-fix solution or a trivial pursuit, but rather as a long-term, foundation-building effort. They also show that establishing common project management practices across an organization at all levels is very difficult, if not impossible, without a sole ownership of those project management business practices being clearly established. This requires that the EPMO must be recognized as an independent business function and its ownership set at the highest management level of the organization. The EPMO needs to have the authority to distribute, monitor, and control the project management business processes and procedures required to achieve enterprise-wide project management best practice capabilities.

Establishing project management in most organizations is very difficult, partly because functional managers are afraid of losing their authority and control over the resources that report to them. In addition, workers are afraid of being held accountable for performing a new set of requirements brought about by organizational changes. This fear, expressed as resistance, comes from lack of information and understanding about how the changes will affect their jobs. Positioning the project management function at the highest management level within the enterprise also provides the measure of autonomy necessary to extend its authority across the organization, while substantiating the value and importance the function has in the eyes of executive management and the other functional organizations.

CHAPTER 4

Integrating Projects with Business Strategies and Objectives

4.1 Methodology

One of the goals of employing enterprise-wide project management and establishing an EPMO is to become more effective and efficient at completing the strategic business objectives set for the enterprise. Realizing this goal requires that the enterprise's projects be aligned with those business objectives.

Incorporating project management process into the enterprise's existing operational business process requires an analysis of how the organization currently develops its business strategies and accomplishes its related business objectives. The next step is to determine what needs to be modified to maintain a better business focus on attaining those objectives.

It is necessary to determine where the enterprise is with respect to effectively employing enterprise-wide project management and to create a clearly documented baseline against which improvements can be measured. Two key points of understanding that can be drawn from the baseline analysis related to strategic and tactical planning and project, program, and portfolio planning and execution are (1) the enterprise has identifiable enterprise environmental factors that are related to achieving its vision and accomplishing its purpose, and (2) it has also developed organizational process assets that directly affect the ability to accomplish the business objectives and successfully perform the associated projects. This baseline needs to include:

- Purpose of the enterprise.
- Vision/mission for the enterprise.
- Current functional organizational structure.
- Organizational process assets.
- Enterprise environmental factors.

This documented baseline is essential to:

- Identify where the operational business processes need to be modified.
- Streamline some of the project-related business operational processes.
- Fold project management business-oriented project processes into the current business management operational processes.
- Oversee the management of portfolio, programs, and projects from the corporate office level.
- Have the capability to quantitatively demonstrate the added value of project management.
- Integrate project management with operations management.
- Institutionalize project management as a core competency.
- Control enterprise operational cost levels (and profits if applicable) while implementing the EPMO.
- Show the benefits gained from establishing an EPMO.
- Achieve the highest level of project management maturity.

The task of a senior manager is to analyze and understand how the management discipline of project management can operate with their other management disciplines and how it can support business operations. In performing the analysis the following is required:

- Identify the key operational aspects of your enterprise.
- Document which aspects are only business management processes.
- Document which aspects are only project management processes.
- Determine which aspects require folding project management business-oriented project processes into the project-related business management operational processes.
- Determine where to integrate project management with operations management.

Many of the business management analysis techniques that support executives in maintaining control in a dynamic and changing environment are based on one premise: break the process or operation down into manageable pieces. The premise is founded on the concept of cascading analysis. The management technique takes the entire process or operation and dissects it into successively lower and lower levels of detail until management understanding and control is possible and, in most processes, until a level of detail is reached where the management actions and activities can be quantified. This analytical concept is used in many management areas, including:

- Business management.
- Management by Objectives (MBO).
- Cascaded/interlocked functional organizational missions.
- Management by Planning (MBP).
- Administrative management.
- Policy, plan, and procedure hierarchy development.
- Project management.
- Work breakdown structuring (WBS).
- Rolling wave planning.

In applying this analytical technique, we will look at the common structural business management components of most enterprises. We will then define each component and determine how each component relates to one or more of the other operational components. The common operational management and project management business components of most enterprises determined through our research are given in Table 4-1. Each of these components has one or more operational business processes and/or project management business processes associated with establishing and executing that component.

Table 4-1. Common Operational Management and Project Management Business Components

Component	Description
Enterprise Business Purpose	The business purpose for which the enterprise was created and is operated.
Enterprise Environmental Factors	All of the external factors in the environment within which the enterprise will operate, and all of the internal environmental factors that the enterprise either creates or adopts.
Enterprise Vision/Mission	What the enterprise aspires to become or what larger goal the enterprise is expected to attain.
Business Strategies	One or more plans, methods, series of actions, or schemes developed by the enterprise to attain its vision/mission.
Strategy Accomplishment Metrics	Those measurable metrics established by the enterprise to determine how well a specific business strategic benefit has been met.
Business Objectives	Something toward which the management and resources of the enterprise are directed, such as a product to be produced or a service to be performed, to accomplish a business strategy.

(continued)

Table 4-1. *(Continued)*

Component	Description
Objective Accomplishment Metrics	Those measurable metrics established by the enterprise to determine how well a specific business objective has been met and the extent to which a specific strategic benefit was delivered.
Organizational Process Assets	All of the assets related to any business, operational, or project process within the enterprise.
Enterprise Resource & Financial Factors	All of the economic assets available to and controlled by the enterprise and all of the human resources, equipment, material, supplies, etc. controlled by the enterprise.
Prioritized & Selected Objectives	Those business objectives prioritized and selected to be pursued based on a set of parameters set by the senior management of the enterprise.
Portfolios	The set of selected business objectives or components of objectives and related work that will be formed into programs and project for execution.
Programs	Sets of related business objectives or related components of objectives and related work
Projects	Either all, or a specific component, of a business objective within a portfolio or program that must be accomplished to attain that business objective.
Continuous Improvement Projects	A series of projects supporting a business objective of improving a process, product, or service within the enterprise.
Project Performance Metrics	Those measurable metrics established by the enterprise to determine how well a specific project has been met and is tied to determining if the business objective has been met.
Business Operations	The enterprise's ongoing processes utilizing the products, services, and results obtained from completed projects and programs.

Figure 4-1 is a graphical analysis of the components identified in Table 4-1. It shows how they interrelate and can be viewed in a hierarchical manner.

4.2 Strategic Planning

Every enterprise is established for a purpose, whether it is a for-profit company created to mine minerals or a government agency created to provide

Figure 4-1. Hierarchy of Business Planning Components

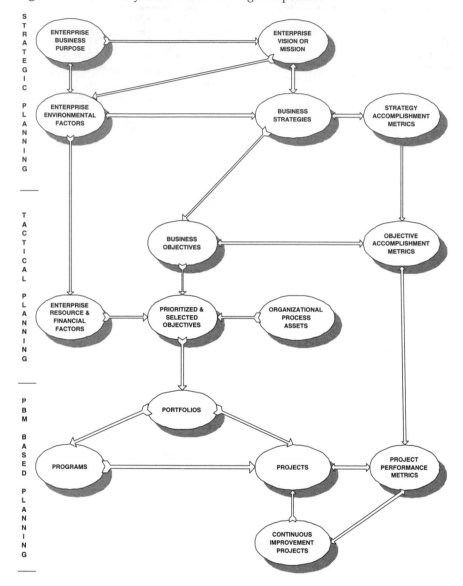

social services. When an enterprise is created or changes, it comes under the influence of a set of *enterprise environmental factors* that affect and sometimes limit how it may operate. Business purpose related enterprise environmental factors include, but are not limited to:

- Government or industry standards, specifications, regulations, and laws.
- Local, regional, national, global, and specific marketplace conditions.
- Stakeholder risk tolerances.
- Culture within the enterprise.
- Culture and social conditions in which the enterprise operates (demographic, ethnic, economic, educational, ethical, religious, and so on).
- Commercial availability of information databases.
- Existing patents held by others.

Every enterprise has a definable vision/mission regardless of whether it is formally documented. To attain or accomplish that vision/mission, the enterprise will need to address additional environmental factors and develop other enterprise environmental factors needed to operate its business. If not understood, some of these factors can limit the enterprise's ability to operate. Vision/mission-related enterprise environmental factors include, but are not limited to:

- Functional organizational structure.
- Physical infrastructure (facilities, and so on).
- Local ecology and geology around the enterprise's physical facilities.
- Globally dispersed operations (time zones, holidays, traveling, and so on).
- Health and safety practices.
- Administrative systems assets (personnel management, procurement, warehousing, legal, and so on).
- Accounting systems assets.
- Work authorization system.
- Information systems and technology.
- Research and development methodologies.
- Manufacturing methodologies.
- Product distribution channels.

The business purpose of the enterprise leads to a vision/mission. The combination of that purpose with the associated vision/mission and management actions addressing them determines what enterprise environmental factors affect how the business operates.

To attain the vision or accomplish the mission, senior management must develop and adopt one or more business strategies (plans, methods, series of actions, or schemes). They should also define the expected associated benefits of those strategies and how achieving these benefits will be measured. However, the ability to execute any strategy is limited by the enterprise environmental factors that pertain to the organization.

4.3 Tactical Planning

Each business strategy is further defined by one or more specific business objectives that, when accomplished, will complete the associated strategies. To determine that a business objective has been achieved, a set of metrics driven by an understanding of the requirements of the strategy and the desired benefits are established to determine how adequately that objective was met.

The set of business objectives are then prioritized using criteria that are meaningful to accomplishing the various strategies. Based on those criteria, a set of objectives are selected that are directly influenced by the enterprise's resources, financial factors, and the organizational process assets.

The enterprise resources and financial factors are a subset of the overall enterprise environmental factors and include, but are not limited to:

- Available funding (authorized funding for governmental enterprises).
- Ability to obtain additional financing for a company (level of indebtedness).
- Availability of existing skilled human resources in the required disciplines.
- Existence and operability of required information systems and technology.
- Availability of required equipment, material, facilities, and so on.

The organizational process assets are those assets related to any business, operational, or project process within the enterprise. They include, but are not limited to:

- Relevant knowledge in the enterprise's databases and files.
- Issued relevant policy statements.
- Applicable plans for managing the work.
- Appropriate and applicable procedures.
- Adequate financial controls.
- Quality assurance and control capabilities.
- Ability to manage the associated risks.
- Defined and approved operational processes.
- Defined and approved project, program, and portfolio management processes.

The combination of specific enterprise environmental factors and the necessary organizational process assets directly affect your ability to reach your objectives and successfully perform the associated projects. The integration of the operational management processes and the related project management process used in prioritizing and selecting business objectives are covered in more detail in Section 5.

4.4 PBM Based Planning

The selected business objectives are assembled into portfolios and then converted into programs and projects that need to be executed. Some of the projects may directly support an existing operational aspect of the enterprise and are called continuous improvement projects. An example is *six sigma* projects that are established as part of the business objectives related to current products or operational and production processes. Some portfolios may be divided into subportfolios, some programs may be divided into subprograms, and some large projects may be divided into subprojects to facilitate the enterprise's management and control of the planned work.

Senior management then formally authorizes the execution of each portfolio, program, and project. Simultaneously, a combination of project and operations management establishes the performance metrics for each program and project and assures that those detailed metrics are a definitive subset of the accomplishment metrics established for the business strategy and related business objectives.

The final output, the deliverables, of the programs and projects are supplied to operations to integrate into ongoing business operations.

4.5 Key Points for Project Business Management Planning Success

The following are the key points on which to concentrate during the planning process and authorizing of the portfolios, programs, and projects related to one's business objectives.

Strategic Planning

- The business strategies must align with the enterprise vision or mission.
- The business strategies must not conflict with the known enterprise environmental factors.

- The corporate culture and organizational structure need to be compatible with, or supportive of, any defined business strategy.
- The expected strategic benefits need to be explicitly defined.
- A business case document needs to be developed for each strategy.

Tactical Planning

- Each business objective must directly relate to a business strategy.
- Objective accomplishment metrics must be designed to measure a set of parameters that are both necessary and sufficient to determine if the objective was attained.
- Prioritization and selection of business objectives must take into account the enterprise's currently available resources and financial assets.
- Objectives selected for accomplishment must be compatible with the currently available organizational process assets.

Portfolio, Program, and Project Planning

- Portfolio's content must fulfill business objectives.
- Program/project charters and project scope statements need to be used in the project authorization processes.
- Program/project scope statements need to reflect the requirement of the related business objectives.
- Performance metrics set to measure project accomplishment must reflect the defined project deliverables. They must also be compatible with and be a further detailing of the objective accomplishment metrics and related strategic benefits.

SECTION 2

Governance

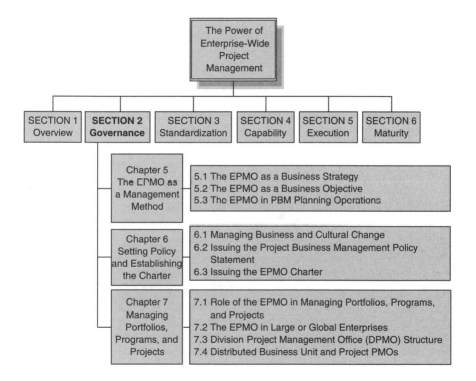

CHAPTER 5

The EPMO as a Management Method

The successful execution of project business management best practices across an enterprise depends on incorporating four related major elements of project business management, the first of which is governance. Governance can be defined as a system or method of management. Organizational governance establishes the roles, responsibilities, and authorities of each position, the rules of conduct, and management protocols. Any management methodology that includes the planning and authorization of projects, programs, and portfolios requires establishing the organizational structures within the enterprise that will institute the planning process and manage the authorization for those portfolios, programs, and projects. This structure, by definition, is an enterprise project management office (EPMO). EPMO organizational governance is employed at different decision-making levels to support implementation of specific strategic initiatives and related business objectives.

5.1 The EPMO as a Business Strategy

It is incumbent on the executives of an enterprise to recognize that portfolio, program, and project management are critical business functions that are necessary to achieve the business strategies.

Embedding project business management as a core competency within an enterprise first requires a business strategy that accepts project management as a business management function. Once accepted, but before embarking on strategically implementing enterprise-wide project management, the enterprise must prepare an organizational business strategy to create the specific organizational structure known as an EPMO at the executive level. The EPMO has the responsibility to instill project management disciplines and manage the processes, procedures, practices, templates, and tools used to apply those disciplines enterprise wide within the organization and to implement project management as a core competency.

The purpose of incorporating project management into the strategic planning of the enterprise's overall operations is to improve the strategic planning processes by adding a project business management perspective. This addition of the EPMO organization to the enterprise can have the following benefits:

- Adding executive level project management planning input into developing business strategies.
- Identifying and implementing the project business management processes applicable to developing the enterprise's business strategies.
- Helping to assure that the business strategies do not conflict with enterprise environmental factors (see Chapter 4) applicable to the organization.
- Helping to assure that any business strategy accomplished by project-related actions and activities will support the enterprise's vision/mission.
- Providing executives with a timely and accurate oversight capability of future portfolios.
- Enabling the maturation of the organization's project business management strategic planning processes.

5.2 The EPMO as a Business Objective

Before the enterprise's management team can effectively prioritize, select, balance, initiate, and authorize portfolios, programs, or projects, business objectives must be defined. The job of the EPMO is to support the definition and successful accomplishment of these business objectives enterprise wide. This task is accomplished by applying project business management practices to the integration of tactical business planning and project management planning activities.

The purpose of incorporating management practices into the enterprise's tactical planning processes is to focus those tactical processes on achieving project-based objectives. This tactical addition of the EPMO organization to the enterprise can have the following benefits:

- Adding executive level project management planning input into developing project-based business objectives.
- Identifying and implementing those project business management processes applicable to defining the enterprise's business objectives.
- Assuring that all project-based business objectives are aligned with and support the business strategies.

- Ensuring that required organizational process assets (see Chapter 4) are available and operational to support all selected project-based business objectives.
- Ascertaining that required resources are available to meet selected project-based business objectives.
- Improving the quality of the project-related portion of the enterprise's budget.
- Providing an integrated enterprise-wide forecast of potential future programs and projects.
- Delineating how tactical business planning integrates with project management planning.
- Enabling the maturation of the organization's project business management tactical planning processes.

5.3 The EPMO in PBM Planning Operations

Before an enterprise can adequately and effective plan, authorize, and charter protfolios, programs, and projects through the project business management planning processes, the organization must create the functional organizational structures that own and provide enterprise-wide project management. The enterprise's management team's greatest organizational asset is an operational enterprise-wide project management office (EPMO) that leads and supports the project business management planning effort.

The purposes of incorporating project business management into the implementation of the enterprise's operations is to ensure that business-based projects are planned, authorized, remain aligned with, and support enterprise business objectives. This addition of the EPMO organization to the enterprise's implementation planning can have the following benefits:

- Adding executive level project management planning input into developing the charter and scope for project-based business objectives.
- Assuring each portfolio, program, and project maintains alignment with related business objectives.
- Developing and establishing project business management as a core competency.
- Providing, with its project management skills, the expertise required for effectively performing detailed planning for projects, programs, and portfolios.
- Providing integrated monitoring and control for projects, programs, and portfolios.

- Owning and maintaining the portfolio, program, and project management processes, procedures, tools, templates, and systems.
- Developing and managing a project management education and training program to ensure that program and project management capabilities are being improved.
- Leveraging limited planning resources to ensure that they are used effectively to achieve major business objectives.
- Identifying and categorizing each business objective into a specific project-based portfolio and/or project-based program.
- Providing a methodology to define the specific scope for each portfolio, program, and project.
- Improving the ability to effectively allocate required resources.
- Establishing the basis for tracking actual versus budgeted costs.
- Improving the capital budget planning processes.
- Providing an enterprise-wide forecast of future projects.
- Facilitating growth of the organization's project business management maturity.

CHAPTER 6

Setting Policy and Establishing the Charter

6.1 Managing Business and Cultural Change

Establishing enterprise-wide project management (EWPM) practices as a mind set improves the communication and cooperation. The value of EWPM is that it focuses the enterprise's resources on the leadership's vision, mission, strategy, and objectives. This focus enables the organization to translate the objectives into executable portfolios, programs, projects, and processes. Establishing EWPM requires successfully making organizational and cultural changes, because it affects every level of the organization from the boardroom to the plant floor.

Implementing EWPM is not easy, but the rewards are significant. The entire organization must recognize and adopt new attitudes that embrace project business management best practices as the normal way of working. The successful adoption of cultural change requires that everyone understand the change being implemented—why is it being done? There are a number of ways for individuals to gain an understanding that will help them to support the changes:

- *Encourage Participation* in implementing the change. This provides a sense of personal ownership.
- *Acknowledge* how the change will improve the organization. What are the benefits for the organization and the individuals?
- *Demonstrate that management has the tenacity* to see change through to successful completion. Implementing an EPMO requires planning and strong management support from start to finish.

Adopting these changes requires the organization to embrace the EPMO:

- *Mission* – explains the degree to which the organization understands why the EPMO exists and what its direction is.

- *Commitment* – spells out the degree to which individuals at all levels of the organization hold that direction as their own and participate in its implementation.
- *Agility* – provides the enterprise with an improved ability to know what customers want, and the degree to which it can respond to external forces and demands.
- *Application* – reinforces the value of consistent utilization of the enterprise's project business management systems and processes that support efficiency and effectiveness in reaching organizational objectives.

Achieving world-class proficiency in managing projects is the target; it is the vision that establishes the organizational ownership required to hit the bulls-eye. World-class proficiency is defined by the organization's customers and the industry in which it practices. Executive management provides the means to demonstrate accountability as part of its leadership responsibilities to the organization as a whole. Accountability is demonstrated in the form of commitment and support of the EPMO's efforts while implementing project business management best practices across the organization. Best practices are defined by the EPMO.

One of the clearest measures of success in achieving a fully distributed application of project business management practices is when the members of the enterprise embrace and use project business management as a practical approach to doing their work. Taking ownership of and embracing new ideas usually does not happen until people experience positive results that are repeatedly proven to be beneficial. It takes time and tenacity to stay the course.

Managers' attitudes can have a positive or negative affect on the working environment. They can create an environment that encourages a positive attitude or not. Actions speak louder than words.

No established approach exists to implementing project business management into the governance structure and culture of an organization. That is not to say that the process itself is not well defined, but rather that the application of the concepts and techniques is different in each environment, especially when the process is guided by experienced professionals . . . the key is *doing it right the first time.* To perform project business management correctly the first time, an enterprise needs to:

- Issue an enterprise policy instituting project business management enterprise-wide.
- Charter the enterprise project management organization (EPMO).

The most important component missing in an enterprise's quest to fully integrate project business management into its business management is the executive's lack of knowledge of and experience with project business management processes and methodologies. This is why executive acceptance of the EPMO value proposition and their ongoing commitment to support the EPMO is the only way to infuse project business management practices into an enterprise's culture.

The EPMO becomes the organization's project management "center of expertise," a core support group of skilled experts who are trained, educated, and experienced in developing and implementing the processes associated with managing projects, programs, and portfolios. This core group can initially provide key project business management support services for strategic mission critical projects, while at the same time mentoring and coaching the business unit project managers by demonstrating the correct application of project business management practices and principles.

A few experienced individuals can provide adequate resources to begin the integration of project management into the enterprise's business processes. The length of time it will take for full integration depends on several variables:

- The organization's project business management maturity level (i.e., general project business management capability across the population).
- Enterprise's size and number of locations.
- Typical portfolio, program, and project sizes and complexities.
- Number of qualified project management staff available or the amount of outsourcing done.

Usually, true acceptance and personal ownership of project management concepts occur only after an individual personally experiences or observes the real value that can be achieved by correctly applying those concepts. This takes time, because cultivating project business management skills is best achieved through personal experience and the best lessons are learned by a successful, repetitive accomplishment of the work.

The governance of the project business management (PBM) processes must be established by institutionalizing and applying PBM policies, plans, and procedures within the enterprise. The first steps in doing this are to issue the Project Management Policy Statement and EPMO Charter.

6.2 Issuing the Project Business Management Policy Statement

The first organizational development action that needs to be taken by senior management is to prepare and formally issue an enterprise level policy statement covering the use of project business management enterprise wide. This policy statement is the format used by the enterprise to issue policies in such areas as human resources, authority levels, quality assurance, procurement, and safety.

The project management policy statement must, as a minimum, cover the following:

- Direct that project business management methodology, principles, and practices will be used throughout the enterprise to manage each and every portfolio, program, and project.
- Establish an enterprise-wide project management functional organization (such as an EPMO) to provide project business management support services to all functional and project organizations.
- Name the executive level position that will head the EPMO.

The policy statement should be no more than one page; two if it is supported by illustrations. The policy needs to be reviewed and agreed to by

Figure: 6-1. Example Project Business Management Policy Statement

PROJECT BUSINESS MANAGEMENT
POLICY STATEMENT

Policy Title:
Application of Project Business Management Methodology and Practices

Policy Statement:
A Project Business Management Methodology developed by and for the <Enterprise Name> shall be applied enterprise-wide in identifying, selecting, initiating, authorizing, planning, managing, monitoring, controlling, executing, and closing of all project-based portfolios and programs, and all stand alone projects.

The <Enterprise Name> shall implement and operate an Enterprise Project Management Office (EPMO) which shall develop and manage the Project Business Management Methodology and practices. The EPMO shall be supervised by the Chief Project Management Officer who shall report to the Chief Executive Officer. The EPMO shall be authorized by, and operated in accordance with, an executive level approved EPMO Charter.

Approved By: _____

               Chief Executive Officer
               (or Chief Operating Officer as appropriated)

Issue Date: _____   *Effective Date:* _____

the executive management team and signed by the CEO of the enterprise. A sample policy statement is shown in Figure 6-1.

6.3   Issuing the EPMO Charter

Establishing an EPMO is a strategic project. As such, the authorization for this project requires a project charter. The charter begins the implementation of the executive direction given in the "Project Business Management Policy Statement." It provides the means to formalize the creation of the EPMO and serves to establish its role, responsibilities, accountability, and requisite authority. It is also the most effective way to communicate to the other functional areas of the organization what the EPMO is all about. The EPMO charter is designed to inform the organization of the purpose for creating the enterprise-wide project management office. It provides the "sizzle" that helps sell the idea to the broader organization. Table 6-1 contains examples of the key elements of an EPMO charter (a complete sample charter is available at www.amacombooks.org/go/EnterpriseWidePM).

The job of creating the EPMO charter belongs to the executive who will own the EPMO. The first important step in establishing the EPMO, after

Table 6-1.   EPMO Charter Key Elements

Element	*Description*
Vision	To create an environment that enables *world-class proficiency* in managing portfolios, programs, and projects enterprise-wide within the enterprise.
Mission	To provide the leadership that will guide the enterprise in performing its portfolios, programs, projects, and services by utilizing *best-in-class* project business management methodologies, tools, templates, and technology.
Strategy	Create an environment within the enterprise that embraces project business management as an *intrinsic enabler* for achieving its business strategies and objectives.
Goals and Objectives	To establish and institutionalize a project business management methodology and practices as the *natural* way to accomplish work and treat the EPMO as a business function to the degree it becomes part of the enterprise's core competency.
Methodology	To establish an internal network to support the EPMO efforts to *distribute* the project business management methodology and practices across the enterprise.

the project business management policy statement is issued, is presenting the EPMO charter to the executive management team to review and formally adopt and to the CEO to approve. These activities must occur before proceeding with the project. Moving ahead without the unanimous support of the executive management team is a risky move that will probably result in failure. Once the management team adopts the EPMO charter, it should be presented to the entire organization as part of the enterprise's communication processes in the EPMO's initiation phase.

CHAPTER 7

Managing Portfolios, Programs, and Projects

Before executive and senior management decide to charter an EPMO, they will want and need to know:

What would the hierarchical structure be for an executive level EPMO functional organization?
What are the roles and responsibilities of the various levels of that organization?
What types of qualified personnel are required to staff each level of the EPMO?
What are the requirements for each position?
What are roles and responsibilities of each position?
What are the authorities of each position?

This chapter answers those key questions and provides the enterprise's executive and senior management with an organizational model for the EPMO that can be customized to meet their business needs and management requirements.

7.1   Role of the EPMO in Managing Portfolios, Programs, and Projects

Figure 7-1 shows the organizational structure of an enterprise project management office (EPMO) that is responsible for developing and implementing project business management as a core competency for the enterprise. The EPMO is located at the highest level of the organization, and its manager reports directly to one of the enterprise's senior executive officers. These officers will have titles such as chief executive officer (CEO), president, or chief operating officer (COO). The EPMO manager should be assigned a title such as "Chief Project Management Officer (CPMO)."

Figure 7-1. Enterprise Project Management Office (EPMO) Organizational Structure

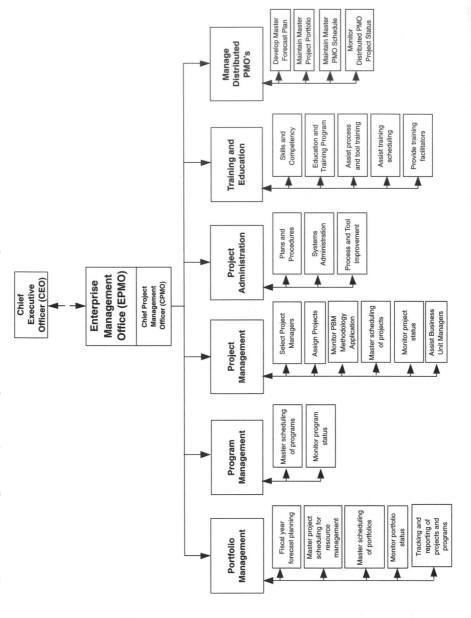

The six primary functions of the EPMO are portfolio management, program management, project management, administration, training and education, and managing distributed project management offices.

Portfolio Management involves:

- Developing and maintaining a prioritized fiscal year forecast plan of portfolios, programs, and projects to meet enterprise business objectives.
- Developing a master schedule of future and current portfolios to help manage resources across all programs and projects.
- Developing and maintaining a master schedule of portfolios planned and in process.
- Monitoring the status of each portfolio on a monthly basis to measure actual performance against performance metrics.
- Tracking and reporting the project status at a portfolio level to the executive management team on a regular basis.
- Monitoring portfolio status on a routine basis to measure performance against objective accomplishment metrics.
- Selecting or recruiting new portfolio managers inside and outside the enterprise.
- Assigning managers to portfolios.

Program Management involves:

- Developing and maintaining a master schedule of programs planned and in process.
- Monitoring program status on a monthly basis to measure performance against performance metrics.
- Tracking and reporting the project status at a program level to the executive management team on a regular basis.
- Monitoring program status on a monthly basis to measure performance against desired benefits.
- Selecting or recruiting new program managers inside and outside the enterprise.
- Assigning managers to programs.

Project Management involves:

- Selecting or recruiting new project managers inside and outside the enterprise.
- Assigning managers to projects.
- Applying project management processes enterprise wide.

- Monitoring the proper application of the project business management methodologies across all projects.
- Developing and maintaining a master schedule of all projects planned and in-process.
- Monitoring project status on a monthly basis to measure performance against project performance metrics.
- Assisting business unit managers with developing and maintaining project schedules and costs through regular status reporting.

Project Administration involves:

- Plans and Procedures: developing plans and procedures governing the management of multisite projects, programs, portfolios, and other issues that affect how project management best practices are applied enterprise wide.
- Systems Administration: Implementing and maintaining a project business management system (PBMS).
- Process and Tool Improvement: planning and managing recommendations for process and tool improvements that are incorporated into the next update release of the project management methodologies.

Training & Education involves:

- Developing and maintaining policies defining program and project management skills and competency level requirements to be applied enterprise wide.
- Developing an education and training program to achieve the skills and knowledge required to meet competency requirements.
- Assisting in project business management process and tool training.
- Assisting Human Resources with scheduling education and training classes and providing facilitators.

Manage Distributed Project Management Offices (PMO) involves:

- Developing and maintaining a master forecast plan for distributed PMOs.
- Developing and maintaining a master budget for distributed PMOs.
- Developing and maintaining a master schedule for distributed PMOs.
- Monitoring distributed PMO project status on a monthly basis to measure performance against project and program performance metrics.

7.2 The EPMO in Large or Global Enterprises

Figure 7-2 illustrates the enterprise project management organization structure that owns and governs the management of portfolios, programs, and projects within the usual three levels of large or global organizations. Table 7-1 defines the various managerial roles and responsibilities of the first two levels of the EPMO organization structure shown in Figure 7-2.

Figure 7-2. EPMO Enterprise Structure Overview

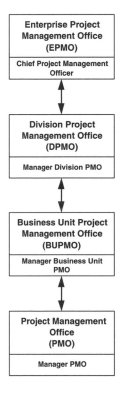

Table 7-1. EPMO Managerial Roles and Responsibilities

Chief Project Management Officer (CPMO) of EPMO: The EPMO head is an executive officer located at the enterprise's headquarters who provides leadership, supervises and manages the EPMO, and reports to the chief executive officer or chief operating officer.

Experience/Education	*Responsibilities*
3 yrs + PM, 15 Yrs. + Industry, MS or MBA	• Direct the preparation and maintenance of policies and procedures that govern organizational relationships, roles and responsibilities.

(continued)

Table 7-1.   *(Continued)*

- Oversee and facilitate executive annual planning of enterprise business strategies and business objectives.
- Oversee and facilitate enterprise portfolio planning.
- Align enterprise-wide portfolios, programs, and projects with prioritized and selected business objectives.
- Oversee the development, adherence, and maintenance of the enterprise portfolio, program and project business management methodology and processes.
- Direct and oversee the development of the summary level of the overall enterprise work breakdown structure.
- Direct the preparation and maintenance of the enterprise-wide master schedule.
- Direct the preparation of the monthly status reports on portfolios, programs, and projects.
- Direct the preparation and maintenance of the definitions of division level program and project management roles and responsibilities.
- Provide governance and direct the development and implementation of the project business management education and training programs at the enterprise level.
- Be the point of control for implementing and changing project tools, such as the enterprise-wide PBMS or procurement system

Manager of Divisional PMO Office (DPMO): The DPMO head is a senior manager located at a division or regional office, or a portfolio manager, who provides leadership of and supervises and manages the Divisional PMO.

Experience/Education	*Responsibilities*
3 yrs + PM, 10 Yrs. + Industry, MS or MBA	• Oversee and facilitate executive annual planning of division-level business strategies and business objectives. • Oversee and facilitate division-level portfolio planning. • Align division-level portfolios, programs, and projects with prioritized and selected enterprise business objectives. • Oversee the adherence of the enterprise portfolio, program and project business management methodology and processes and methodologies. • Direct and manage division level portfolio, program, and project managers. • Direct and oversee the development of the portfolio level of the enterprise work breakdown structure. • Direct the preparation and maintenance of the division-level master schedule. • Direct the preparation of the monthly status reports on portfolios, programs, and projects for the EPMO. • Oversee development and implementation of portfolio, program, and project management education and training programs at the division level.

7.3 Division Project Management Office (DPMO) Structure

Figure 7-3 shows the organizational structure of a division (or regional or portfolio) project management office (DPMO) that is responsible for developing and implementing project business management best practices as core competencies enterprise wide within a division, region, or major facility—or for a single portfolio. The DPMO is managed by a senior manager who reports directly to the Chief Project Management Officer or to the division general manager. If the DPMO reports to the division general manager, then it has an indirect reporting interface to the enterprise project management office on matters relating to portfolio, program, and project management.

Figure 7-3.   Division Project Management Office (DPMO) Structure

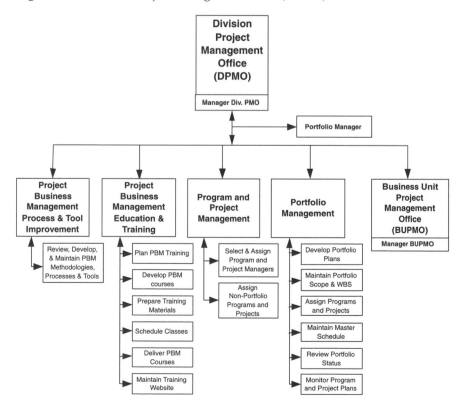

The five primary responsibilties of a DPMO are project business management process and tool improvement, project business management education and training, portfolio/program management, overseeing business unit PMOs, and overseeing program PMOs. A program management office supports an individual major program and the program manager and program management team. Table 7-2 defines the various managerial roles and responsibilities of the third level of the EPMO organization structure shown in Figure 7-2, as well as the portfolio and program managers.

Table 7-2.   BUPMO and Portfolio Managerial Roles and Responsibilities

Manager of Business Unit PMO Office (BUPMO): The BUPMO manager is a senior or midlevel manager located in a business unit office that provides leadership of and supervises and manages the BUPMO.

Experience/Education	*Responsibilities*
3-5 yrs + PM, 5-7 Yrs. + Industry, BS, PMI-PMP	• Assist executive management in the development of business plans, and business cases for programs.
	• Understand the applicable enterprise environmental factors and organizational process assets applicable to the program.
	• Support, and participate in negotiations with potential customers.
	• Provide leadership and supervision of the PMO staff.
	• Facilitate a forum for regular communications between all project managers.
	• Provide project management expert assistance as a mentor or coach. Participate in internal project management training as needed.
	• Apply the enterprise project business management methodology (PBMM) and processes to the program.
	• Validate that program aligns with portfolio or business objectives.
	• Manage major program and project scope changes and view them as potential opportunities to better achieve business objectives.
	• Manage the authorization of projects within the program.
	• Direct and manage project managers.
	• Direct and oversee the development of the program level of the enterprise work breakdown structure.
	• Ensure all projects are planned in accordance with the PBMM process.
	• Tie each project and subproject to the program business objectives.

(continued)

Table 7-2. (*Continued*)

- Define and approve the business plan budget for the program and related projects.
- Acquire funding approval from program sponsor.
- Oversee the coordinated planning, prioritization, and execution of the projects.
- Manage risks (threats and opportunities) and all program interdependencies.
- Review all in-process projects at least monthly to assess their risk, cost and schedule impacts, continued value, and priority for resource allocation.
- Manage program and project scope changes and schedule changes to better achieve program business objectives.
- Optimize, as necessary, shared project personnel, suppliers, and dedicated program personnel across the program.
- Minimize the funds and time needed to achieve the defined program business objectives.
- Approve supplier invoices for work on the program.
- Deliver specific program business objectives and benefits within the constraints set for the program.
- Recommend projects for closure or termination by the portfolio manager or other executive manager.
- Submit program updates for maintaining master schedule for business unit.
- Prepare monthly business unit program status reports and provide reports to the business unit manager and the DPMO.
- Review and approve project schedule and report status.

Portfolio Manager: The portfolio manager (who may also be the head of a major business unit or division) is responsible for overall management of all programs and projects within the portfolio and for focusing on the portfolio-specified objectives. This manager demonstrates leadership and management skills, is a member of the EPMO, and reports to either a BUPMO or a DPMO, as appropriate. In smaller enterprises, the roles of executive management and portfolio management may be within the same area of responsibility.

Experience/Education	*Responsibilities*
10-12 yrs + PM, 5 Yrs. + Industry, BS	• Assist executive management in the development of strategic business plans, sales strategies, and business cases for portfolios. • Identify and select potential programs and projects on the basis of business criteria such as strategic business alignment, organizational impact, cost/benefit results, risk/reward categories, regulatory priority, and cost containment opportunities.

(*continued*)

Table 7-2. *(Continued)*

- Understand the applicable enterprise environmental factors and organizational process assets applicable to the portfolio.
- Tie each program and project to the overall portfolio business objectives.
- Address specific portfolio business mandates that include an enterprise-wide perspective.
- Manage overall risk, overall opportunity, and overall portfolio work priorities and interdependencies.
- Define and approve the business plan budget for the portfolio.
- Acquire funding approval from portfolio sponsor.
- Balance the programs and projects among incremental or radical investments.
- Manage the overall business plan budget for the portfolio.
- Initiate and terminate (close) projects and programs.
- Initiate and authorize programs and projects within portfolio to balance overall enterprise risks and meet budget or funding targets.
- Ensure centralized management of the portfolio's programs and projects.
- Oversee the coordinated prioritization and execution of the projects and projects across the portfolio.
- Optimize, as necessary, shared program personnel, suppliers, and dedicated project personnel across the portfolio.
- Optimize the enterprise's return on investment or minimize the funds needed by the programs and projects to achieve a broader set of defined strategic business objectives.
- Develop and maintain the specific portfolio work breakdown structure portion of the enterprise work breakdown structure.
- Manage major program and project scope changes and schedule changes as potential opportunities to better achieve business objectives.
- Ensure the review of all in-process programs and projects at various stages of their life cycle to assess their risk, continued value, and priority for resource and funds allocation.
- Manage overall risk (overall threats and opportunities) and all portfolio-level interdependencies.
- Close completed projects or programs and terminate projects or programs to keep the business objectives consistent.
- Provide central monitoring of all portfolio, program and project timelines and budgets, usually at the portfolio enterprise level.

7.4   Distributed Business Unit and Project PMOs

Figure 7-4 shows a typical organizational structure for a business unit project management office (BUPMO). This office is responsible for developing and implementing the project business management core competencies for a major business unit within a specific division or region, which manages a significant number of programs and projects. Some BUPMOs may also function as a program PMO for large programs. The manager of the business unit PMO reports directly to either the DPMO or the business unit manager. If the BUPMO reports to the business unit manager, then it has an indirect reporting interface to the senior manager of the division project management office on matters relating to program and project management.

Business units within an organization, if they are small, may be provided the services and support of a BUPMO by the division project management office (DPMO), rather than establishing a separate BUPMO; however, in all cases, some form of the DPMO/BUPMO must be established at all divisions, regions, or major facilities.

If projects are significant enough to the enterprise, then a project management office (a project PMO, see Figure 7-4) can be established and either managed by the project manager or by a separate PMO manager. The example PMO staff shown in Figure 7-4 can be for a project PMO or for a BUPMO. The level of effort of PMO support personnel will vary from program to program or project to project based on the technical complexity of the programs and project and where the program or project is within its life cycle. In general, the PMO level of effort over time will be higher during the planning phase, will have a few peak days during the routine status cycle, and will have some basic ongoing effort. To be effective, PMO personnel need to be familiar with the business units that are the performing organizations and the program and projects being managed. PMO personnel need to be, from time to time, where the actual project work is being performed to view the progress of the work and provide an independent project progress assessment.

As indicated in Figures 7-3 and 7-4, there may be a combination of Business Unit PMOs (BUPMO) and Project PMOs below the Division PMO (DPMO). If a division or portfolio has a few large projects and no programs, then there could be a set of project PMOs and no Business Unit PMO.

Where can the BUPMO fit into the enterprise organization chart?

The BUPMO can fit into almost any organization structure. However, the strong matrix organization structure provides the best environment. There are two important elements that are significant factors affecting the

Figure 7-4. Typical Business Unit PMO or Project PMO Organizational Structure. Note that not all of these functional roles are found in every BUPMO or PMO. They are shown as examples only. The size of a BUPMO or PMO staff is usually determined by the number of concurrent projects and the workload capability of the staff.

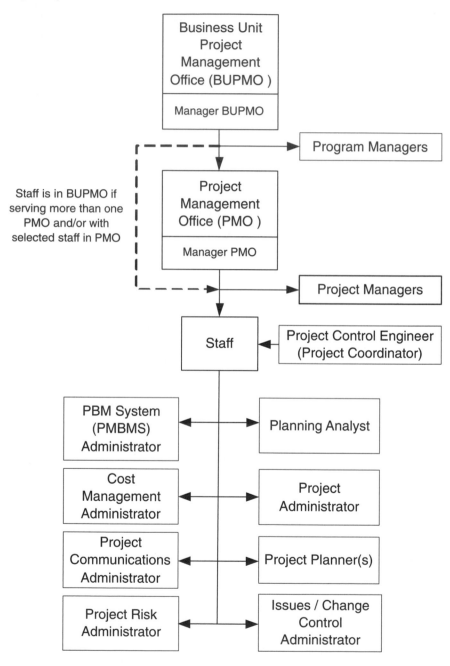

role of the project manager and the project manager's relationship to the business unit PMO or the project PMO.

1. In many companies, project managers are not assigned as part of the BUPMO or PMO staffs, but continue to report to a functional manager. This direct reporting relationship can remain intact in this configuration, because of the project manager's technical subject matter expertise. The project manager's project-related activities, however, are directed and supervised by the BUPMO manager.

2. The interface between some projects and the BUPMO is coordinated by a PMO Project Coordinator staff position, such as a Project Control Engineer, whose primary job is to provide project management skills expertise. This is achieved by mentoring and coaching the business unit project managers and project team members. The project coordinator acts as the primary liaison between the project team and the BUPMO and coordinates communications between the two groups. This position usually exists when the project managers are not in the BUPMO/PMO and report directly to business unit managers.

It might be argued that in a true project-oriented matrix organization the project managers would report only to the BUPMO manager or manage a PMO reporting to the BUPMO. This is based on a concern for the loss of political autonomy that insulates the project manager from undue influences from a business unit functional group that may wish to compromise decisions or disposition actions. This concern has some legitimacy. However, greater political benefits can be gained by having the project manager remain in his/her functional organization, where his/her sphere of influence and knowledge are the greatest. We suggest that this arrangement is the best initial approach, especially in the early stages of implementing enterprise-wide project management and the EPMO organization. This position will reduce or eliminate a business unit manager's resistance for establishing the EPMO.

This scenario for locating project managers in the organization also eliminates a major element of the change process that probably has the greatest impact on most workers—that of changing bosses. More importantly, the distribution of project management knowledge, skills, and experience is the main objective and moving the project managers under new organizational leadership will not in and of itself ensure that specific business objective will be met. Neither will a corporate-wide education and training program on its own achieve the objectives. It may make sense to move the project managers under the direct supervision of the BUPMO manager after operating for a period of one to two years.

You may not have yet deployed a BUPMO or PMO or started implementing project business management processes and methodologies in your business unit. If so, you may be interested in how a typical BUPMO might be organized and staffed. To assist you, Table 7-3 provides the roles and responsibilities for the staff positions shown in the model given in Figure 7-4. The roles and responsibilities of PMO staffs will vary from one organization to the next and the number of staff may also change as the organization matures in its competence for managing projects.

Table 7-3.   BUPMO and PMO Staff Roles and Responsibilities

Program Manager: The program manager is responsible for overall management of a program and its related projects and for focusing on the delivery of program-specified objectives and benefits. The program manager is a member of the EPMO and can report to a portfolio manager, a BUPMO manager, or a business unit manager as appropriate, or may also be a BUPMO manager.

Experience/Education	*Responsibilities*
3-5 yrs + PM, 5-7 Yrs. + Industry, BS, PMI-PMP	• Assist executive management in the development of business plans and business cases for programs. • Understand the applicable enterprise environmental factors and organizational process assets applicable to the program. • Support, and participate in negotiations with potential customers. • Provide leadership and supervision of the program staff. • Facilitate a forum for regular communications between all project managers. • Provide project management expert assistance as a mentor or coach. Participate in internal project management training as needed. • Apply the enterprise project business management methodology (PBMM) and processes to the program. • Validate that program aligns with portfolio or business objectives. • Manage major program and project scope changes and view them as potential opportunities to better achieve business objectives. • Manage the authorization of projects within the program. • Direct and manage project managers. • Ensure all projects are planned in accordance with the PBMM process. • Tie each project and subproject to the program business objectives. • Define and approve the business plan budget for the program and related projects.

(continued)

Table 7-3.   (*Continued*)

- Acquire funding approval from program sponsor.
- Oversee the coordinated planning, prioritization, and execution of the projects.
- Manage risks (threats and opportunities) and all program interdependencies.
- Review all in-process projects at least monthly to assess their risk, cost and schedule impacts, continued value, and priority for resource allocation.
- Develop and maintain the specific program work breakdown structure portion of the enterprise work breakdown structure.
- Manage program and project scope changes and schedule changes to better achieve program business objectives.
- Optimize, as necessary, shared project personnel, suppliers, and dedicated program personnel across the program.
- Minimize the funds and time needed to achieve the defined program business objectives.
- Approve supplier invoices for work on the program.
- Deliver specific program business objectives and benefits within the constraints set for the program.
- Recommend projects for closure or termination by the portfolio manager or other executive management.
- Submit program updates for maintaining master schedule for business unit.
- Prepare monthly program status reports and provide reports to the business unit manager and the DPMO.
- Review and approve program schedule and report status.

Manager PMO: The PMO manager is a senior or midlevel manager located in a business unit office that provides leadership of and supervises and manages the PMO. The PMO manager reports to the BUPMO manager or, if there is not a BUPMO, to the Division PMO manager.

Experience/Education	*Responsibilities*
3-5 yrs + PM, 3-5 Yrs. + Industry, BS, PMI-PMP	- Assist BUPMO manager in the development of business plans and business cases for projects. - Understand the applicable enterprise environmental factors and organizational process assets applicable to the project. - Support, and participate in negotiations with potential customers. - Provide leadership and supervision of the PMO staff. - Facilitate a forum for regular communications among all project team members. - Provide project management expert assistance as a mentor or coach. Participate in internal project management training as needed.

Table 7-3.   (*Continued*)

- Apply the enterprise project business management methodology (PBMM) and processes to the project.
- Manage major project scope changes and view them as potential opportunities to better achieve business objectives.
- Manage the authorization of subprojects.
- Direct and manage project managers, PMO staff, and project team members.
- Direct and oversee the development of the project level of the enterprise work breakdown structure.
- Ensure project is planned in accordance with the PBMM process.
- Tie the project and each subproject to the program business objectives.
- Define and approve the business plan budget for the project.
- Acquire funding approval from program manager or project sponsor if stand alone project.
- Oversee the coordinated planning, prioritization, and execution of the project.
- Manage risks (threats and opportunities) and all project interdependencies.
- Review all in-process project components at least monthly to assess their risk, cost and schedule impacts, continued value, and priority for resource allocation.
- Manage project scope changes and schedule changes to better achieve program business objectives.
- Optimize, as necessary, shared project personnel, suppliers, and dedicated project personnel across the project's components.
- Minimize the funds and time needed to achieve the defined project deliverables.
- Approve supplier invoices for work on the project.
- Produce specific project deliverables within the constraints set for the project.
- Recommend project for closure or termination by the BUPMO manager or other executive management.
- Review and approve project schedule development and report status.
- Submit project updates for maintaining master schedule for business unit.
- Prepare monthly business unit project status reports and provide reports to the business unit manager and the BUPMO.

(*continued*)

Table 7-3. *(Continued)*

Project Manager: The project manager is responsible for managing a single project and focusing on the specified business objective and deliverables for that project. Whether an employee of the enterprise or a supplier, the manager is responsible for accomplishing on schedule and within budget a designated unit of work, which is funded as part of the project.

Experience/Education	*Responsibilities*
3-5 yrs + PM, 3 Yrs. + Industry, BS, PMI-PMP	• Plan, execute (manage and direct), and control (implement corrective actions) project work. • Create project staffing plan, select and obtain project team members. • Obtain/define with customer the project constraints and deliverables. • Develop project scope statement. • Guide development of project baseline plans and monitor schedule performance. • Facilitate project schedule progress review meetings. • Develop project budgets and monitor expenditures. • Develop a project risk plan and monitor risks. • Develop and monitor on-going application of the project communications plan. • Guide and monitor project team activities. • Monitor project issues resolution and change control requests. • Develop the plan for performance of the project work using the PBMM processes. • Balance the competing demands for scope, time, budget, quality, and special requirements. • Apply selected knowledge, skills, disciplines, methodologies, tools, and techniques to planned project activities to produce desired results. • Manage and direct assigned project resources to best meet the project business objectives. • Develop and maintain the specific project work breakdown structure portion of the enterprise work breakdown structure. • Direct and oversee the development of supplier contract work breakdown structures. • Oversee the management of the work packages and schedule activities. • Approve supplier invoices for work on their project. • Routinely and at least monthly report on schedule status, percent physical work completed, and either estimate-to-complete or estimate-at-completion for all project work in-process.

(continued)

Table 7-3.   (*Continued*)

• Deliver specific project business objectives and deliverables within the constraints set by portfolio or program management.
• Document project success for inclusion in project closure documentation.

Project Control Engineer: The project control engineer (PCE) is either a business unit person or a person provided by a supplier and is an experienced professional with technical expertise in applying the project business management methodology and operating the project business management system (PBMS) (Chapter 15). The PCG must be capable of completing complicated tasks independently. The PCE position is common in the architectural, engineering, and construction industries and can also be a project coordinator role in other application areas. The PCE reports to a BUPMO manager, PMO manager, portfolio manager, program manager, or project manager, as applicable.

Experience/Education	*Responsibilities*
3-5 yrs + PM, 3 Yrs. + Industry, BS, PMI-PMP	• Assist business unit managers, program managers, and project managers in the successful implementation, monitoring, control, and execution of projects.
	• Provide the planning, progress, and status information for all projects on a program to the program manager and associated project managers.
	• Provide project control support and assistance to the program and project managers.
	• Support the uniform application and implementation of the project business management methodology (PBMM) in planning program and project work.
	• Support program and project business plan budget development and reporting.
	• Establish and administer a planning and budgetary process that ensures cost flow control on both annual and multiyear bases.
	• Prepare supplier invoices for project work for approval by affected project managers and program managers.
	• Provide the integration, manipulation, and analysis of the requisite project control information needed to allow project management to make project decisions and effectively control the ongoing project work.
	• Measure and monitor the project execution so that corrective actions can be taken when required to ensure the project work is performed in accordance with the established project management plan.
	• Provide the annual, monthly, and weekly performance reporting of budget, schedule, actual cost, accrued costs, progress status, and earned value parameter data to the program manager and project managers.

(*continued*)

Table 7-3.   (*Continued*)

• Tailor PBMS reporting capabilities to meet specific project requirements.
• Accumulate and access historical data such as performance experience, for use in maintaining a realistic basis for future planning and forecasting.
• Interface with suppliers and enterprise subcontractors.
• Attend regular project management and project controls status meetings and give statistical reports.
• Provide guidance, direction, and specialized assistance for the resolution of difficult project control problems.
• Develop and maintain critical path logic networks and bar charts utilizing the PBMS schedule processor.
• Acts as the primary interface with enterprise and supplier accounting for actual and accrued costs.
• Analyze, evaluate, and forecast current status against an established baseline budget and schedule.
• Utilize earned value analysis.
• Assess the impact(s) of scope changes and schedule slippages.
• Report cost and schedule status to appropriate project managers and program manager and recommend corrective action if required.
• Monitor and report on performance relative to the cost effective and timely achievement of strategic, operational, and regulatory requirements.
• Operate as a project business management system (PBMS) administrator.
• Implement PBMS change management for the program and related projects to maintain fiscal year and total budgets to current status.
• Utilize the PBMS to document budgets, capture actual costs, analyze trends, forecast estimates at completion and schedule the project activities.

Planning Analyst: An individual who provides trend and variance analysis of program and project schedules, as well as recommendations for corrections and preventive actions to eliminate or reduce cost and schedule variances. Reports to a BUPMO manager or a PMO manager and indirectly to program and project managers.

Experience/Experience	*Responsibilities*
3 yrs PM,	• Assist with project business management training development.
3 yrs. + Industry,	• Utilize project business management process design.
BS/MS, PMI-PMP	• Assist in resource management.
	• Assist in the development of complex project EWBSs.
	• Conduct complex project assessments.
	• Utilize earned value analysis.

(*continued*)

Table 7-3.   *(Continued)*

- Assist in developing team leadership skills.
- Utilize proposal development skills.
- Assist project administrators in project start-up plan implementation.
- Assist in identification and development of risk management plans.
- Assist in preparation and participate in project audit reviews.
- Assist in creation of work breakdown structures & WBS dictionaries.
- Assist the project administrator in developing the project schedule.
- Monitor the mapping of all project deliverables in project scope to the project baseline schedule.
- Assist project team leaders in the development of project baseline schedules.
- Assist the project manager in developing a project communications plan.
- Monitor project schedule progress and update communications between PMO project planner(s) and the various project functional groups.
- Assist project managers with documentation of project successes for inclusion into a close-down announcement and success story.

PBM System (PBMS) Administrator: Provides the latest industry direction on project management software applications. Provides daily supervision of the project business management system for the PMO and reports to a BUPMO manager or a PMO manager.

Experience/Education	Responsibilities
3 yrs + PM, 3-5 Yrs. + Industry, BS, PMI-CAPM	• Act as the PMO project business management system (PBMS) subject matter expert. • Oversee the application of information systems technology for the PMO and its use on all projects. • Manage the preparation of system documentation and maintenance. • Establish the methods to be used for project communications. • Document project business management processes. • Coordinate periodic documentation revisions and releases. • Create and maintain the electronic and hard copy versions of the project information for each project. • Oversee periodic back-up and archiving of the project information files for each project.

(continued)

Table 7-3.   (*Continued*)

Project Administrator: An individual who provides clerical support for developing and maintaining program and project records, reports, presentations, meeting minutes, travel arrangements, and coordination the BUPMO manager's daily schedule, and reports to a BUPMO manager or a PMO manager.

Experience/Education	*Responsibilities*
1-3 yrs. PM, 1 yr. Industry, Associates or BS, PMI-CAPM	• Provide administrative services to the PMO manager and staff. • Develop and maintain phone and distribution lists. • Prepare travel itinerary and make all arrangements. • Maintain office supplies. • Assist with scheduling meeting arrangements. • Assist with distribution of project information.

Cost Management Administrator: An individual who provides assistance to the BUPMO and PMO Managers in the development of business unit budgets, as well as in analyzing earned value cost variances for programs and projects. Reports to a BUPMO Manager or PMO Manager.

Experience/Education	*Responsibilities*
3 yrs + PM, 3-5 Yrs. + Industry, BS, PMI-PMP	• Act as the risk management subject matter expert. • Provides latest industry direction on project cost management. • Utilize *PMBOK® Guide* for cost management guidance. • Employ project cost management involving multiple projects. • Employ earned value implementation. • Participation in corporate focus groups. • Provide cost performance reports to management. • Establish cost standards and procedures. • Document all estimating and cost assumptions. • Monitor project spending to the project baseline budget.

Project Planner: An individual who provides expert assistance to program and project teams in the development of schedules and estimates. Works with cost management administrator and business unit estimators in the development of cost estimates and schedules. Reports to a BUPMO Manager or a PMO Manager.

Experience/Education	*Responsibilities*
3 yrs. PM, 1 yr. Industry, Associates or BS, PMI-CAPM	• Employ computing hardware and scheduling software systems. • Perform graphic generation. • Prepare status review presentations. • Receive weekly progress update information from the project administrator. • Coordinate and communicate schedule status. • Update, produce, and distribute schedules and reports.

(*continued*)

Table 7-3.   (*Continued*)

Project Communications Administrator: An individual who develops and manages the knowledge database for the PMO and coordinates updates to the enterprise knowledge database on a periodic basis. Assists program and project managers with the development of their program/project communications plans. Assists the BUPMO Manager with preparation and distribution of periodic status reports to the DPMO. Reports to the BUPMO Manager.

Experience/Education	*Responsibilities*
3 yrs. PM, 1 + yrs. Industry, BS/BA, PMI-CAPM	• Develop PMO communication plans with support from project managers. • Determine all audiences requiring PMO project communications. • Determine message strategies and modes of communication for delivery of project communications. • Interface with external organizations as required to deliver project communications. • Ensure timely communications of all project accomplishments such as major implementation milestones. • Develop and maintain a PMO project visibility area.

Issues/Change Control Administrator: An individual who develops and maintains the issue /problem reporting database for all programs and projects. Monitors activities and progress of issue and problem resolution, maintains change control log, and provides status reports to the program and project managers on a regular basis.

Experience/Education	*Responsibilities*
3 yrs. PM, 1 + yrs. Industry, BS	• Establish and maintain the PMO issues/change control system with a common PBMS repository database for all projects. • Establish issues/change control standards and procedures. • Produce and distribute project open issues reports. • Facilitate issues/change control review meetings, keep minutes and update PBMS database.

Project Risk Administrator: An individual who develops and maintains the risk management processes and provides training support for the business unit. Analyzes program and project risk management response plans and coordinates the implementation of risk mitigation activities for all programs and projects in the business unit. Reports to a BUPMO Manager or a PMO Manager.

Experience/Education	*Responsibilities*
3-5 yrs + PM, 3 Yrs. + Industry, BS, PMI-PMP	• Assist the project team through the risk planning process. • Monitor schedule variances and change requests. • Identify impacts to the quantified risks. • Act as the risk management subject matter expert.

SECTION 3

Standardization

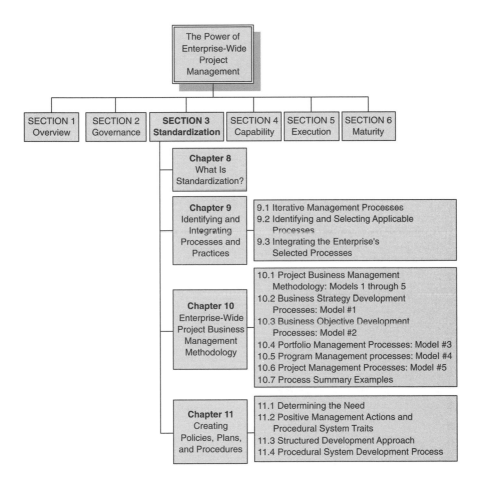

The Power of Enterprise-Wide Project Management

| SECTION 1 Overview | SECTION 2 Governance | **SECTION 3 Standardization** | SECTION 4 Capability | SECTION 5 Execution | SECTION 6 Maturity |

Chapter 8
What Is Standardization?

Chapter 9
Identifying and Integrating Processes and Practices

9.1 Iterative Management Processes
9.2 Identifying and Selecting Applicable Processes
9.3 Integrating the Enterprise's Selected Processes

Chapter 10
Enterprise-Wide Project Business Management Methodology

10.1 Project Business Management Methodology: Models 1 through 5
10.2 Business Strategy Development Processes: Model #1
10.3 Business Objective Development Processes: Model #2
10.4 Portfolio Management Processes: Model #3
10.5 Program Management processes: Model #4
10.6 Project Management Processes: Model #5
10.7 Process Summary Examples

Chapter 11
Creating Policies, Plans, and Procedures

11.1 Determining the Need
11.2 Positive Management Actions and Procedural System Traits
11.3 Structured Development Approach
11.4 Procedural System Development Process

CHAPTER 8

What Is Standardization?

Successfully developing and executing project business management best practices across an enterprise depends on integrating four related elements of project business management, the second of which is standardization. Standardization means establishing a project business management methodology (PBMM) model composed of a set of defined and integrated project management and business management processes. These processes are aligned with the development processes of the enterprise's products and services and are supported by associated written procedures.

Standardization includes the activities required to develop:

- Project business management governance policies.
- Business management policies, processes, and procedures.
- Strategic business management policies, processes, and procedures.
- Tactical business management policies, processes, and procedures.
- Portfolio management policies, processes, and procedures.
- Program management policies, processes, and procedures.
- Project management processes and procedures.
- Business and project management plans, systems, tools, and templates that support the project business management processes, including:
  - Project Business Management System (PBMS) (decribed in Section 4).
  - Project Business Management Information System (PBMIS) (described in Section 4).

Standardization requires the formal issuance, acceptance, and implementation of policies, processes, systems, plans, and procedures that are used consistently across the enterprise to authorize and manage all portfolios, programs, and projects. To have formally authorized and issued policies, plans, and procedures in project business management is not different from having them for the practice areas and functional organizations of accounting, human resources, or safety. Standardization is the best way to effectively spread the competencies and skills of project business management throughout an enterprise to achieve maximum benefit.

What purposes are served and what benefits are derived from standardizing the project business management processes?

Incorporating project management into the enterprise's overall business operations process serves two purposes:

- The business purpose is to have standard process models, methods, and techniques that can be applied to all portfolios, programs, and projects.
- The enterprise-wide project management vision purpose is to achieve a world-class proficiency in the consistent application of well-defined project business management practices, processes, procedures, tools, and techniques.

The goal is to support inculcating project business management as a core capability and discipline that is part of the fabric of the enterprise's work. From an enterprise business perspective, standardized processes offer the following benefits:

- Improving efficiency and shortening the learning curve for new portfolio, program, and project managers.
- Supporting schedule improvement and cost reductions.
- Enhancing planning and management skills.
- Enabling consistent tracking of actual versus planned schedule and cost.
- Facilitating regular management reviews of status.
- Aiding in maturing the organization's project business management methods.
- Improving the effectiveness and capability of the enterprise to manage portfolios, programs, and projects.
- Providing standardized management models and tools that support profitability and business growth.
- Improving the ability to achieve strategic business objectives and obtain the related benefits.
- Improving operational business processes.
- Providing standardized material supporting project management career path development.

Experiencing the benefits that can be derived from a standardized project business management methodology requires that it become integrated into the operations of the business. The actual benefits are directly related to the extent that the project business management processes are considered a natural and regular part of the work culture and day-to-day business processes.

How much implementation effort will be required?

An effective enterprise-wide implementation of a standardized project business management (PBM) methodology model will require greater effort and will encounter greater resistance in organizations that have a low level of PBM maturity. Regardless of the extent of the role PBM will play within the organization, it will change the way work is currently managed. Change of any kind is usually met with some level of resistance, and PBM is no different. However, the amount of resistance is in proportion to how much people are kept informed about and involved in the development and implementation of the standardized processes. Implementing just the technological improvements related to standardized project business management is a relatively easy task; forging the cultural changes that affect the way business is done is far more challenging.

Our experience has shown that the development and documentation of a project business management methodology (PBMM) can usually be accomplished in three-to-six months, whereas the successful integration of project management processes into the business processes can require from one to three years. It is important to note, however, that many improvements can be realized almost immediately.

Project, program, and portfolio management concepts and techniques taken one at a time are not particularly complicated. What is challenging is their effective implementation and integration into business processes. The functions and elements of a project business management methodology are intended to be the foundation of an enterprise's project business management solution, which becomes documented as processes and procedures. These processes and procedures, when developed, address the specific requirements of the enterprise that are the result of variations in product, organizational structure, maturity, and organizational culture.

CHAPTER 9

Identifying and Integrating Processes and Practices

9.1 Iterative Management Processes

The enterprise should develop and issue an integrated model methodology for portfolio, program, and project management. This model should describe all the processes applicable to the enterprise's overall project business management operations. The overall methodology develops the "big picture" and establishes the extent to which portfolio, program, and project management practices will be integrated into the business operations. This standardization requires the formal issuance, acceptance, and implementation of policies, processes, systems, plans, and procedures that are to be used consistently across the enterprise to authorize and manage all portfolios, programs, and projects. Integrating the various disparate processes listed in Chapter 8 so they work together is only slightly less challenging for management than integrating personnel from different cultures into an effective team.

The work to complete a portfolio, program, or project is accomplished by progressing through a series of basic interrelated project business management processes. Those processes are initiating, planning, executing, monitoring, analyzing, reporting, controlling, replanning, and closing. Managing changes to a portfolio, program, or project requires a repetition of planning, executing, monitoring, analyzing, reporting, and controlling processes, because execution actions usually involve making changes that require replanning. This results in modified execution of the work. Figure 9-1 illustrates this iterative PBM processes wheel.

The simpler and more commonly portrayed plan-do-act version of this process wheel is applicable to all human endeavors that require forethought and planning. Similarly, this more detailed set of processes is applicable to accomplishing any project-based endeavor beginning with managing a strategic initiative down through its smallest supporting project.

Figure 9-1. Iterative PBM Processes Wheel

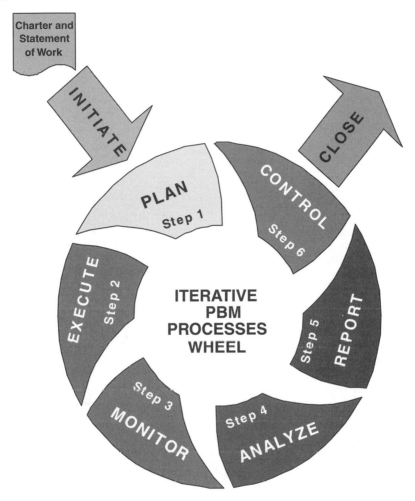

9.2 Identifying and Selecting Applicable Processes

It is incumbent on a fledgling enterprise project management office (EPMO), working with the enterprise's management team, to identify and select a set of processes that will form the basis for the organization's project business management operations. The EPMO's first step in this activity is to determine what current business processes of the organization will also be used as part of the future project business management operations. This requires the following evaluation:

- Identification of the current business processes associated with strategic, tactical, and objective planning and execution.
- Review of current procedures documentation or preparation of a rough draft procedure for those identified business processes.
- Extraction of a list of the scopes of responsibility and operational activities for the business processes.
- Preparation of flowcharts of the major steps required to complete the identified business processes.
- Determination of the functional responsibility assigned to complete each step of the business processes.
- Construction of a hierarchical diagram of the management functions owning the identified business processes.

The EPMO's second step is to determine what project related processes should be included in establishing the enterprise's new project business management methodology. Less than ten years ago this activity could have been fairly difficult. The general management discipline did not recognize the documented definitions of project management processes, which are now generally considered good practices, because they were not acknowledged as common practices among the practitioners in general business management.

However, today the discipline of project management has taken its place within the set of defined disciplines that make up general business management. Many current books and standards identify and document project management processes that are both necessary and sufficient to support the enterprise's future project business management methodology. The standards promulgated by the Project Management Institute (PMI®) are good examples of the body of knowledge that is available:

- A Standard for Portfolio Management.
- A Standard for Program Management.
- A Guide to the Project Management Body of Knowledge (*PMBOK® Guide*).
- Construction Extension to a Guide to the Project Management Body of Knowledge (2000).
- Government Extension to A Guide to the Project Management Body of Knowledge (2000).
- Organizational Project Management Maturity Model (OPM3).
- Practice Standard for Earned Value Management.

- Practice Standard for Work Breakdown Structures.
- Project Manager Competency Development (PMCD) Framework.

These standards, in addition to other documentation issued by other professional organizations outside of the United States, including business case studies related to establishing an enterprise-wide project business management operation, can be used by the EPMO to:

- Identify what business processes could be used.
- Determine what project-related processes could be used.
- Assist the management team in deciding which of the identified business and project-related processes are to be used.
- Document the scope and operational content of the selected processes.
- Prepare flowcharts of the major steps required to complete the selected processes.
- Determine the responsibility for each major step within the processes.
- Build a hierarchy of the management actions associated with the processes.

The processes promulgated in the PMI® standards are meant to be generally recognized good practices that are applicable to managing most projects, programs, and portfolios most of the time. The standards imply that the application of those processes have been shown to enhance the potential for success over a broad range of projects, programs, and port folios. However, the enterprise's management team and the EPMO must still determine what processes are appropriate and the extent to which each process will be applied.

Standards are a "what to do" and not a "how to do." Therefore, the enterprise must implement the "how to" in a customized manner, as noted by Mr. Byham of the University of South Florida in his foreword to this book. The customization is based on the enterprise's interpretation of the standards and its governance structures, related business processes, and so on.

Therefore, in identifying, selecting, and developing the project business management processes, the enterprise's management team and the EPMO may substitute a process that they have found to be a best, rather than a good, practice. The enterprise may also add other processes that it deems necessary to meet its business needs or may decide not to use a specific process promulgated in a standard if that process is not applicable to their successful ways of doing business. The identified and selected process may also be related and sequenced in the order the enterprise finds effective and efficient.

9.3 Integrating the Enterprise's Selected Processes

The integration of the selected project management process with the identified related general business processes is accomplished through a set of fairly common business operation development steps. There is also a simple progressive process inherent in project business management: strategic planning defines the business strategies that evolve into business objectives with desired benefits that become a set of portfolios, programs, and projects. This hierarchy can be used as the basic structure on which to build a set of integrated project and business management processes that will create the basis for a project business management methodology. The business development integrating activities are:

- Identifying the common points and steps between the documented scope and operational content of the selected project processes and identified business processes.
- Building a single flowchart for the major steps within the related project and business processes, highlighting the common steps, and showing the interface points to other processes.
- Determining the appropriate responsibility for each major step within each of the integrated processes.
- Building a hierarchy of the management actions associated with each process.
- Documenting a formal procedure for each process.
- Issuing and implementing each procedure in the order as defined by the process flowchart steps.

CHAPTER 10

Enterprise-Wide Project Business Management Methodology

Most organizations recognize the management value of the Project Management Institute's (PMI®) *A Guide to the Project Management Body of Knowledge* (*PMBOK® Guide*) in identifying good project management practices. PMI® has also recently issued *A Standard for Program Management* and *A Standard for Portfolio Management* to complete the set of good project management practices. However, executives at all levels still struggle with how to implement these practices and processes within their organizations.

The key is translating the PMI® *PMBOK® Guide* and the program and portfolio standards or other non-United States standards into a methodology, which is a set of standard processes that integrates the processes with the enterprise's product and services development processes. Many organizations view the PMI standards as methodologies; this is not the case. PMI standards are intended to serve as the basis for developing a methodology. Enterprises must struggle with how to translate those standards into usable methodologies. This book provides a model for completing those translations by providing five sets of processes that integrate strategic, tactical, portfolio, program, and project management into an integrated methodology. How the results of this integration will be applied is different for every enterprise because all of these processes are influenced by the organization's culture and other enterprise environmental factors.

We have adapted the project management practices and processes in those referenced three PMI® standards in this chapter to create a basic business management oriented model that can be used by any enterprise to guide the management of portfolios, programs, and projects in a consistent and reliable manner. This model is referred to as the Project Business Management Methodology Model.

For an enterprise to develop a Project Business Management Methodology, familiarity with the PMI® *PMBOK® Guide* and the program and

portfolio standards is strongly recommended, as is some basic project management training. This training can be obtained from any one of the PMI®
Registered Education Providers listed on the PMI® website <www.pmi.org>
under the Professional Development and Careers menu.

The Project Business Management Methodology developed in this section and applied in Section 5 is, we believe, faithful to the intent of the PMI
standards, while providing executive and senior managers with a usable
model of how those standards could successfully be implemented.

The PBM model is meant to be a simple, easy-to-follow, top-down hierarchically integrated blend of strategic, tactical, portfolio, program, and project planning and execution processes. It is a means to take the many management processes and the complex principles and concepts of portfolio
management, program management, and project management, and blend
them with the better understood (by executives and very senior managers)
principles, concepts, and varied processes of general business management
to create what we call the concept of project business management (PBM).

The model is by necessity simple so it can succinctly communicate
the major concepts. It also needs to be customized before implementation, since we do not cover the nuances of all the "what" that are presented clearly in the three standards. However, this PBM methodology
and model can be clearly understood by executive management and provide the general ideas and a roadmap of "how" they might incorporate
all the "what" of the three PMI standards as core competencies within
their enterprises.

10.1 Project Business Management Methodology: Models 1 Through 5

The Project Business Management Methodology (PBMM) model is composed of five components that create a blueprint for planning project-
related business strategies, business objectives, portfolios, programs, and
projects; monitoring schedule, scope, and resource information; controlling
the schedule, scope, and resources based on information collected; and reporting on progress. The PBMM model identifies the basic processes to be
followed to complete the work during various stages of the enterprise's business cycle. The PBMM model is a contiguous framework of processes, each
relying on the proper application of the others. At the same time, each
process is a separate, definable process that can stand alone. These processes
can and should be scaled to suit the requirements of the enterprise's portfolio, program, and project classifications. That set of scaled defined processes should be incorporated into a manual with the following focuses:

- *Scope:* The enterprise PBM manual defines the model processes and their application in managing the organization's portfolios, programs, and projects.
- *Purpose:* The manual contains the project business management best practices methodology for managing all portfolios, programs, and projects to ensure consistent and effective project business management practices across the enterprise.
- *Applicability:* Use of the manual is mandatory for all portfolios, programs, and projects.
- *Usage Guidelines:* The manual defines what processes are to be applied to portfolios, programs, and project management. The manual uses common project business management terminology and is used in conjunction with the specific documents developed by each of the business units that compares local (division, region, facility) standard definitions of terms with those contained in the manual. The specific document should also contain references to internal local policies and other requirements that would apply to parts of the defined processes and identify local processes that would be substituted for the model processes.
- *Procedures:* The manual is supported by a set of process procedures that defines how each process is to function and provides best practice guidance on how to apply that process.
- *Governance:* The manual is owned by the enterprise executive responsible for institutionalization of the EPMO and project business management practices across the organization. It is the responsibility of each business unit manager to ensure compliance.

Development, distribution, implementation, and maintenance of a project business management methodology is the responsibility of the EPMO. The EPMO is also chartered to coach and mentor project team members in the proper application of project management practices as defined by a standard set of processes that will be applied in all areas of the organization. Enterprise-wide acceptance and adoption of the enterprise's project business management methodology model as a standard will help establish a mature environment that enhances the capability for continuous improvement through effective applications of lessons learned. A basic knowledge of project management processes is needed to understand and properly apply the processes identified in a project management process manual and effectively utilize the information contained in supporting procedures and templates.

A simple hierarchy is inherent in project business management: strategy, objective, portfolio, program, project. This hierarchy can be used as the basic structure on which to build the set of integrated project and business management processes that will create the basis for a project business management methodology. From this simple hierarchy, we produce five related components of the PBMM model:

1. Business Strategy Development Process Model.
2. Business Objective Development Process Model.
3. Portfolio Management Process Model.
4. Program Management Process Model.
5. Project Management Process Model.

The PBMM processes within each of the five model components are organized into the five common business management categories identified as process groups in the PMI® *PMBOK® Guide* and *A Standard for Program Management*. We have used the five process group format for our models, not only to be consistent with those two PMI® standards, but also to allow the processes in all five PBMM model components to be similarly presented, even though the higher level components may not have many specific processes associated with one or more of the process groups. In addition, we have added, as is permissible by the PMI® standards, those additional processes for portfolio management that we have actual physical experience in performing with our successful executive clients. The model also uses the common simple *input-process-output* format to describe the function of each PBMM model component.

The model emphasizes the initiation and authorization steps in the business strategy development model, the business objective development model, and the portfolio management model, as these processes comprise the first two of the five common process groups associated with program and project management.

Who initiates a project or a program and what documentation do they use?

In our model, as in the PMI® *PMBOK® Guide,* each project or program is initiated and authorized using a statement of work and a charter provided by the enterprise's management outside of and above the manager of the project or program—sometimes that is by a portfolio manager, but only for a project within a portfolio; or by a program manager, but only for a project within a program.

In our model, as in the portfolio standard, the portfolio manager and portfolio management team employ the "Aligning Process Group" process to develop the supporting components for the portfolio. They can initiate and authorize a program or project from within the portfolio, which we chose to do using a statement of work and a charter for simplicity and uniformity of process.

Who initiates a portfolio, when is it authorized, and what documentation is used?

This first answer is simple and obvious to most executives and senior managers. The person who initiates a portfolio is the same executive management that initiates and authorizes a project or program if there is no related program or portfolio. The reason is also very simple: no effective executive is ever going to allow any portfolio manger to self-initiate his/her own portfolio.

Portfolios are initiated at the end of the enterprise's Business Strategy Development Model and Business Objective Development Model processes, which are usually performed as part of an enterprise's business cycle planning. They are the higher planning levels at which processes similar to the portfolio standards, Aligning Process Group process, are applied to develop the Strategic Business Objectives, which support the enterprise's Strategic Initiatives. After the business objectives have been developed, we model how to identify, categorize, evaluate, prioritize and select the supporting standalone projects (i.e., not part of a program or a portfolio) and standalone programs (i.e., not part of a portfolio), and the portfolios. Each selected portfolio is then initiated and authorized by the appropriate executive or senior manager in our chosen manner which, for simplicity and uniformity of process, is by issuing a statement of work and a charter

For each of the PBMM model components, we have selected a set of processes that should be applicable to most enterprises regardless of application area or industry. Each process is entered into one of the five process groups in a tabulation. A description of the basic purpose and major activities for each process is developed, and the processes are then ordered within each process group according to the sequence in which they are most commonly performed. This sequence and the interrelatedness among the process and model components are then presented as input-process-output formatted flow-charts. These can be found in Section 5, where the execution of the PBMM model is presented. A set of procedures is then identified that will document how each process should be routinely performed. Those procedures are then prepared using the guidance provided in Chapter 11.

10.2 Business Strategy Development Processes: Model #1

Strategic business planning is common and performed to some extent in all enterprises. Some enterprises have a rigorous methodology while others have a more ad-hoc approach. The result in each case is some sort of strategic business plan for the enterprise's next business cycle. The implementation of each strategy is then managed and monitored and closed when completed or terminated.

Table 10-1 identifies the few basic processes that must be performed to have a simple documented model that will provide the products and information needed to support an effective PBM methodology. These few processes should be applicable regardless of how extensive an enterprise's overall strategy development methodology may be.

Business strategy initiating processes are as follows:

1A-1 Update Enterprise Vision and Mission: The enterprise's executives document the vision and mission statements that define the purpose of the enterprise and its value proposition. This process also involves updating the vision and mission statements as they evolve to address changing business and market conditions.

1A-2 Develop Business Strategies for the Next Business Cycle: The enterprise's executives perform strategic planning that documents the business strategies for the next business cycle. This includes updating the business strategies as required by new business and changes in market conditions.

1A-3 Identify Applicable Enterprise Environmental Factors: The EPMO documents existing and new factors that can affect the accomplishment of identified strategies and related implementation processes. This also involves defining and updating enterprise environmental factors as a result of business and industry changes.

1A-4 Define Strategy Prioritization Criteria: Develop and document the criteria that will be used to prioritize business strategies and objectives and specify their method of application.

1A-5 Develop Strategy Accomplishment Metrics: The EPMO develops and documents an enterprise strategy metrics set that includes a list of the performance measurements that define the metrics, as well as data gathering and reporting requirements.

Business strategy planning processes are as follows:

1B-1 Prepare Strategic Business Plan: The management team develops a strategic business plan for the next business cycle that documents the basis for each strategic initiative.

1B-2 Prepare Business Cases: A business case is prepared for each business strategy in the business plan.

Table 10-1. PBMM Business Strategy Development (Strategic Planning)–Model Processes

Strategy Initiating Processes (A)	*Strategy Planning Processes (B)*	*Strategy Executing Processes (C)*	*Strategy Monitoring & Controlling Processes (D)*	*Strategy Closing Processes (E)*
1A-1 Update Enterprise Vision and Mission	*1B-1* Prepare Strategic Business Plan	*1C-1* Implement Strategy	*1D-1* Manage Strategy Change	*1E-1* Close Strategy
1A-2 Develop Business Strategies for Next Business Cycle	*1B-2* Prepare Business Case	*1C-2* Perform Strategy Status Reviews	*1D-2* Monitor Strategic Metrics Performance	
1A-3 Identify Applicable Enterprise Environmental Factors	*1B-3* Prioritize Business Strategies			
1A-4 Define Strategy Prioritization Criteria				
1A-5 Develop Strategy Accomplishment Metrics				

1B-3 Prioritize Business Strategies: The enterprise executives use the prioritization criteria developed in process 1A-4 to document a prioritized list of business strategies.

Business strategy executing processes are as follows:

1C-1 Implement Strategy: The further planning and implementation by the business units of each strategy is authorized and overseen, and possible threats and opportunities are identified that may require revision of the strategic business plan.

1C-2 Perform Strategy Status Reviews: The executive officers and possibly the board of directors of the enterprise periodically review the progress toward accomplishing each business strategy.

Business strategy monitoring and controlling processes are as follows:

1D-1 Manage Strategy Change: Possible changes to a strategy resulting from identified threats or opportunities are monitored and documented. The PBM change request process is used to document, review, approve/reject, and manage the implementation of approved strategy changes.

1D-2 Monitor Strategic Metrics Performance: Implements metric data collection, analysis, reporting, and response actions.

Business strategy closing processes are as follows:

1E-1 Close Strategy: The EPMO chief project management officer prepares the closing report for the strategy. The closing report includes a summary of the lessons learned. The report is submitted to executive management and states if and how the strategy was accomplished and the benefits that were accrued to the enterprise, if any.

The process procedures listed in Table 10-2 support the model processes in Table 10-1 and are used by executive, business unit, and EPMO management in the business strategy development, as is appropriate within the enterprise.

10.3 Business Objective Development Processes: Model #2

The second stage of most business planning models and of the PBM methodology model is to develop the business objectives that support each business strategy and then to identify, document, and authorize the proj-

Table 10-2. PBMM Business Strategy Development Procedures Listing

Process No.	Title
1A-1	Prepare/Update Enterprise Vision and Mission Development Procedure
1A-2	Business Strategic Planning Procedure and template
1A-3	Enterprise Environmental Factors Development Procedure
1A-4, 1B-3	Strategy Prioritization Criteria Procedure and template
1A-5, 1D-2	Strategy Metrics and Accomplishment Procedure with template
1B-1, 1B-2	Strategic Business Plan and Business Case Procedure with template
1C-1	Strategy Implementation Procedure with template
1C-2	Strategy Status Reviews Procedure with templates
1D-1	Strategy Change Management Procedure
1E-1	Strategy Closure and Lessons Learned Procedure with template

ect-related portfolios, programs, and projects that will be employed to accomplish each objective. The implementation of each objective is managed, monitored, and closed when completed or terminated. The business objective development processes are shown in Table 10-3.

Business objective initiating processes are as follows:

> *2A-1 Obtain Enterprise Vision/Mission and Business Strategies for the Next Business Cycle:* Copies of the purpose, vision, and mission statements,

Table 10-3. PBMM Business Objective Development (Tactical Planning)–Model Processes

Objective Initiating Processes (A)	Objective Planning Processes (B)	Objective Executing Processes (C)	Objective Monitoring & Controlling Processes (D)	Objective Closing Processes (E)
2A-1 Obtain Enterprise Vision/Mission and Business Strategies for the Next Business Cycle	2B-1 Document Business Objectives	2C-1 Implement Objective	2D-1 Manage Objective Changes	2E-1 Close Objective
2A-2 Develop Business Objectives for the Next Business Cycle	• Prepare Project Profiles	2C-2 Issue Charters	2D-2 Monitor Objective Metrics Performance	
2A-3 Identify Applicable Enterprise Environmental Factors	• Perform impact Studies	2C-3 Perform Objective Status Reviews		
2A-4 Identify Applicable Organizational Process Assets	2B-2 Prioritize Business Strategies			
2A-5 Define Objectives Prioritization Criteria				
2A-6 Develop Objectives Accomplishment Metrics				

the current strategic business plan, and supporting business cases for the next business cycle are obtained and reviewed.

2A-2 Develop Business Objectives for the Next Business Cycle: The enterprise executives perform tactical planning that develops and documents the business objectives that support the identified strategies for the next business cycle. This includes updating the business objectives to reflect changes in the strategic business plan during the next business cycle.

2A-3 Identify Applicable Enterprise Environmental Factors: The EPMO documents existing and new factors that can impact the accomplishment of the identified business objectives and related implementation processes. This process also involves defining and updating enterprise environmental factors as a result of new business and industry requirement changes.

2A-4 Identify Applicable Organizational Process Assets: The EPMO identifies existing assets and documents new assets that can affect the accomplishment of the identified business objectives and related implementation processes. This process also involves defining and updating organizational process assets as a result of new business requirements and project management asset advancements.

2A-5 Define Objectives Prioritization Criteria: Develop and document any additional criteria that will be used to prioritize business objectives and specify their method of application.

2A-6 Develop Objectives Accomplishment Metrics: The EPMO develops and documents an enterprise objective metrics set that includes a list of the performance measurements that define the metrics, as well as data gathering and reporting requirements.

Business objective planning processes are as follows:

2B-1 Document Business Objectives: The management team and EPMO staff develop a set of scope and related documentation for each business objective that includes an objective/project profile document and an impact study document.

2B-2 Prioritize Business Strategies: The enterprise executives and EPMO staff use the prioritization criteria developed in process A-6 to prepare a prioritized list of the business objectives.

Business objective executing processes are as follows:

2C-1 Implement Objective: The further planning and implementation by the enterprise business units and the EPMO of each business objective are overseen. A set of portfolios, programs, and projects to be implemented during the next business cycle is identified, selected, and documented with a prepared statement of work and performance metrics. Possible threats and opportunities are identified that may require the revision of the business objective or modification of the supporting portfolios, programs, and projects.

2C-2 Issue Charters: Prepare and issue a charter for each portfolio to be authorized for work during the next business cycle. Prepare and issue charters for each program and project that are not part of a portfolio and for each project that is not part of a program or portfolio.

2C-3 Perform Objective Status Reviews: The executive officers and possibly the board of directors of the enterprise periodically review the status of progress toward accomplishing the enterprise's business objectives.

Business objective monitoring and controlling processes are as follows:

2D-1 Manage Objective Change: Possible changes to an objective resulting from identified threats or opportunities and implementation actions are monitored and documented. The PBM change request process is used to document, review, approve/reject, and manage the implementation of approved objective changes.

2D-2 Monitor Objective Metrics Performance: Implements business objective metric data collection, analysis, reporting, and response actions.

Business objective closing processes are as follows:

2E-1 Close Objective: The EPMO chief project management officer prepares the closing report documentation for the business objective. The closing report includes a summary of the lessons learned. The report is submitted to executive management and states if and how the objective was accomplished and what benefits were accrued to the enterprise versus those planned.

The process procedures listed in Table 10-4 support the model processes in Table 10-3 and are used by executive, business unit, and EPMO management in the planning and implementation of business objectives, as is appropriate within the enterprise.

10.4 Portfolio Management Processes: Model #3

Recent literature includes a significant amount of discussion about planning and managing portfolios in commercial businesses. The focus is usu-

Table 10-4. PBMM Business Objective Development Procedures Listing

Process No.	Title
2A-1	Obtaining Strategic Planning Documents Procedure
2A-2	Business Objective Planning Procedure and template
2A-3	Enterprise Environmental Factors Development Procedure
2A-4	Organizational Process Assets Development Procedure
2A-5, 2B-3	Objectives Prioritization Criteria Procedure and template
2A-6, 2D-2	Objectives Accomplishment Procedure with template
2B-1	Document Business Objectives Procedure
2B-1-a	Objective/Project Profile Procedure with template
2B-1-b	Objective/Project Impact Study Procedure with template
2B-2	Prioritize Business Objectives Procedure
2B-3	Tactical Planning Procedure with template
2C-1	Implementing Objectives Procedure with checklist
2C-2	Portfolio, Program and Project Authorization Procedure with template
2C-3	Strategy Status Reviews Procedure with templates
2D-1	Objective Change Management Procedure
2D-2	Monitor Business Objective Metrics Procedure
2E-1	Objective Closure and Lessons Learned Procedure with template

ally on assembling various enterprise business objectives and related business unit action items, with the objectives and action items being constrained by budget and/or funds. This type of portfolio is managed or overseen by an executive or senior manager who usually resides in the business unit most involved with the work to be accomplished and is most interested in a successful outcome.

Project portfolio management is concerned with project-related portfolios and is a subset of enterprise-wide project management. It is an ongoing business function, as well as an ongoing management process. This discipline of portfolio management can be described in terms of its component processes, defined by PMI® in *A Standard for Portfolio Management*. Project business management includes the standardized application of those principles, practices, and processes on an enterprise-wide basis. Table 10-5 lists the processes included in the portfolio management portion of the PBMM model.

Portfolio management initiating processes are as follows:

3A-1 Obtain Portfolio Charter: The document prepared by the sponsor overseeing the portfolio and issued to the portfolio manager to provide the formal authorization to start the portfolio. The charter provides the authorization to expend the organization's resources on the activities.

Table 10-5. PBMM Portfolio Management Model Processes

Portfolio Initiating Processes (A)	Portfolio Planning Processes (B)	Portfolio Executing Processes (C)	Portfolio Monitoring & Controlling Processes (D)	Portfolio Closing Processes (E)
3A-1 Obtain Portfolio Charter	3B-1 Develop Portfolio Scope Statement	3C-1 Manage Portfolio	3D-1 Monitor & Control Portfolio	3E-1 Document Portfolio Lessons Learned
3A-2 Identify Applicable Enterprise Environmental Factors	3B-2 Develop Portfolio WBS	3C-2 Issue Program/ Project Charters	• Manage Configuration Management System	3E-2 Close Portfolio
3A-3 Identify Applicable Organizational Process Assets	3B-3 Develop Portfolio Management Plan	3C-3 Perform Portfolio Status Reviews	• Manage Change Control System	
3A-4 Develop Portfolio Performance Metrics			3D-2 Monitor Portfolio Metrics Performance	
3A-5 Implement Configuration Management				

3A-2 Identify Applicable Enterprise Environmental Factors: The EPMO identifies existing factors and documents new factors that impact the PBM portfolio, program, and project processes.

3A-3 Identify Applicable Organizational Process Assets: The EPMO identifies existing assets and documents new assets that impact the PBM portfolio, program, and project processes.

3A-4 Develop Portfolio Accomplishment Metrics: The portfolio manager assisted by the EPMO develops and documents a list of the portfolio performance metrics and reporting requirements.

3A-5 Implement Configuration Management: The EPMO implements the integrated PBMS change management processes (see Monitoring and Control Processes – D-1) for portfolio documentation version control.

Portfolio management planning processes are as follows:

3B-1 Develop Portfolio Scope Statement: Portfolio management prepares and issues a scope statement for the portfolio using the same preparation guidelines as for a project scope statement.

3B-2 Develop Portfolio WBS: Portfolio management prepares and issues the portfolio portion of the enterprise work breakdown structure.

3B-3 Develop Portfolio Management Plan: Portfolio management prepares and issues a document using the guidelines for a project management plan containing as a minimum a communication subplan, a risk management subplan, cost management subplan, and change management subplan.

Portfolio management executing processes are as follows:

3C-1 Manage the Portfolio: Portfolio management oversees the further planning and execution of the portfolio. The components of the portfolio (program, projects, and other work) for the next business cycle are further identified, categorized, evaluated, selected, prioritized, and balanced. Portfolio management develops and prepares the statement of work for the programs and standalone projects contained within the portfolio. Possible threats and opportunities are identified that may require revision of the portfolio plan or modification of the supporting programs and projects.

3C-2 Issue Program/Project Charters: Portfolio management prepares and issues a charter for each program to authorize the program work to be performed and issues charters to authorize the work for each project in the portfolio that is not part of a program.

3C-3 Perform Portfolio Status Reviews: Portfolio management conducts periodic reviews of the progress toward accomplishing the intent of the supported business objective.

Portfolio management monitoring and controlling processes are as follows:

3D-1 Monitor and Control Portfolio: Portfolio management monitors the portfolio execution and uses integrated change management, which is composed of configuration management and change control systems.

Configuration Management System: A configuration management process is implemented at the start of the portfolio to manage development and revisions of portfolio documentation.

Change Control System: The PBMS change request process is used to document, review, approve/reject, and manage the implementation of approved changes.

Table 10-6. PBMM Portfolio Management Process Procedures Listing

Process No.	Title
3A-1	Obtaining Portfolio Charter and Other Initiating Documents Procedure
3A-2	Enterprise Environmental Factors Development Procedure
3A-3	Organizational Process Assets Development Procedure
3A-4, 3D-2	Portfolio Performance Measurement Procedure with template
A-5	Configuration Management Implementation procedure
3B-1, 3B-2, 3B-3	Portfolio Scope, WBS, and Management Plan Procedures with templates
3C-1	Manage Portfolio Procedure with checklist
3C-2	Program and Project Charter Authorization Procedure with template
3C-3	Portfolio Status Reviews Procedure with templates
3D-1	Monitor and Control Portfolios Procedure
3D-1-A	Manage Configuration Management System Procedure
3D-1-B	Manage Change Control System Procedure
3D-2	Monitor Portfolio Performance Metrics Procedure
3E-1	Portfolio Closure and Lessons Learned Procedure with template

3D-2 Monitor Portfolio Metrics: Implements portfolio metric data collection, analysis, reporting, and response actions.

Portfolio management closing processes are as follows:

3E-1 Close the Portfolio: The portfolio manager prepares the closing report documentation for the portfolio. The closing report includes a summary of the lessons learned and what benefits were accrued to the enterprise versus those planned.

The process procedures listed in Table 10-6 support the model processes in Table 10-5 and are used by portfolio management in the planning and execution of portfolios, as is appropriate within the enterprise.

10.5 Program Management Processes: Model #4

The concept of a program is familiar to any person who has worked with or for the United States Department of Defense on various military programs or, on a worldwide basis, for those who have worked in information technology on software or hardware programs. In both commercial business and government organizations, the focus is on assembling various related and sometimes interdependent enterprise business objectives and related business unit actions items. A program is normally managed or overseen by a senior manager who resides in the business unit that is charged with its successful completion and is heavily involved with the work to be accomplished.

Program management is a subset of enterprise-wide project management and is an ongoing business function as well as an ongoing management process. The discipline of program project management can be described in terms of its component processes, as defined by PMI® in *A Standard for Program Management.* Project business management includes the standardized application of those program management principles, practices, and processes on an enterprise-wide basis. Table 10-7 lists the processes included in the program management portion of the PBMM model.

Table 10-7. PBMM Program Management Model Processes

Program Initiating Processes (A)	Program Planning Processes (B)	Program Executing Processes (C)	Program Monitoring & Controlling Processes (D)	Program Closing Processes (E)
4A-1 Receive Program Charter	4B-1 Refine Program Scope Statement	4C-1 Manage Program	4D-1 Monitor & Control Program	4E-1 Archive Program Information
4A-2 Assemble Program Core Team	4B-2 Define Program Work Breakdown Structure	4C-2 Issue Project Charters	• Manage Developmental Configuration Management System	4E-2 Transition to Operations
4A-3 Implement Integrated Change Management Plan	4B-3 Develop Program Schedule and Management Plan	4C-3 Manage Program Budget & Schedule	• Manage Change Control System	4E-3 Write Closing Report
4A-4 Receive Program Statement of Work	4B-4 Develop Program Budget and Management Plan	4C-4 Manage Program Resources	4D-2 Monitor Program Metrics	4E-4 Close Program
4A-5 Develop Preliminary Program Scope Statement	4B-5 Define Program Metrics and Management Plan	4C-5 Manage Program Communications	4D-3 Monitor & Control Program Risk	
4A-6 Perform Program Initiating Gate Review		4C-6 Manage Program Issues and Problem Reporting Systems	4D-4 Document Program Lessons Learned	
		4C-7 Manage Program Procurement Contracts		

(continued)

Table 10-7. (*Continued*)

Program Initiating Processes (A)	Program Planning Processes (B)	Program Executing Processes (C)	Program Monitoring & Controlling Processes (D)	Program Closing Processes (E)
	4B-6 Define Issues and Problem Reporting Systems	*4C-8* Perform Program Execution Gate Review		
	4B-7 Define Program Resource and Management Plan			
	4B-8 Establish Program Communications and Management Plan			
	4B-9 Define Risks and Management Plan			
	4B-10 Develop Procurement and Management Plan			
	4B-11 Consolidated Program Management Plan			
	4B-12 Perform Program Planning Gate Review			
	4B-13 Obtain Full Program Authorization			

Program management initiating processes are as follows:

4A-1 Receive Program Charter: A document prepared by the portfolio manager or program sponsor overseeing the program if the program is standalone and issued to the program manager to provide the formal authorization to start the program. The charter provides the authorization to expend the organization's resources on the activities.

4A-2 Assemble Program Core Team: The program manager negotiates with the functional department managers and third party suppliers to assign the program core team members.

4A-3 Implement Integrated Change Management Plan: The program team implements the integrated change control management system that includes project configuration management and change control management.

4A-4 Receive Program Statement of Work: A document that identifies all program requirements (functional, technical, and performance) that involve combining customer requirements (normally provided by a customer statement of work) with all internal stakeholder requirements.

4A-5 Develop Preliminary Program Scope Statement: A document that defines how the program requirements will be met, the boundaries of the program, and the deliverables to be produced.

4A-6 Perform Program Initiating Gate Review: A gate review that uses a checklist to ensure that all requirements for initiating a program have been properly completed so that the core team can proceed with detailed program planning.

Program management planning processes are as follows:

4B-1 Refine Program Scope Statement: Refine and create a baseline for the preliminary program scope statement that defines how the project requirements will be met, the boundaries of the program, and the deliverables to be produced. Provide input to the development of the program work breakdown structure.

4B-2 Define Program Work Breakdown Structure: Program management prepares the program's portion of the enterprise work breakdown structure to manage the program work and deliverables.

4B-3 Develop Program Schedule and Management Plan: Program team generates activity sequences, durations, resource requirements, and schedule constraints to create a program schedule that is approved by the program core team as the baseline schedule. Develop a program schedule management plan that defines how the schedule will be updated and establish criteria to amend the baseline of the program schedule.

4B-4 Develop Program Budget and Management Plan: Program manager creates the program budget and defines how it will be managed.

4B-5 Define Program Metrics and Management Plan: Program manager assisted by the EPMO identifies the metrics and benefits to be delivered that will be measured and defines how they will be managed.

4B-6 *Define Issues and Problem Reporting Systems:* Develop a systematic method for recording and resolving action items and problem reports.

4B-7 *Define Program Resource and Management Plan:* Develop the program resources and management plan to identify how resources will be added and released from the program.

4B-8 *Establish Program Communications and Management Plan:* Identify the information and communication needs of the program stakeholders: who they are, what their information requirements are, what their influence on the program is, when information is required, and how it will be delivered. The program communications management plan defines the systems that will be used to gather, store, and disseminate program information as well as to identify any security requirements related to the dissemination of program information.

4B-9 *Define Risks and Management Plan:* Define program risks and how the risks will be managed.

4B-10 *Develop Procurement and Management Plan:* Plan what program work will be subcontracted and determine how it will be managed.

4B-11 *Consolidated Program Management Plan:* A document containing the subsidiary plans developed in processes 4B1 through 4B10 and updated through the PBMS integrated change management.

4B-12 *Perform Program Planning Gate Review:* Reviewing and approving the program management plan, with a checklist to ensure that all requirements for program planning have been properly completed.

4B-13 *Obtain Full Program Authorization:* The program manager prepares this document after the program management plan and the gate review have been approved, to authorize release of program funding to start program execution activities. Subsequent addendums are issued as required for rolling-wave planned programs.

Program management executing processes are as follows:

4C-1 *Manage the Program:* Program management oversees the further planning and execution of the portfolio. Portfolio management develops and prepares the statement of work for the projects to be contained within the program. Possible threats and opportunities are identified that may require the program plan to be revised or modifications be made to the supporting projects.

4C-2 *Issue Project Charters:* Program management prepares and issues a charter for each project to be authorized for work during the next business cycle.

4C-3 Manage Program Budget and Schedule: Analyze program cost and schedule variances, establish variance criticality, identify variance drivers, and make adjustments to keep the program within budget. Hold regularly scheduled team status meetings to anticipate and avoid program schedule variances and adjust resource allocations and activity dependencies to maintain the critical path changes to a minimum.

4C-4 Manage Program Resources: Analyze program cost and schedule variances on a regular basis and make adjustments in resource allocations as needed to maintain program cost and schedule baseline goals.

4C-5 Manage Program Communications: Establish regularly conducted program team meetings, technical reviews, management reviews, and exchanges of information. Establish internal reviews to ensure that the various elements of the program core team are properly coordinated and that the proper communication is in place.

4C-6 Manage Program Issues and Problem Reporting Systems: Document and resolve program action items and problem reports.

4C-7 Manage Program Procurement Contracts: Coordinate the program work of suppliers and subcontracts.

4C-8 Perform Program Execution Gate Review: A program review that verifies that all of the required program deliverables and other requirements have been met before beginning the closing activities.

Program management monitoring and controlling processes are as follows:

4D-1 Monitor & Control Program: Program management monitors the program execution and uses configuration management and change control management systems.

Configuration Management System: A program configuration management process, which is implemented at the start of the program and manages development and revisions of program documentation.

Change Control System: The change request process is used to document, review, approve/reject, and manage the implementation of approved changes.

4D-2 Monitor Program Metrics: A process that implements program metrics data collection, analysis, reporting, and response actions.

4D-3 Monitor and Control Program Risk: A process that monitors known program risks, identifies new risks, and implements response plans.

4D-4 Document Program Lessons Learned: Documents program lessons learned after each gate review for summarization in the program closing report.

Program management closing processes are as follows:

4E-1 Archive Program Information: Defines what types of program information and artifacts will be archived at the end of the project. It also defines how the information will be collected and stored during the program's lifecycle.

4E-2 Transition to Operations: The products involving mass production that are produced by the program are transferred to the manufacturing operations for market production. The program manager facilitates the transfer of pertinent program data and artifacts that are necessary for the manufacturing process.

4E-3 Write Closing Report: The program manager prepares the program closing report. The closing report includes a summary of the program lessons learned.

4E-4 Close the Program: The program manager closes the program contracts and finalizes all customer product or service deliverables including all associated documentation.

The process procedures listed in Table 10-8 support the model processes in Table 10-7 and are used by program management in the plan-

Table 10-8. PBMM Program Management Process Procedures Listing

Process No.	Title
4A-1, 4A-4	Obtaining Program Charter and Other Initiating Documents Procedure
4A-2	Program Team Member Assignment Procedure
4A-3	Integrated Change Management Procedure
4A-5, 4A-6, 4B-13	Program Initiation Procedure and template
4B-1, 4B-11	Program Scope and Management Plan Development Procedure
4B-2	Program WBS Development and Maintenance Procedure
4B-3, 4B-10	Program Management Sub-Plan Development Procedure with template
4B-12, 4C-7	Program Gate Review Procedure with template
4C-1, 4C-6	Program Execution Procedure with templates
4D-1	Program Monitoring and Control Procedure
4D-1-a	Configuration Management System Procedure
4D-1-b	Change Control System Procedure
4D-2	Monitor Metrics Procedure with template
4D-3	Program Risk Procedure with template
4D-4	Program Lessons Learned Procedure with template
4E-1	Program Information Archive Procedure with template
4E-2	Closing Report Procedure with template
4E-3	Transition to Operations Procedure
4E-4	Program Closure Procedure with template

ning and execution of programs, as is appropriate within the enterprise. This set, or a similar set, of procedures are developed by the EPMO to establish the program management portion of the PBMM.

10.6 Project Management Processes: Model #5

Almost all executives and managers generally understand the concept of a project in the form of developing a new product, implementing reorganization, improving a production process, and so on. In the context of integrating business management with project management, a project is either all of, or a specific component of, a selected business objective necessary to attain that objective. As with portfolios and programs, a project (specific business objective) is usually accomplished with limited resources, which include time and funds. The management goal is to produce the desired results that will create the project deliverables and meet the project's business objective. In most business management processes and in all project management process, a project is usually managed or overseen by a single project manager who provides the focus for the planning, organizing, directing, and controlling of all project activities.

Project management is a subset of enterprise-wide project management and is an ongoing business function as well as an ongoing set of management processes. The discipline of project management can be described in terms of its component processes as defined in the Project Management Institute's (PMI®) *A Guide to the Project Management Body of Knowledge (PM-BOK® Guide)*, which is universally recognized and accepted as the project management standard. As such, it provides the guiding principles on which an enterprise methodology for management of a single project can be based. Project business management includes the standardized application of those project management principles, practices, and processes on an enterprise-wide basis. Table 10-9 lists the project management processes included in the PBMM model. This set, or a similar set, of processes are developed by the EPMO to establish the project management portion of the PBMM model.

Project management initiating processes are as follows:

5A-1 Receive Project Charter: A document prepared by the project sponsor, portfolio manager, or program manager overseeing the project and issued to the project manager to provide the formal authorization to start the project. The charter provides the authorization to expend the organization's resources on the activities.

Table 10-9. PBMMM Project Management Model Processes

Project Initiating Processes (A)	*Project Planning Processes* (B)	*Project Executing Processes* (C)	*Project Monitoring & Controlling Processes* (D)	*Project Closing Processes* (E)
5A-1 Receive Project Charter	5B-1 Refine Project Scope Statement	5C-1 Manage Project Schedule	5D-1 Monitor & Control Project	5E-1 Archive Project Information
5A-2 Assemble Project Core Team	5B-2 Define Project Work Breakdown Structure	5C-2 Manage Project Budget	• Manage Configuration Management System	5E-2 Write Project Closing Report
5A-3 Implement Integrated Change Management Plan	5B-3 Develop Project Schedule and Management Plan	5C-3 Manage Project Resources	• Manage Change Control System	5E-3 Transition to *Operations*
5A-4 Receive or Develop Project Statement of Work	5B-4 Develop Project Budget and Management Plan	5C-4 Manage Project Communications	5D-2 Monitor Project Metrics	5E-4 Close Project
5A-5 Develop Preliminary Project Scope Statement	5B-5 Define Project Metrics and Management Plan	5C-5 Manage Issues and Problem Reporting Systems	5D-3 Monitor & Control Project Risk	
5A-6 Perform Project Initiating Gate Review	5B-6 Define Issues and Problem Reporting Systems	5C-6 Manage Procurement Contracts	5D-4 Document Project Lessons Learned	
	5B-7 Define Project Resource and Management Plan	5C-7 Perform Project Execution Gate Review		
	5B-8 Establish Project Communications and Management Plan			
	5B-9 Define Project Risk and Management Plan			
	5B-10 Develop Project Procurement and Management Plan			
	5B-11 Consolidated Project Management Plan			
	5B-12 Perform Project Planning Gate Review			
	5B-13 Obtain Full Project Authorization			

5A-2 Assemble Project Core Team: The project manager negotiates with the functional business unit managers or third party suppliers to assign the project core team members.

5A-3 Implement Integrated Change Management Plan: Implement the PBMS integrated change control management system that includes project configuration management and change control management.

5A-4 Receive or Develop Project Statement of Work: A document that identifies all project requirements (functional, technical, and performance) that involves combining customer requirements (normally provided by a customer statement of work) with all internal stakeholder requirements.

5A-5 Develop Preliminary Project Scope Statement: A document that defines how the project requirements will be met, the boundaries of the project, and the deliverables to be produced.

5A-6 Perform Project Initiating Gate Review: A gate review that uses a checklist to ensure all requirements for initiating the project have been properly completed so that the project core team can proceed with detailed project planning.

Project management planning processes are as follows:

5B-1 Refine Project Scope Statement: Refine and create a baseline for the preliminary scope statement that defines how the project requirements will be met, the boundaries of the project, and the deliverables to be produced. Provide input to the development of the project work breakdown structure.

5B-2 Define Project Work Breakdown Structure: Prepare the project portion of the enterprise work breakdown structure to manage the project work and deliverables.

5B-3 Develop Project Schedule and Management Plan: Generate activity sequences, durations, resource requirements, and schedule constraints to create a project schedule that is approved by the project core team as the baseline project schedule. Develop a project schedule management plan that defines how the schedule will be updated and establish criteria to revise the project baseline schedule.

5B-4 Develop Project Budget and Management Plan: Create the project budget and define how it will be managed.

5B-5 Define Project Metrics and Management Plan: Identify the performance metrics that will be measured on the project and define how they will be managed.

5B-6 Define Project Issues and Problem Reporting Systems: Develop a systematic method for recording and resolving action items and problem reports.

5B-7 Define Project Resource and Management Plan: Develop the project resources and management plan to identify how resources will be added and released from the project.

5B-8 Establish Project Communications and Management Plan: Identify the information and communications needs of the project stakeholders: who they are, what their information requirements are, what their influence on the project is, when information is required, and how it will be delivered. The management plan defines the systems that will be used to gather, store, and disseminate project information as well as identification of any security requirements related to the dissemination of project information.

5B-9 Define Project Risk and Management Plan: Define risks and how they will be managed.

5B-10 Develop Project Procurement and Management Plan: Plan what work will be subcontracted and determine how it will be managed.

5B-11 Consolidated Project Management Plan: A document containing the subsidiary plans developed in processes 5B1 through 5B10 and updated by approved integrated change management.

5B-12 Perform Project Planning Gate Review: Review and approve the project management plan with a checklist to ensure all requirements for project planning have been properly completed.

5B 13 Obtain Full Project Authorization: The project manager prepares this document after the project management plan and the gate review have been approved, to authorize release of project funding to start project execution activities. Subsequent addendums are issued as required for rolling-wave planned projects.

Project management executing processes are as follows:

5C-1 Manage Project Schedule: Hold regularly scheduled team status review meetings to anticipate and avoid project schedule variances and adjust resource allocations and activity dependencies to maintain the critical path changes to a minimum.

5C-2 Manage Project Budget: Analyze cost and schedule variances, establish variance criticality, identify variance drivers, and make adjustments to keep the project within budget.

5C-3 Manage Project Resources: Analyze cost and schedule variances on a regular basis and make adjustments in resource allocations as needed to maintain project cost and schedule baseline goals.

5C-4 Manage Project Communications: Establish regular project team meetings, technical reviews, management reviews, and exchanges of information. Establish internal reviews to ensure that the various elements of the project core team are properly coordinated and that the proper communication channels are in place.

5C-5 Manage Issues and Problem Reporting Systems: Document and resolve action items and problem reports.

5C-6 Manage Procurement Contracts: Coordinate the work of suppliers and subcontracts.

5C-7 Perform Project Execution Gate Review: A project review that verifies that all of the required project deliverables and other requirements have been met prior to beginning the closing activities.

Project management monitoring and controlling processes are as follows:

5D-1 Monitor and Control Project: An integrated change management process that uses configuration management and change control systems.

> *Configuration Management System:* A project configuration management process is implemented at the start of the project to manage developing and revising project documentation.

> *Change Control System:* The change request process is used to document, review, approve/reject, and manage the implementation of approved changes.

5D-2 Monitor Project Metrics; A process that implements project performance metrics data collection, analysis, reporting, and response actions.

5D-3 Monitor and Control Project Risk: A process that monitors known risks, identifies new risks, and implements response plans.

5D-4 Document Project Lessons Learned: Documents lessons learned after each project gate review for summarization in the project closure report.

Project management closing processes are as follows:

5E-1 Archive Project Information: Defines what types of project information and artifacts will be archived at the end of the project. It also defines how the information will be collected and stored during the project lifecycle.

5E-2 Write Project Closing Report: The project manager prepares the project closing report, which will include a summary of the project lessons learned.

5E-3 Transition to Operations: The products involving mass production that are produced by the project are transferred to the manufacturing operations for market production. The project manager facilitates the transfer of pertinent project data and artifacts that are necessary for the manufacturing processes.

5E-4 Close the Project: The project manager closes the project contracts and finalizes all customer product or service deliverables, including all associated documentation.

The process procedures listed in Table 10-10 support the model processes in Table 10-11 and are used by project management in the planning and execution of projects, as is appropriate within the enterprise. This set, or a

Table 10-10. PBMM Project Management Process Procedures Listing

Process No.	Title
5A-1	Project Charter Initiating Procedure with template
5A-3, 5D-1	Project Developmental Configuration Management Procedure
5B-6	Project Issues Item Management Procedure
5B-6	Project Problem Reporting Management Procedure
5A-3, 5D-1	Integrated Change Management Procedure
5A-5	Project Statement of Work Procedure with template
5A-6, 5B-13, 5C-7	Gate Review Procedure with template
5C-6	Project Lessons Learned Management Procedure with template
5A-5, 5B-1	Project Scope Statement Procedure with template
5B-2	Project Work Breakdown Structure Procedure
5B-3, 5C-1	Project Schedule Management Procedure
5B-4, 5C-2	Project Budget Management Procedure
5B-5, 5D-2	Project Metrics Management Procedure with template
5B-8, 5C-4	Project Communications Management Procedure
5B-9, 5D-3	Project Risk Management Procedure with template
5B-10, 5C-6	Project Procurement Management Procedure with templates
5B-11	Project Management Plan with template
5D-1	Project Configuration Management Procedure
5D-1	Project Change Control Management Procedure
5D-4	Project Lessons Learned Management Procedure
5E-1	Project Archive Information Procedure with template
5E-3	Project Closing Report Procedure with template

similar set, of procedures are developed by the EPMO to establish the project management portion of the PBMM model.

10.7 Process Summary Examples

To document the processes in your PBMM model, various formats such as those below are used. Table 10-11 and Table 10-12 are two examples of a format that can be used to summarize the processes in the PBMM model. A summary contains the important components of each process.

   These process summaries, along with the process flowcharts (see Section 5), provide guidance on what procedures can effectively contain which process to minimize the number of procedures and also to have procedures that can be used for similar processes at each level of the PBMM model hierarchy. This is just one step in addressing a common problem that frustrates and plagues management's control of resources, facilities, and projects. That is the lack of a simple, properly integrated, formal procedures system that supports safe, prudent, and cost-effective project business management practices. The next chapter addresses how EPMO management can support the enterprise in developing that set of simple integrated policies, plans, and procedures.

Table 10-11.   Process 5A-1 Receive Project Charter

RECEIVE PROJECT CHARTER

OBJECTIVE: Provide formal authorization for the project manager to start a project and begin expending resources.

ENTRANCE CRITERIA:	*TYPICAL INPUTS:*
• Management approval to proceed	• Proposal phase documentation (proposal/contract/project material including customer's statement of work if available)
• Project charter	• Customer schedule requirements

ACTIVITY DESCRIPTION:

The project charter is prepared by the project sponsor or a program manager assigned to manage the project and is received by the project manager. See additional activity description below.

EXIT CRITERIA:	OUTPUTS:
Project charter is received	

ROLES	*RESPONSIBILITIES*
Sponsor or program manager	Prepare and issue project charter
Project manager	Review project charter and request additional information if required

ID NUMBER	*PROCEDURE*
100	Project charter procedure with template

Additional Activity Description

The project charter is the document that formally authorizes the project. The project charter provides the project manager with the formal authority to apply organizational resources to project activities. The project charter typically contains, but is not limited to, the following information:

Project ID number	Program manager	Target start date
Project name	Project manager	Strategy supported
Charter date	Project description	Project risks
Charter issued date	Project rational	Business case objectives
Customer	Proposal number	Project constraints
Customer buyer	Sales order/contract no.	Project assumptions
Customer prime contact	Bid manager	Critical milestones & dates

Additional issues to be considered:

Some additional issues need to be considered when preparing the charter such as:

• Special resources not currently available within the organization or in limited supply.
• Current projects underway that may be impacted by the startup of this new project because of a direct or indirect connection to development of a product or service.

Table 10-12. Process 5A-4 Develop Preliminary Project Scope Statement

---

DEVELOP PRELIMINARY PROJECT SCOPE STATEMENT

OBJECTIVE: To draft the preliminary project scope, including obligations, deliverables, and limitations. To establish an initial definition of what will and what will not be done.

ENTRANCE CRITERIA:	*TYPICAL INPUTS:*
Project charter	• Product line strategic guidance
Approved project statement of work	• Project statement of work
	• Proposal/negotiations material/contract
	• Lessons learned
	• Historical information

ACTIVITY DESCRIPTION:
 • Develop the preliminary project scope statement
 • Identify specialist resources required to meet project requirements
 • Provide input to the development of the project work breakdown structure (WBS)
See additional activity description below.

EXIT CRITERIA:	*OUTPUTS:*
Approved preliminary project scope statement	Preliminary project scope statement

ROLES	*RESPONSIBILITIES*
Customer	Participates in the development of the preliminary project scope statement and approves the document
Project manager	Leads the project core team in the development of the preliminary scope statement

ID NUMBER	*PROCEDURE*
300	Project Scope Statement Procedure with template

Additional Activity Description:
The preliminary project scope statement defines how the project requirements will be met, the boundaries of the project, and the deliverables to be produced. The creation of the preliminary project scope statement is the initial version of the project scope statement that will be baselined during the planning process. The project scope statement may be a standalone document or a section within the project management plan itself as determined by the project core team. The preliminary project scope statement includes, but is not limited to:

Project justification	Project constraints
Project's product	Project assumptions
Project deliverables	Initial project organization
Project objectives	Initial defined risks
Product characteristics	Initial work breakdown structure
Product acceptance criteria	Order of magnitude cost estimate
Project boundaries	Project configuration management requirements
Project baseline and deliverables	Customer schedule milestones

CHAPTER 11

Creating Policies, Plans, and Procedures

11.1 Determining the Need

Why should executive and senior managers care about having formal, institutionalized procedures for the enterprise's operational and project business management processes?

A large number of litigations and a significant number of regulatory actions have challenged the prudence of various management actions and projects. Such litigation and regulatory findings come from customers, alleged victims, regulatory bodies, and shareholders. A judgment of no-fault or fault is based on the documented objective evidence that the work was or was not performed in accordance with all applicable requirements. Experience has shown that a simple and properly structured set of vision/mission statements, policies, plans, and procedures improves management's effective control and efficient application of resources on portfolios, programs, and projects, and ensures that applicable industry, local, state, and federal requirements, and professional discipline, industry, and practice standards are met.

A properly integrated policy and procedure system is useful to management, accommodates the numerous business and management factors driving portfolios, programs, and projects, helps avoid accidents, eliminates regulatory findings of procedural deficiencies and fines, and reduces lost time. It enhances the psychological and occupational work environment and improves the physical environment in which we all live and work. In today's competitive and litigious business and project environments, this structured, communicated, and concise set of current policies, plans, and procedures is a simple, effective means of showing prudent management. It is also an enterprise's first and best defense against unwelcomed litigation and a proven means of helping sustain profitability.

Formal policies, plans, and procedures exist so that an organization will not generate informal undocumented policies and procedures as a result of repeatedly making the same decisions and performing the same tasks. Policies, plans, and procedures establish a large portion of the business environment in which operational and project personnel work, and they are an important determinant of organizational effectiveness. They direct or influence how personnel resources perform work and how other types of resources are used. From a human and organizational effectiveness standpoint, those policies, plans, and procedures also determine how personnel reach decisions; how personnel behave in doing the work; and the enterprise's reaction to the actions of portfolio, program, and project personnel.

Policies and procedures are usually indicative of an enterprise's value system—its beliefs about employee behavior and its concepts of community and professional responsibility. What an enterprise espouses establishes how the enterprise is perceived by its employees, customers, suppliers, regulators, shareholders, and community. Therefore, enterprises must ensure that policies and procedures are consistent with their vision, mission, values, culture, beliefs, and long-term business strategies and objectives.

Enterprises operating without comprehensive and integrated written policies, plans, and procedures are at risk operationally and financially, and they may not obtain the most from limited enterprise resources. Uncontrolled repairs, reworks, lost time, fines, accidents, inefficiency, and lawsuits directly impact the enterprise's bottom line. In addition, process problems and dysfunctional management interactions and organizational interfaces, over a period of time, can seriously impact operations, projects, and profitability.

As we understand more about the types of competition we face, the impact of industry and practice standards, regulatory requirements, and how to remain profitable, we must thoughtfully examine and revise our missions, policies, plans, and procedures. The following illustrates these points.

For example, some commercial nuclear power facilities have been forced into extended shutdowns by the Nuclear Regulatory Commission (NRC) for what the NRC termed "inadequate management" of safety-related activities. In each case, an identified root cause of the management problems was inadequate management systems, administrative processes, and procedural controls. Although the specific processes and procedures varied across those facilities, all displayed similar weaknesses in the fundamental philosophy and approach to providing management direction to working personnel and establishing procedural controls for the work. In addition, the forced outage of each of those facilities cost those enterprises significant profits.

Conversely, a review of the literature and various studies shows that when good policies, plans, and procedures are available, errors can be significantly reduced. In addition, project and operations personnel effectiveness and performance efficiency are measurably improved. This means that the application and use of effective policies, plans, and procedures can also lead to reduced costs and increased profits.

11.2 Positive Management Actions and Procedural System Traits

What are some common management actions and procedural system traits that have fostered developing integrated, focused, and cost-effective systems of procedures?

A review of the literature and various studies shows the following traits for the more successful project and operational procedural systems:

- Top management did not directly blame lower-level line managers, personnel, or a myriad of management process symptoms for the enterprise's technical, operational, and project process problems.
- Most line managers viewed the defined processes and procedures as real management tools and provided procedural or process changes based on user feedback, performance trends, or root cause analysis of problems.
- Senior managers of the major organizational functions were chastised when necessary for any lack of management interaction, technical process integration, or focus on a common enterprise objective.
- Overall primary responsibility for preparing policies, plans, and procedures and for defining the associated technical and administrative processes was centralized and *not* split among the major organizational functions.

The set of key operational, organizational, and management traits common to successful policy, plan, and procedure systems were and are:

- The missions of each major functional organization were defined, well documented, and integrated with the related organizational missions.
- Modification of the procedural system was also considered when setting enterprise strategies, key objectives, or resource planning.
- The policy, plan, and procedure system evolved over a period of years using a master plan.
- The elements of the policies, plans, and procedures control system and their hierarchical relationships were clearly defined and understood.

- In most cases, the responsibility and authority for the procedural system was not spread across major organizational elements and was not controlled by each of those fiefdoms. Therefore, the enterprise did not produce organizationally unique policies, procedures, and records that are of limited value to the overall enterprise.
- Important task information that was only found in the memory of experienced personnel was documented. As a consequence, the overall work process flow was well integrated with the enterprise's policies and was represented in the procedural system.
- Multiple layers of documents were reduced and redundancy and overlap were eliminated from the various documents in the system. Employees then performed similar tasks on similar projects or operations.
- Applicable requirements were identified and clearly understood and documents did not just pass responsibility for interpretation and implementation to the next layer of the operation.
- Plans and procedures did not include explanation-type information (which belongs in training documentation), thereby increasing usability and reducing problems with updating the documents.
- Working personnel were able to identify all plans and procedures applicable to their work. In addition, most personnel did not feel the procedures were an insult to the employee's intelligence. This led in most cases to an attitude among project and operations personnel that the procedures and documentation were of great value.
- Identification and handling of the potential impact of new or revised requirements or of new upper-tier documents on lower-tier documents was well managed.

Plans and procedures preparation was *not* viewed as a nontechnical or basic administrative task. Consequently, personnel performing this task were highly regarded by their peers or management and senior personnel. Technical writers with appropriate understanding and personnel who made the grade in their line organization were assigned to the work. In many cases, these individuals had, or received, training in requirements analysis, overall process understanding, and known methods of implementing industry-proven procedural systems. They were usually given a schedule and adequate time to prepare the procedures. The result was a necessary and sufficient number of procedures and procedural steps with a focus on supporting the enterprise's mission, procedural integration, and minimal procedural redundancy, accountability, reduced training cost, interchangeability of personnel among portfolio, programs, projects, or operations, limited but adequate documentation and records, and good information automation.

11.3 Structured Development Approach

Enterprises with good operational, project, and regulatory compliance histories have recognized that clearly written and concise policies, plans, and procedures are vital to their operations. They found their old policies and procedures do not support the new and changing environment in which an enterprise now operates. Therefore, these organizations took a more business-oriented look at restructuring and upgrading their policies, plans, and procedures.

The analysis of the results of many of these efforts has led to a structured management approach that has been successful in restructuring and upgrading or modifying a set of policies, plans, and procedures that is useful to management, enhances the work environment for personnel, and accommodates the numerous business and project management factors driving enterprise operations and project business management.

The structured approach implements the concept of doing work/tasks simply, efficiently, and correctly the first time, in full compliance with all requirements. After an enterprise establishes a structured and integrated set of clear policies and procedures and trains its employees, the following benefits become apparent:

- Costs of development and implementation are quickly offset by facilities and production operations being on-line additional days and projects having better adherence to schedule.
- Quantity of policies and procedures is limited.
- Employees performing tasks have both the necessary general and specific procedures.
- Work proceeds without delays caused by repetitive training of employees or employee cross-training on different procedures for the same task. Training time for all personnel is reduced.
- Employees need not stop work to consult disjointed volumes of procedures or ask questions of experienced personnel.
- Personnel trust the procedures and plans and maintain a habit of using them.
- Employee morale and job performance improve.

The structured approach to developing policies, plans, and procedures is useful for those who must ensure that their enterprise's policies, plans, and procedures meet strategic business objectives, project goals, government regulations, and the needs of their employees. The approach applies system engineering methods to the development process to substantially reduce the potential for failure. This integrated approach completely defines all requirements on the system and establishes a system configuration that is proven, early on, to be capable of meeting those requirements. Another key component to success has been the active involvement of the chief executive officer and senior management in structuring and developing the policies, plans, and procedures system.

This approach is successful because it also requires that management understand why policies, plans, and procedures are prepared; what benefits they provide; and how and by whom they must be developed and maintained. In addition, it requires portfolio, program, and project managers to know how the enterprise's vision/mission, policies, plans, and procedures can be communicated and used to show prudent management and help sustain profitability.

An analysis of successful structured procedural development processes shows that they have the following sixteen common attributes, which can also be considered the requirements for a successful procedural system:

- Strong senior management leadership.
- Qualified development/modification team.
- Structured and implemented top down.
- Established enterprise and organizational missions.
- Documented local, state, and federal agency requirements being addressed.
- Documented discipline and practice standards being addressed.
- Enterprise policies set by major external/internal requirements.
- Procedures driven by technical and administrative work processes.
- All processes covered.
- Employee participation and responsibility.
- Staged implementation.
- Effective and focused communication.
- Management of change used to implement restructuring.
- Extensive enterprise-wide training.
- Established performance assessment program.
- Enterprise commitment to modify and upgrade.

The most common questions asked related to these requirements are as follows:

Who initiates the development or restructuring?

The impetus for this can come from the executive level, but senior management's support and insistence that it be performed is necessary for a successful development or restructuring and modification process.

How does management involvement help?

Strong leadership is required by senior management to develop and maintain a procedural system. Management must recognize that developing policies, plans, and procedures is a major effort that affects all functions and requires coordination. All members of the management team must understand their roles in creating, modifying and upgrading the procedural system. Management must show they recognize that an effective policy and procedural system requires a significant commitment of resources, development time, follow through, and training. The CEO must visibly support and drive the development program by continuous involvement—recognizing that all employees, not just management, have full responsibility for implementing and maintaining a cost-effective, quality-supporting procedural system. Management must also establish consequences for organizations and personnel who do not produce cost-effective procedures.

Who manages a development restructuring/upgrade procedures project?

A procedural development or restructuring and upgrade process is a senior management-directed activity, but it is not a common task and requires planning and a disciplined effort. The individual senior manager chosen to head the effort must be able to manage a group of individuals with very different interests and technical and managerial capabilities. This project manager must understand the overall vision/mission of the enterprise and be able to champion the new structure and revised procedural content.

Who prepares this documentation?

The actual task of reviewing, developing, and restructuring the policies and procedures can be assigned to any group management chooses. However, this task force should be a team of individuals from various organizations and functions in the enterprise to bring diverse perspectives to the development, restructuring and upgrade project. Developing an integrated set of policies, plans, and procedures is a highly technical and top-level administrative task. Personnel performing this task must be seasoned and experienced individuals who are highly regarded by their peers and senior management. An enterprise should recognize that specialists in various disciplines can provide help with the planning and production of policies, plans, and procedures. They should be qualified senior technical personnel, expert technical writers, subject matter specialists, and consultant personnel who can make up an integrated team with a limited life span to accomplish an explicit mission. The use of consultants and external procedure preparation experts has proven effective for many enterprises. These specialists can:

- Perform unbiased reviews.
- Translate and document technical information obtained from work process experts.
- Ensure procedures meet external requirements.
- Identify ways to meet local, state, and federal regulations.
- Identify ways to meet discipline and practice standards.
- Develop graphical representations to reduce the volume of words.
- Maintain consistency among procedures and across functions.
- Conduct usability tests.
- Design and conduct procedure verifications and validations.
- Set up efficient methods of preparation.

Consultants or experienced internal personnel should be used to train all team members in requirements analysis, overall process understanding, and known methods of implementing industry-proven procedural systems.

What are external/internal requirements?

External requirements are derived from the enterprise environmental factors that include a broad range of mandatory and optional requirements, such as pertinent laws and statutes established by local, state, and federal regulatory agencies and discipline and practice standards promulgated by professional organizations. Internal requirements are derived from the organizational process assets that include enterprise missions, organizational goals, executive directives, and upper-level procedural documentation. These requirements are illustrated in Figure 11-1, which shows an enterprise environmental factors umbrella that both supports and flows down to drive an enterprise's policy, plan, and procedures system. In addition, it illustrates that those external requirements addressed in the internal procedural documentation at one level of the documentation hierarchy also flow down as requirements to the documentation in the next level of the hierarchy.

Why use a top down approach?

The structuring of a procedural system lends itself to development through use of a cascading analysis process, which allows for structured review from the top external/internal requirement to the lowest implementing step. Each applicable requirement must be identified, properly and clearly documented, and placed within a hierarchy of requirements.

Figure 11-1. Top Down Relationship Hierarchy and Requirements Flow Down

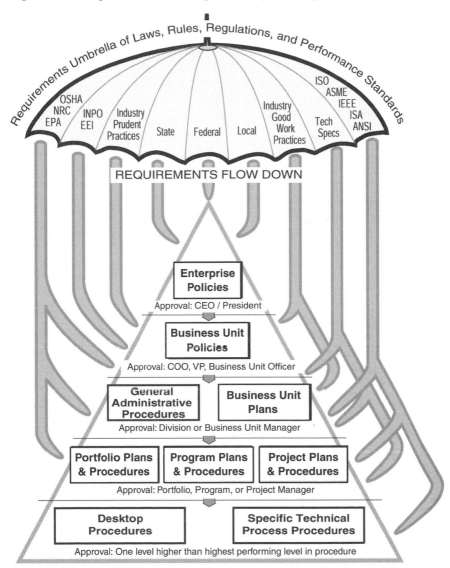

Each policy, plan, or procedure should explicitly address one or more of those requirements. This ensures the procedural system will be defined in terms of sound realistic implementing steps that have been sequentially developed and logically and properly verified.

Why is focused and effective communication necessary?

Effective communication, both oral and written, is required for successful project business management. Policies, plans, and procedures cover a broad area of written communication. They also represent the largest volume of permanent and reused written communication on a portfolio, program, project, or any operation.

Why use management of change?

Because any change within an organization can be traumatic, senior management must manage both the implementation of the change and the cultural impacts of that change. Personnel normally tend to reject and not support any initiative, whether a procedural or process change, that affects the status quo. Therefore, a management of change process operated by change management professionals will help ensure a smooth and effective implementation of a restructured and upgraded procedural system.

What value does a performance assessment program provide?

A routine performance assessment program covering the procedural system can provide essential data related to productivity, trends, timeliness, costs, and root causes of failures. This can be accomplished through quality circles, employee suggestions, periodic review of how well requirements are being met, third-party reviews of the procedural system and requirements analysis, empowerment of employees, evaluation of project business management maturity (see Section 6), and so on. This knowledge of performance effectiveness can support a continuous procedural process improvement as an integral part of the daily work routine. This will also lead to more mature and institutionalized processes.

11.4 Procedural System Development Process

The structured approach for developing procedures has proved highly effective from the standpoint of acceptance, timeliness, and effectiveness. As stated previously, the process uses the concepts of system engineering for complex interdisciplinary systems. This combination of scientific method supplemented with administrative technique can be broadly summarized as follows:

- Establish requirements and parameters.
- Define interfaces at all levels.
- Identify end use requirements.

- Define system.
- Establish plans and system design to meet requirements.
- Test the system.
- Determine if results satisfy system design.
- Implement system.

This method incorporates flow charts of the process, identification of needed monetary and personnel resources to implement the process, and the obtaining of management awareness and commitment to the process before writing begins.

The following are the major steps and considerations in developing or restructuring and upgrading a procedural system. These points may prove useful to those responsible for defining, developing, modifying, managing, or administering a set of policies, plans, and procedures. These steps will also help ensure alignment of the procedures with the enterprise's vision/mission and values and will eliminate organizational barriers to effectiveness.

Setting Vision/Missions and Objective

The senior management team sets, revises, or reaffirms the enterprise vision/mission and long-range objectives. Each senior manager in turn sets, revises, or reaffirms his or her organizational mission to interface to and integrate with the other organizational missions. The integrated set of organizational missions should not overlap or omit any area. All together, it must support the enterprise's mission. This team also defines and documents any philosophy or value statements. Each mission is approved by the enterprise officer representing the organizational function, and all affected officers and general managers approve the philosophy and value statements.

Analyzing Requirements and Defining Topics

Either the procedural review task force or another team will, as its first activity, identify and document all internal and external requirements to be met by the integrated set of policies, plans, and procedures. This includes the pertinent local, state, and federal laws and regulations and the relevant discipline and practice standards. These are then reviewed to establish a set of ten to thirty topic areas for which policy statements will be developed. Examples of common policy topic areas are:

- Project Business Management.
- Safety.

- Quality.
- Conduct of Business.
- Human Resources.
- Licensing and Regulatory Issues.
- Training and Qualifications.

Individual requirements that the enterprise must consider for both policies and procedures are then identified and recorded. This can be accomplished by highlighting the requirements to be met on the requirements document. This identification can also be automated within a relational database management system, with the full text of each specific requirement captured as well as the information related to the requirement source document name, number, revision, and so on.

Reviewing and Setting Policies

A policy is a brief statement set forth by senior management that defines those courses of action selected to influence or direct management and employee decisions, actions, and other related matters. It is a guiding principle or philosophy, usually based on internal and external requirements, considered to be prudent, expedient, or advantageous for the enterprise. The examination sequence for policies should be a systematic six-step process:

Step 1: Identify affected business functions and develop a policy checklist. The checklist for the review process should include:

- Enterprise purpose and vision statement.
- Enterprise and organizational mission statements.
- Enterprise philosophy and value statements.
- Organizational objectives.
- Current approved policies and their purposes.
- Desired policy topic areas.
- Identification of each organization involved in each policy area.
- Documented enterprise environmental factors.
- Documented organizational process assets.
- Questions to be asked on usage, application, acceptance, and benefit.

Step 2: Interview selected key managers to obtain a composite view of policy process.

Step 3: Review both formal and informal policies for compliance with applicable checklist items. Formal policies are documented and easily examined, but informal policies are embedded in the everyday work processes of the organization. They are less visible, more difficult to find, and may completely contradict the organization's formal values. The review team must determine to what goal each policy is directed. What are the legal requirements or implications? If a policy is issued to satisfy a labor contract, law, standard, or government regulation, it may be difficult to alter its content, but it should be examined for possible improvement within the intent of the requirements.

Step 4: Review both formal and informal policies for salient content and compliance with the following list of requirements for a good policy. The content of each policy should:

- Be consistent with and support the enterprise mission and principles.
- Seek benefits not easily quantified.
- Support the long-term enterprise objectives.
- Be compatible with the enterprise's vision of tomorrow.
- Align with key enterprise and management concepts.
- Clearly explain why the policy is necessary.
- Be written in appropriate language and form.
- Be brief, concise, unambiguous, and complete.
- Contain no procedural-type steps.
- Be stated in positive terms, if possible.
- Diminish barriers between functional groups.
- Assume people will act responsibly and are trustworthy.
- Promote employee self-esteem.
- Encourage team work and leadership.
- Promote desirable behaviors.
- Enhance employees' ability to take pride in their work.
- Minimize one employee inspecting another employee's actions or behavior.
- Foster decision making at an appropriate level.
- Create conditions that foster innovation and improvement.

Step 5: Examine the clarity of the policy and the effectiveness of its implementation. Clarify and state the intent(s) of each policy. Is one intent more important than another? Is the policy ignored or altered in practice? If so, examine the need for the policy's existence.

Step 6: Document effectiveness, noncompliances, policy overlaps, and missing topics, and describe needed modifications. Identify and describe informal policies. The review report should also answer questions such as: Is the policy necessary? Is the policy complex, and will it be easy to administer? Will it be easily understood by the organizations and personnel affected? Does it address the intended requirement, and can it produce the desired results? When the analysis is complete, the review team should be able to demonstrate where the policies do not meet the checklist, the requirements for a good policy, and how any proposed new policy or modification will benefit the organization.

Analyzing Work Processes, Reviewing Existing Procedures, and Documenting Work Processes

Senior management must first set the objectives and expected results and provide a formal commitment in the form of a review or development charter. The organizational scope of the review must also be set (i.e., just one function or the entire organization). The review team can then perform a systematic six-step review process to identify the problems and shortcomings of current procedures and develop potential improvements.

Step 1: Identify affected work processes, define and list applicable procedures, and develop a checklist. The review process checklist should include:

- Enterprise and organizational mission statements.
- Current approved policies.
- Organizational objectives.
- Current approved procedures and their intended purposes.
- Identification of every work process.
- Applicable internal requirements (organizational processes assets).
- Mandatory external requirements (enterprise environmental factors).
- Optional external requirements.
- Good business practices.
- Recommended industry, discipline, and practice standards.
- Glossary of terms.
- Questions to be asked on usage, utility, application, acceptance, and benefit.

Step 2: Interview selected key employees to obtain a composite view of the procedural system.

Step 3: Review procedures for salient content, compliance with applicable checklist items, and compliance with the following list of requirements for a good procedure. The procedural content should:

- Consider total cost.
- Benefit the mission and goals of the entire enterprise.
- Reference and not repeat policy or other requirements.
- Enhance employees' ability to take pride in their work.
- Enhance employee self-esteem.
- Encourage teamwork and leadership.
- Be presented in a language and form appropriate to the situation.
- Be brief, concise, unambiguous, complete.
- Minimize one employee inspecting another employee's actions or behavior.
- Foster decision making at an appropriate level.
- Limit an employee's need to do extra work.
- Limit authorizations for routine actions.
- Communicate that employees are trusted.
- Contain no barriers to cross-functional cooperation.
- Promote employee self-esteem.
- Ensure personnel can be managed effectively.
- Define performance qualifications.
- Have a high graphical content.

Step 4: Describe all organizational interfaces, each organization involved in the work processes, functional work responsibilities, and points of organizational integration/interaction.

Step 5: Create a flow diagram of the optimum procedural steps and sequence, indicating performance responsibility.

Step 6: Document noncompliances, document unnecessary redundancies, and describe potential modifications. When the analysis is complete the review team should be able to demonstrate how the procedures meet the checklist and requirements for a good procedure, or how any proposed improvement modification will benefit the organization.

Creating Revised Documentation Hierarchies

A key step in the restructuring process is the development of a documentation hierarchy. The structure must be developed from the top down and have a limited number of levels. This is the most managerially difficult and organizationally sensitive step because of the number of factors that must be accommodated in creating the structure. The concept is to identify the applicable external requirements documents and their flow-down relation to the enterprise's policy, plan, and procedure structure. Each level should stand by itself and must also implement the requirements addressed in and flowed down from the level above. (An example of a summary hierarchy is provided in Figure 11-1.) The hierarchical structure should ensure the mission is at the top, followed by the policies, intermediate general administrative procedures and project plans, and the unique and task-specific implementing procedures at the bottom. In addition, the managerial level needed to administer and approve each level should decrease as we move down the structure. This hierarchy should be issued and maintained as part of the documented procedural system.

Designing Documentation Formats

Firm documentation formats should be defined and mandated for each document type. This produces a series of benefits:

- Maintains consistency among procedures and across functional organizations.
- Establishes an effective format for the organization.
- Defines appropriate language.
- Limits document size.
- Establishes uniform page layouts for each document type.
- Minimizes undesirable or legally dangerous content.
- Promotes enterprise's image.

The following are the essential features, accepted by most organizations, for simple and effective procedural documentation:

Mission and Values: Each vision/mission is usually a one to three sentence statement. Philosophy or value statements are usually one paragraph to one page long. Vision/mission, philosophy, and value statements are usually presented together in a single page, sometimes oversized, graphic format with high text content and associated management signatures.

Policies: Each policy is a single-topic, concise, one-page document. The policy number, effective date, policy title, issue date, revision number, and page number should be inserted into a preprinted form. The body contains five major sections followed by an authorization.

- *Policy Statement:* Simple, direct statement of the policy, excluding qualifiers about intention, applicability, or implementation. The maximum length should be three sentences.
- *Policy Intent:* Statement of policy goal provided by using an action verb at the beginning of each sentence to designate what the policy should accomplish.

- *Applicability:* Statement of which organizational element(s) are governed by the policy.
- *Implementation:* Statement of how policy is to be implemented and maintained, including what must be established, how policy will be communicated, and the activities to implement the policy.
- *Source Documents:* Identification of internal or external requirements documents that define, identify, or establish the policy requirements and are incorporated by reference into the policy.
- *Approval Authority:* Title and signature.

Plans: The formats for plans are the most variable, and, therefore, a set of annotated content outlines and formats, each with a purpose, will need to be established. The key to useful plans is that they follow the outline and include all content items specified in the external or internal requirements document that mandated their generation. When properly created, a good plan:

- Has limited objectives and a well-defined set of parameters and requirements.
- Is closed and well defined to provide a management guide for directing the work.
- Limits detail to that needed for the level of control expected to be exercised.
- Provides sufficient alternatives so that it will still function when changes occur.
- Defines and integrates desired scope with technical, cost, quality, and schedule requirements.
- Defines the most effective and logical sequence of actions for successful achievement of specified objectives.

Procedures: Each procedure is a document that specifies or describes how a process or an activity is to be performed. The procedure number, effective date, title, issue date, revision number, page number, and approval authority with signature should be inserted on a preprinted form. The body contains eight major sections and may include methods to be employed, equipment or materials to be used, and a sequence of operations. The major sections are:

- *Purpose and Scope:* Brief statements of the subject and intended purpose of the procedure, plus the activities, processes, or other process features covered.
- *Applicability:* Statement of affected personnel and organizational elements and activities to which it applies.
- *Definitions:* Definition of terms which are not contained in the enterprise's general glossary of terms, which have a specific meaning

within the procedure, or which are repeated (this is discouraged) for full understanding of the procedure.

- *Requirements:* Identify specific requirements from the source document items that must be met in performing the work; to the extent they reflect all relevant requirements so the user need not research source documents.
- *Responsibilities:* Identify position or organization and describe responsibilities of those affected.
- *Procedural Steps:* A step-wise set of declarative statements of the tasks or actions that must be performed to meet the intent of the procedure, including the associated performing organization or position; this preferably includes a procedural flow chart.
- *Records:* Statements of the records that must be generated, as well as their administrative disposition.
- *Sources and References:* Clear identification of internal or external requirements documents that define, identify, or establish the requirements, and administrative identification of the supporting or interfacing procedures referenced in the procedure.
- *Attachments:* Identification of forms, instructions, samples, and so on, included.

The presentation style is terse and concise, using action verb declarative sentence fragment statements with an assumed performer. The length should be short (two to four pages) and include at least one page of graphics such as the procedural step flow chart. Flow charts are used to answer the questions "what, by whom, how, and when" and should be focused at management direction, not at detailed methods for implementation.

Develop Policy, Plan, and Procedure Documentation

The physical preparation is actually one of the easiest—although the most time-consuming—steps in a structured development approach. The manager in charge should carefully plan and schedule this step in detail to ensure sufficient time is allowed to produce the set of policies, plans, and procedures documentation in a timely and cost-effective manner. Personnel assignment should consider that most enterprise subject matter experts are not usually skilled writers. Therefore, this step is usually more effective and economically performed when some of the consultant resources described previously are also employed. Plans and procedures should be written to be implemented by trained and qualified personnel. The level of detail should be limited to only that required by the least qualified employee.

Before proceeding with the preparation, one of the many adequate and available electronic publishing programs and a graphics or flow chart program should be selected and implemented. This will obviously speed the development or revision process and reduce costs. This step uses as input the already documented output of the previous review and analysis steps to initiate the development or modifications. Each document is developed through a basic eight-step sequence.

The policy planning steps are:

- Identify and select specific topic area.
- Identify and select applicable requirements.
- Prepare annotated outline.
- Accept outline.
- Produce working draft.
- Upgrade draft to meet content requirements (described previously) for a good policy.
- Acquire senior management comments.
- Create executive approval draft.

The plan preparation steps are:

- Identify and select applicable requirements.
- Outline plan based on requirements.
- Prepare annotated outline.
- Accept outline.
- Produce working draft.
- Upgrade draft to meet content specified in requirements document.
- Acquire project and technical comments.
- Create management approval draft.

Procedure preparation steps are:

- Identify and select applicable requirements and project plans.
- Prepare procedure flow chart based upon work process flow chart(s) and project plans.
- Prepare annotated outline.
- Accept outline and flow chart.
- Produce working draft.
- Upgrade draft to meet content requirements described above for a good procedure.

- Acquire user comments.
- Create business unit manager approval draft.

Staged Implementation

Sequentially staging the implementation of a new procedural system in terms of both time and specific actions is the most cost-effective and prudent approach. This is a three-part operation:

Set Plan: Key decisions that must be made to support an efficiently staged implementation include:

- Which policies and procedures will be tested or validated?
- How many new or revised policies or procedures can be released at one time without negatively affecting the organization?
- When will new or revised policies and procedures be issued?
- When will new or revised policies and procedures be effective?
- Who will communicate new or revised policies to the enterprise?
- Which organizations need training?
- How often must individuals be retrained or when must a newly assigned employee be trained?

Test: All major policies and complex procedures should be tested prior to management approval and implementation. This validation and verification may include:

- Testing usability.
- Clarifying intent.
- Verifying requirements.
- Implementing on a trial basis.
- Verifying desired results are obtainable.

Training: Training should be incorporated into the staged implementation between the procedure issue and effective date. A revised procedural system will be of greatest economic value after the implementing personnel are trained to perform successfully. Consultants can also be used and controlled effectively to develop and present this selected training and to train internal trainers.

SECTION 4

Capability

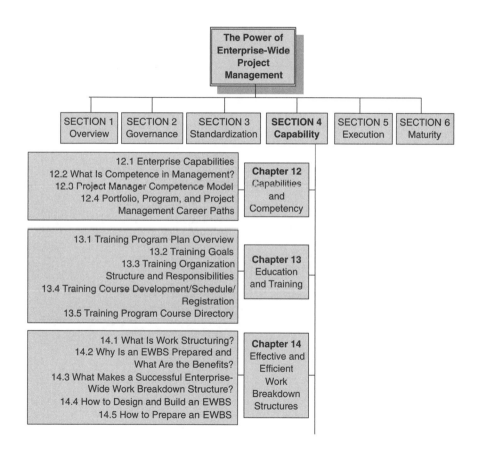

The Power of Enterprise-Wide Project Management

| SECTION 1 Overview | SECTION 2 Governance | SECTION 3 Standardization | **SECTION 4 Capability** | SECTION 5 Execution | SECTION 6 Maturity |

Chapter 12 Capabilities and Competency
12.1 Enterprise Capabilities
12.2 What Is Competence in Management?
12.3 Project Manager Competence Model
12.4 Portfolio, Program, and Project Management Career Paths

Chapter 13 Education and Training
13.1 Training Program Plan Overview
13.2 Training Goals
13.3 Training Organization Structure and Responsibilities
13.4 Training Course Development/Schedule/Registration
13.5 Training Program Course Directory

Chapter 14 Effective and Efficient Work Breakdown Structures
14.1 What Is Work Structuring?
14.2 Why Is an EWBS Prepared and What Are the Benefits?
14.3 What Makes a Successful Enterprise-Wide Work Breakdown Structure?
14.4 How to Design and Build an EWBS
14.5 How to Prepare an EWBS

CHAPTER 12

Capabilities and Competency

The third of the four major pillars in the enterprise-wide project management house of excellence is the part of the structure that evaluates the impact that individual and corporate capabilities have on the establishment of enterprise-wide project management. The following chapters visit the topics of personnel competency, capability measurement, development, and education and training with career path development, the use of the work breakdown structure tool, project business management system implementation, earned value methodology application, and the utilization of communications and risk management. These are all key ingredients to successfully building enterprise-wide project management practices within businesses of all sizes.

12.1 Enterprise Capabilities

To have capabilities in project business management implies that specific requisite capabilities are identified, developed, and maintained over time. Much of this book discusses those specific *organizational process asset* capabilities.

What is also needed is management and staff qualified to implement project business management. To confirm that this competency exists, personnel at all levels should be assessed. If personnel capabilities are missing, the enterprise needs to have a training and education program. This program is most effective when integrated as part of the career path development for individuals qualified to become project, program, or portfolio managers.

In recent years, for example, enterprises in the aerospace, automotive, and construction industries wanted to improve time to market, cost to market, and quality to market. One approach was to reduce their list of suppliers to a few selected companies. Each selected enterprise became a business partner and an an integral part of a total solution, rather than a component product supplier or single service provider. This action focuses on suppliers with the capability to rapidly plan, award, and perform work. This saves time, resources, and funds. If those enterprises and their suppliers successfully shift the way they do business, it will also change the nature of how people within those enterprises perform their work. Effective employment of project business management best practices is another key element in their achieving and maintaining a competitive advantage in the global market, where being a preferred supplier or using preferred suppliers is becoming a common business management practice. These enterprises understand that their portfolios, programs, and projects are only as successful as the people who manage them, and they understand the need to increase their organization's project business management capability and competency.

Besides focusing on the competency and capabilities of an enterprise's personnel, most of the discussion emphasizes the key organizational process assets (see Subchapter 4.3)—policies, procedures, and management processes capabilities—needed to be effective and successful in applying project business management. In addition, certain methodologies, systems, and practices are also key enterprise environmental factors (see Subchapters 4.2 and 4.3) that are critical to effectively implementing project business management.

These other factors are breakdown structure, a project business management system, the earned value technique, and project cost accounting methodology. When effectively implemented, these factors are the primary reasons many enterprise-wide project management implementations succeed. Conversely, when an enterprise attempts to implement these project management oriented systems, tools, and methodologies without simultaneously developing the requisite project business management processes and enterprise project management office, that attempt at implementing enterprise-wide project management usually fails. The simple reason is management is done by people through the use of tools—people manage, tools do not.

12.2 What Is Competence in Management?

In *A Global Approach to Project Management Competence* (AIPM, 1997), Dr. Lynn Crawford states:

> Competence is a term which is widely used but which has come to mean different things to different people. It is generally accepted, however, as encompassing knowledge, skills, attitudes and behaviors that are causally related to superior job perform-

ance (Boyatzis, 1982). This understanding of competence has been described as attribute-based inference of competence (Heywood, Gonczi et al, 1992). To this can be added what is referred to as the performance-based approach to competence, which assumes that competence can be inferred from demonstrated performance at pre-defined acceptable standards in the workplace (Gonczi, Hager et al, 1993). The performance-based approach is the basis for what has become known as the Competency Standards Movement that underpins the National Vocation Qualifications in the United Kingdom, the Australian National Competency Standards Framework [linked to the Australian Qualifications Framework], and the National Qualifications Framework of the New Zealand Qualifications Authority (NZQA).

Our example of a project business management competency model is based on the requirements found in the Project Management Institute's (PMI®) *Project Manager Competency Development Framework* (PMCDF) standard that was published in 2002. The working definition the PMCD used for development of its standard is based on Scott Parry's (1998) definition; a competency is a cluster of related knowledge, attitudes, skills, and other personal characteristics:

- That affects a major part of one's job (i.e., one or more key roles or responsibilities);
- That correlates with performance on the job;
- That can be measured against well-accepted standards;
- That can be improved via training and development; and
- That can be broken down into dimensions of competence.

Evaluating project business management personnel competencies can identify persons who are, or have the potential to become, superior portfolio, program, or project managers. These evaluations can determine what is needed in the way of training, education, and career development to raise the performance level of each person. When project management personnel have superior competency levels, programs and projects are managed more effectively, increasing the probability of project success and a higher return on project investment. The development of project management skills will enable an organization to build a team of experienced and trained managers capable of taking on multiple projects and helping their customers achieve their goals.

Measuring portfolio, program, and project management competencies and benchmarking them against recognized project business management best practices is the first step in developing an effective project business management training program to achieve the highest level of competency in all areas.

12.3 Project Manager Competence Model

Our project business management methodology model is based on the PMI®'s *PMBOK® Guide,* which has become the de facto standard for managing individual projects, and PMI's new *A Standard for Program Management,* and *A Standard for Portfolio Management.* It is logical therefore that a project management competency model should also be based on another PMI® Standard, the *Project Management Competency Development Framework (PMCDF).*

The first step in applying project management best practice principles at the organizational level is to assess the organization's project management competency to establish a baseline against which to measure progress. Table 12-1 contains a list of project business management competency elements that are organized into five categories that assign target competency levels for eight project management job classifications.

Figure 12-1 shows an example of a competency model and provides a competency rating system that establishes the competency target for the eight project business management position classifications for each of the elements within each category.

1 = BASIC: The employee has been exposed to the concepts of project business management, is familiar with the terms, and demonstrates a basic knowledge and skill in the competency. The employee may begin to increase development of knowledge and skill competency through training, day-to-day activities, and project assignments. The employee should be aware of the self-development required to meet expectation, as defined in the employees' development plan.

2 = DEVELOPMENT: The employee exhibits a limited level of the knowledge and understanding expected for this competency. Im-

Table 12-1. Competency Elements

Team Skills	Professional Skills	Technical Skills
Personal characteristics	Analytical skills	Core skills
Working characteristics	People management	Experience and certifications
Communication skills	Client service	Education

Figure 12-1. Project Business Management Competency Model

Project Business Management Competency Elements	Project Management Classifications							
Competency Scores 1 = Basic, 2=Development, 3=Proficient, 4=Mastery, 5=Expert	Proj. Admin.	Technical Leader	PM Level 1	PM Level 2	PM Level 3	Program Manager	Portfolio Manager	EPMO Manager
TEAM SKILLS								
Personal Characteristics								
Working Characteristics								
Communication Skills								
PROFESSIONAL SKILLS								
Analytical Skills								
People Management								
Client Service								
TECHNICAL SKILLS								
Core Skills								
EXPERIENCE and CERTIFICATIONS								
EDUCATION (D = Desired, R = Required)								

provement can be attained by the completion of specific training and activities, as defined in the employee's development plan. The employee is expected to display significant progress in the basic knowledge of the competency.

3 = PROFICIENT: The employee exhibits an exceptional level of knowledge and understanding of this competency in a skillful and consistent manner. The employee confidently takes on opportunities to exhibit or use the skill. The employee should progress to the mastery stage with additional time and experience.

4 = MASTERY: The employee demonstrates the competency in a highly proficient and consistent manner. The employee exhibits mastery of the competency in a wide variety of situations and circumstances. Management, other employees, and customers regard the employee as an authority in the competency area.

5 = EXPERT/MENTOR/TEACHER: The employee demonstrates competency with a high degree of knowledge. The employee exhibits mastery of the competency in a wide variety of complex situations and cir-

Figure 12-2.   Project Business Management Competency Score Card

Name: _____   Date: _____

Classification: _____

Project Management Competency Elements	Score			
Personal Competency Scores 0 = Not rated 1 = Minimally effective - barely exhibits this competency the way expected 2 = Effective - exhibits an adequate example of this competency 3 = Highly effective - exhibits a very good example of this competency				
TEAM SKILLS				
Personal Characteristics				
Working Characteristics				
Communication Skills				
PROFESSIONAL SKILLS				
Analytical Skills				
People Management				
Client Service				
TECHNICAL SKILLS				
Core Skills				
EXPERIENCE and CERTIFICATIONS				
EDUCATION (D = Desired, R = Required)				

cumstances. Management, other employees, and customers regard the employee as an expert in this area. The employee is capable of leading customer, branch, regional, and national activities, which provide the employee with an opportunity to teach or mentor others.

Figure 12-2 illustrates a score card that is used to evaluate a person's project management competency as defined in Figure 12-1. Project management competency evaluations are part of the annual employee performance review process.

12.4 Portfolio, Program, and Project Management Career Paths

The performance of project business management processes and activities requires that project team members, referred to as project human resources, provide the skills and experience required to complete the technical work of projects to produce the products, services, or results for which the project was authorized. These knowledge and skills are usually obtained through formal technical training or on-the-job training that is provided or paid for by the enterprise.

Project business management is usually the responsibility of the individual manager selected to head the project. Project managers lead project teams, but in many cases they also often perform project activities that directly produce deliverables. Project managers oversee and coordinate the project work and productive interaction among team members (technical resources). Until recently, individual managers received specialized training on the job. In the last ten years, however, many earned Bachelor, Masters, and Doctorial degrees in project management.

In 1984, the Project Management Institute (PMI®) began a certification program with the designation of Project Management Professional (PMP®). It is the first such program of its kind to achieve ISO-9000 certification, and that certification is respected by organizations worldwide. An increasing number of enterprises uses the PMP® as a baseline requirement for assigning or hiring project managers. Many of these same organizations have also developed their own internal qualification and certification programs. The knowledge and experience required to obtain PMP® certification is not specific to any one industry, but rather focuses on the application of the processes, tools, and techniques contained in the *PMBOK® Guide.* Therefore, internal programs usually include PMP® certification, as well as additional industry-specific training in the application of project management practices.

A proposed framework for a Project Business Management Competency Model, which was provided in Subchapter 12.3, identifies eight role classifications:

1. Project Administration Support
2. Technical Leader
3. Project Manager – level one
4. Project Manager – level two
5. Project Manager – level three
6. Program Manager
7. Portfolio Manager
8. EPMO Manager

Development of a portfolio, program, and project management career path program involves the integration of three important components:

- A competency model that identifies the project business management roles and the capabilities associated with those roles (See Section 2).

- A qualification and certification program that provides a method to plan an individual's career path and have the individual gain the knowledge and skills required to advance along the path.
- An education and training program that identifies the knowledge and skills required to meet the competency requirements defined in the model (see Chapter 13).

One of the responsibilities of the enterprise-wide project management office (EPMO) is to work with human resources (HR) to establish a career path program to facilitate the growth and advancement of individuals. Establishing such a career path requires support and commitment from senior managers. Selling the concept of establishing a project management career path to those executives and managers involves answering the following questions:

1. Why create a project business management career path?
2. What value is provided, and how does the enterprise benefit?
3. What are the benefits to the individuals?
4. How will the qualification/certification program be structured and managed?
5. What are the components of a program?

Why create a project management career path?

Most enterprises have some form of career advancement process associated with its business and technical positions. Generally, advancement is usually aligned with an increase in knowledge, skills, and experience in a discipline that is recognized as a profession. Such disciplines are accounting, engineering, quality control, and information technology. Establishing a career path for the project management discipline is directly associated with and is in support of the establishment of a Project Business Management Competency Model. Developing a project business management career path facilitates the delineation of specific skills, knowledge, and experience that provides the ability to measure the competencies defined in the Project Business Management Competency Model.

The HR business unit usually has the responsibility and authority to develop programs for employee development, while the EPMO can and should provide a supporting role to facilitate the development of a career path within the enterprise's project business management employment environment. It is not the job of the EPMO to implement the program as an initiative, but rather to become an advocate that plays a key role contributing the knowledge associated with the project management profession. The EPMO's primary contribution is its role as a subject matter expert in the ongoing career maturation of the project management roles defined in the Project Business Management Competency Model. HR will facilitate the program through its insight into personnel management practices. Therefore, a collaborative effort between the EPMO and HR is the best approach to creating guidelines for planning, developing, implementing, and managing the project business management career path.

What value is provided and how does the organization benefit?

Establishing project business management position levels requires defining the individual skill, knowledge, and experience necessary for specific roles and responsibilities. Distinguishing among the capabilities and competencies for the various project business management positions makes it easier to identify qualified individuals as management positions or assignments become available.

Establishing a project business management career path enables the EPMO to:

- Recognize the project management discipline as a profession.
- Develop professional recognition and career planning.
- Provide incentives and encourage participation in career planning.
- Expand business roles and responsibilities.
- Retain valuable resources and attract new talent.
- Raise competitiveness in the marketplace.
- Improve achievement of business goals and objectives.
- Establish equity with other business areas.
- Ensure alignment in the marketplace.
- Adopt project business management methodology best practices as a core competency.
- Satisfy governmental agency and regulatory skill requirements or business needs.

Establishing a career path for project business management provides the following benefits to the enterprise and various business units:

- Formal documentation of the roles and responsibilities for all project business management positions.
- Specific advancement requirements for each project business management position.
- Improved retention of key human resources by providing a defined means for professional advancement.
- A higher degree of confidence in identifying the right personnel for specific portfolio, program, and project assignments.
- Increasing employee morale, motivation, and performance enterprise-wide.

- Improving cooperation and information sharing among personnel, as well as within and among business units.

What are the benefits to the individual staff member?

Career advancement provides rewards and recognition. Promotions usually bring added responsibilities, increases in pay, and professional recognition by peers. Progression up the career ladder increases a person's economic and technical values both inside and outside the enterprise as a project business management resource with verifiable capabilities that qualify them for future opportunities.

Developing a career path for project business management positions will have the following positive effects on current project business management human resources management operations. For each position it will:

- Define the roles.
- Establish the level responsibilities.
- Identify authority and accountability.
- Provide a basis for pay and benefits.
- Provide levels of professional recognition.
- Set up qualification and certification requirements.

The business units with the affected personnel will experience the following positive effects:

- Defined administration of the career path program.
- Support from other affected business units.
- Controlled stakeholder reaction to the changes.
- Managed change within the organization.

How will it be structured and managed?

The EPMO selects the applicable portfolio, program, and project business management standards, develops and implements the project business management methodology, and creates the criteria used to measure acceptable performance as required for career advancement. This includes any internal or external professional or technical certification that is required.

The EPMO mentors and coaches individuals through the process of career advancement. Establishing a project business management career path creates equal opportunities for everyone within an enterprise and reinforces executive management's position that project management is a professional discipline requiring specialized skills, knowledge, and experience.

HR can own the career path program as a part of its business function. The EPMO can assist HR in developing and implementing the career path program by providing knowledge in:

- Defining portfolio, program, and project management position responsibilities.
- Establishing the capabilities that define skill, education, and experience for the roles of the various positions.
- Identifying benchmark study data establishing pay grades and benefits.
- Defining requirements to improve capabilities through training, education, and certification programs.
- Performing an evaluation of project business management maturity level to establish a baseline.
- Preparing a plan for project maturity improvements related to human resource competency.

The enterprise's project business management maturity will affect its ability to sustain the changes that come with the implementation of a project business management career program. When developing the project career path for individual positions, the following elements need to be defined and formally documented:

Position title: Be consistent in using titles that are already part of the enterprise's structure and that are commonly used in other organizations within the industry.

Roles and responsibilities: Consider identifying performance objectives and the degree to which they are affected by the type of work performed.

Authority and accountability: Identify and define direct and indirect reporting within the hierarchical structure of the overall enterprise and with the EPMO. Establish the authority and level of control over budgets, work authorization, assigned personnel, internal and external procurement or contracting for goods and services, and any other specific function applicable to that position.

Experience requirements: Establish the number of years of experience, as well as the requisite level of responsibility, required to perform the work.

Education and training requirements: Establish formal, informal, technical, and professional education and training that includes any required professional certifications.

Compensation and benefits: Establish annual salaries or hourly wage ranges. Include details about benefits beyond those provided to all employees of the organization. This usually includes specialized training, membership in professional organizations, and reimbursement of costs to obtain professional certification, if required, for the position or advancement to the next level of one's career path.

What are the components of a qualification/certification program?

The following is an example of a competency development program. Note that each role is developed with a three-stage program that involves a qualification and certification process at each stage. The components of the project management career path program are illustrated in Figure 12-3.

In the qualification step, participants validate that they have the skills and knowledge required to meet the qualification criteria for the position or to obtain instruction through education and training programs provided or supported by the enterprise. The criteria defining the qualification requirements are developed by the joint efforts of the EPMO and the HR business unit. Table 12-2 contains information about the requirements and timeframes for the three-level program shown in Figure 12-3.

Figure 12-3.   Internal Career Path Program

Table 12-2.   Career Qualification Requirements

Career Stage	Knowledge Assessment	Skills Assessment
Entry Level	Validate achievement capabilities defined in the Competency Model by testing.	Validate achievement capabilities defined in the Competency Model by testing.
Intermediate Level	Validate achievement capabilities defined in the Competency Model by testing.	Validate achievement capabilities defined in the Competency Model by testing.
Advanced level	Validate achievement capabilities defined in the Competency Model by testing.	Validate achievement capabilities defined in the Competency Model by testing.

The certification step of the program requires that participants demonstrate the required skills and knowledge requirements by performing the work assigned to them during the certification period. Table 12-3 contains information about the requirements and timeframes for the three levels shown in Figure 12-3.

The third critical component of the career path program is developing a comprehensive education and training program. Chapter 13 describes an education and training program that provides the skills and knowledge required to satisfy the competency objectives defined in the Project Business Management Competency Model described in this chapter.

Table 12-3. Career Certification Requirements

Career Stage	Certification Requirements	Duration
Entry Level	Complete the work assigned under close supervision.	Three projects, but not less than six months.
Intermediate Level	Complete the work assigned under minimal supervision.	Three projects, but not less than 12 months.
Advanced level	Complete the work assigned under close supervision.	Three projects, but not less than 24 months.

CHAPTER 13

Education and Training

An enterprise that intends to accomplish significant strategic plan objectives through completing portfolios, programs, and projects needs to develop and deliver education and training programs that effectively provide the requisite knowledge, skills, and capabilities. The organization should clearly communicate enterprise-wide that it wants and has a comprehensive education and training program that offers an internal qualification and certification for the development of portfolio, program, and project managers and that offers education and training opportunities in project business management at all levels of the organization.

Purpose: Establish a comprehensive education and training program to enable to the enterprise to effectively and consistently apply the enterprise's project business management methodology to achieve continuous improvement.

Benefits: Among the key benefits are the following:

- Improving new product and/or services time to market, quality to market, and cost to market.
- Reducing project schedule and cost.
- Improving planning and management skills.
- Aiding the growth of the organization's project business management maturity.
- Increasing personnel capabilities, which, in turn, increases their value to the enterprise.
- Improving employee job satisfaction.
- Improving employee retention.

13.1 Training Program Plan Overview

The project business management training plan identifies the strategy for creating the courses that teach the necessary skills to the personnel respon-

Figure 13-1. Training Program Development Process

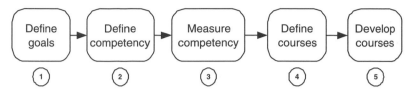

sible for portfolios, programs, and projects. The plan describes the process for identifying the training needs and skills and the responsibilities for executing the plan. The focus of this plan is to achieve the training goals of the eight project management roles identified in Figure 12-1. One process for developing such a program is shown in Figure 13-1.

Information on how to download a copy of an example project management training program plan document is available at www.amacom books.org/go/EnterpriseWidePM. This plan implements the policy of holding each business unit responsible for identifying employee training and development needs within its operation.

The plan is designed to describe the project business management training program (PBMTP), whose objective is to ensure that all project personnel are properly trained in the use of project business management best practices. This objective applies to all personnel but the training plan applies specifically to project business management. It does not include nonspecialist training. The PBMTP also assumes that the minimal requirements identified by the enterprise-wide project management office (EPMO) for each position are satisfied.

13.2 Training Goals

Table 13-1 provides guidelines that define the following six types of enterprise goals for project team members, portfolio, program and project managers, and business unit managers.

Business objective goals define training outcomes that influence institutionalized project business management best practices enterprise wide.

Performance goals establish training outcomes that can improve organizational performance.

Competency goals identify training outcomes that can improve individual performance.

Knowledge goals define training outcomes that quantifiably improve individual knowledge in the subject area.

Skill goals establish training outcomes that increase individual proficiency in using a process or tool.

Attitude Goals identify training outcomes that support project business management best practices as a core competency.

These goals are the basis for establishing project business management competencies. Such a model can be used to measure an individual's project business management maturity. Developing a project business management training program requires an assessment of the organization as a whole. Defining the types of education and training courses to be offered

Table 13-1.   Education and Training Goals

	PROJECT MANAGEMENT ROLES		
General Population	*Project Team Members*	*Project, Program, and Portfolio Managers*	*Business Unit Managers*
BUSINESS OBJECTIVE GOALS			
Obtain enterprise-wide support to establish project business management best practices as a core competency.	Obtain enterprise-wide support and consistent use of project business management best practices as a core competency.	PMP® Certification of all project managers. Ensure all projects are managed using project business management best practices utilizing a common project business management methodology.	Ensure corporate strategic planning objectives are achieved through effective use of project business management best practices.
PERFORMANCE GOALS			
Establish general knowledge of the project business management methodology (PBMM).	Institute a consistent use of the PBMM.	Ensure a consistent use of the PBMM to manage portfolios and projects.	Proactively support the use of PBMM on all projects.
COMPETENCY GOALS			
Establish the consistent use of project business management best practices to manage work.	Demonstrate effective application of the PBMM to manage projects.	Demonstrate the ability to consistently complete portfolios, programs, and projects by applying the PBMM effectively.	Ensure all projects are managed effectively utilizing the PBMM.

(continued)

Table 13-1. *(Continued)*

General Population	Project Team Members	Project, Program, and Portfolio Managers	Business Unit Managers
KNOWLEDGE GOALS			
Establish enterprise-wide familiarity with project business management terms and acronyms.	Achieve practical knowledge of the PBMM processes.	Demonstrate a working knowledge of proper application of PBMM processes to manage portfolios, programs, and projects.	Demonstrate a working knowledge of proper application of PBMM processes to manage portfolios, programs, and projects.
SKILLS GOALS			
Exhibit a basic capability of the PBMM processes.	Confirmed ability to effectively apply PBMM and the processes contained within.	Verified ability to effectively lead others in the application of PBMM processes.	Demonstrated ability to effectively support and enforce the application of processes contained within the standard PBMM methodology.
ATTITUDE GOALS			
Acceptance of executive management's goal to establish project business management practices as a core competency across the enterprise.	Verifiable desire to effectively apply project business management practices at a core competency level.	Confirmed desire to effectively apply project business management practices at a core competency level.	Visible support and encouragement of the adoption of project business management practices as core competency goal to achieve.

is determined by analyzing the results of an evaluation and comparing that results with the competency model. The primary goal of an education and training program is to improve the organization's project business management maturity level so that the company meets its strategic plan objectives by delivering programs and projects on schedule and within budget.

13.3 Training Organization Structure and Responsibilities

An example of an enterprise-wide project management office (EPMO) structure, shown in Figure 13-2, contains a function that manages all aspects of project business management education and training development and implementation. Table 13-2 is a responsibilities matrix that lists typical responsibilities for developing and managing the execution of a project business management education and training program.

Individual Training Plans: Business unit managers are responsible for evaluating the skills of all new employees against the requirements of the competency model. They also prepare and implement a training plan for each employee for the first year of employment.

In the training plan, the business unit manager identifies the specific training method that best meets the needs of the employee. This can vary because individuals have different backgrounds and experiences. Changes in technology or the introduction of new or updated tools may necessitate training for individuals outside the annual appraisal process. This training is the responsibility of the business unit manager, with input from the employees.

Maintaining Training Records: The EPMO maintains records of the training received by each employee, unless those records are maintained by an enterprise-level training organization or HR. Each business unit manager communicates these details to the EPMO. Table 13-2 lists other training-related responsibilities as they are applied to specific roles.

Training Methods: The logistics used to deliver the training programs vary from course to course. Training can be obtained in a number of

Figure 13-2. Project Management Training Structure

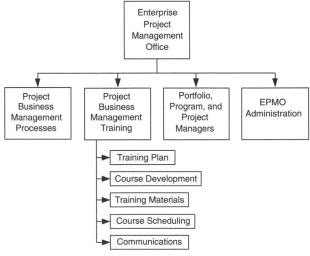

Table 13-2. Responsibility Matrix

Symbol Table R: Responsible I: Informed S: Support A: Approved *Responsibilities*	*Business Unit Manager*	*Business Unit Director*	*EPMO*	*Human Resources*
Conduct employee skill assessment.	R	S	S	I
Identify skill deficiencies.	R	S	S	S
Develop personalized employee training plan.	R	S	S	I
Execute employee-training plan.	S	A	R	I
Coordinate all business unit PBMM Manual training.	S	S	R	I
Coordinate all business unit PBMM Process Handbook training.	S	S	R	I
Maintain training records.	S	S	R	I
Maintain and update the business unit Training Plan.	R	S	S	I
Identify and evaluate training options for design tool skills.	S	S	R	S
Plan business unit training budgets.	R	A	S	I

different ways. The same information may be contained in part or whole in more than one course. The following is a list of the various ways training can be provided:

- Internal classes presented by internal personnel or contract consultants.
- External classes provided by PMI® Chapters, PMI® Registered Education Providers (R.E.P.), or local training providers.
- Distance Learning provided on the Internet by PMI® R.E.P. companies.
- Guest speaker workshops.

13.4 Training Course Development/ Schedule/Registration

The first step in developing project business management training is to determine if the planned training course are still relevant. Therefore, the training course synopsis, which defines the content of a training course, should be reviewed. Table 13-3 is an example of a training course synopsis.

The course training plan details how to create an internal course and provides guidelines for selecting external options. The process steps for developing a course are as follows:

Table 13-3. Example Training Course Synopsis

1.1 Introduction to Project Management	
Purpose:	Provide an overview of project business management and it's benefits.
Knowledge objectives:	Establish enterprise-wide familiarity with the Project Management Institute (PMI®) standards.
Learning objectives:	Establish enterprise-wide familiarity with project management as a profession.
Assessment method:	General awareness of PMI® defined knowledge areas and the benefits of project management.
Prerequisite:	None
Topics covered:	Introduction to PMI® defined knowledge areas, process groups, and processes; and project management benefits
Course length:	Approximate 15 minutes
Logistics:	Available any time
Class Size:	None—self-learning
Facilities and equipment:	Access presentation on enterprise's server
Course materials:	PMI® provided presentation materials
Reference:	None
Facilitator:	Self-Learning

Step 1: Decide if the course will be offered internally or externally.

Internal course: select course developer from internal personnel or contract developer.

- Develop and approve course presentation materials.
- Develop course workbook/handout materials, if required.

External course: select PMI® R.E.P. and determine the desired delivery method.

- E-learning: Internet-based self learning.
- Off-site: delivered by R.E.P at prescheduled locations.
- In-house: delivered by R.E.P at enterprise's facility.

Step 2: Implement schedule and registration process.

The training course scheduling and registration process involves the following steps:

Step 1: Establish a list of the intended participants.

Step 2: Determine the number of training sessions required and reserve a training room for the date(s) the course will be delivered.

Step 3: Enter the course information into the EPMO PBMIS training database.

Step 4: Send an email message to the intended participants providing course information and registration instructions.

Step 5: Send a reminder email two days before to the class participants.

Step 6: Have the participants sign in when entering the room. The completed list must be turned in to EPMO for its audit files.

Step 7: Have participants complete the course evaluation sheet and compile the responses into a summary report. File the report and provide a copy to EPMO for its records.

Step 8: Complete course completion certificates and email them to the class participants.

13.5 Training Program Course Directory

The training program course directory identifies classes for the target audiences identified in Subchapter 13.2. These are the general population, project team members, project managers, program managers, portfolio managers, and business unit managers. Some of the courses are offered on a recurring basis, while others are available on an "on-demand" basis. Further, additional courses sponsored by the EPMO may be listed separately.

The EPMO, business unit managers, and others use the directory to inform personnel of the training courses currently offered and planned. The directory does not list courses provided on a one-time basis, but it does identify training that may be delivered outside of the standard classroom. Such alternative methods include on-the-job training, formal mentoring, videotapes, and computer-based training. Near-term needs would include the following categories:

- Leadership.
- Operating in a project management team.
- Introduction to project business management methodology processes.
- Process training.
  - PMI® A Standard for Portfolio Management terminology and processes.
  - PMI® A Standard for Program Management terminology and processes.
  - PMI® *PMBOK® Guide* terminology and processes.
- PMP® certification examination preparation.

Table 13-4 lists training courses that could form the project business management training program.

Table 13-4. Project Business Management Training Program Example Course Directory

PROJECT BUSINESS MANAGEMENT TRAINING PROGRAM COURSE DIRECTORY

Core Competency Training	Process Training	Skills Training	Tools Training	Organization Training	Project Orientation Training
1.1 Introduction to Project Business Management	2.1 Project Management Integration	3.1 Program and Project Leadership	4.1 Scheduling Program	5.1 Program and Portfolio Management	6.1 Project Product Orientation
1.2 Introduction to EPMO Processes, Tools, Templates, Systems	2.2 Project Scope Management	3.2 Project Requirements Definition	4.2 Software Spreadsheet	5.2 Strategic Planning	6.2 Project Customer Orientation
1.3 Technical Lead Workshop (Project Business Management Methodology Overview)	2.3 Introduction to Project Schedule Development	3.3 Project Negotiation Skills	4.3 Data Base	5.3 Data Security	6.3 Team Building and Chartering
1.4 Project Initiation Process Group Processes	2.4 Project Cost Management	3.4 Project Reporting Requirements		5.4 PMP® Certification Exam Preparation	6.4 Project History Orientation

1.5 Project Planning Process Group Processes

1.6 Project Execution Process Group Processes

1.7 Project Monitoring & Controlling Process Group Processes

1.8 Project Closing Process Group Processes

1.9 Integrated Change Management

2.5 Project Quality Management

2.6 Project Human Resource Management

2.7 Project Communications Management

2.8 Project Risk Management

2.9 Project Procurement Management

2.10 Project Earned Value Management

2.11 Baseline Change Management Process Training

3.5 Project Estimating

5.5 Program Management Office

6.5 Project Lessons Learned Orientation

6.6 Project Management Plan Orientation

CHAPTER 14

Effective and Efficient Work Breakdown Structures

14.1 What Is Work Structuring?

What relationship does work breakdown structure development and usage have with project business management?

Work breakdown structure (WBS) development is a technique that supports integrated project business management planning and control. It is a technique that has been used successfully in managing portfolios, programs, and projects. The work breakdown structure is at the heart of project business management (PBM) planning efforts, as it defines the basic project business management structure that provides the framework for development and maintenance of scope, schedule, budget, status data collection, and performance evaluation. The PBM-WBS is used to produce integrated project management plans in which all project business operations and actions are accomplished with reference to the work breakdown structure. The benefits to the enterprise are streamlined information flow, improvement in communication, reduction in redundancy, and improved operational visibility. The work breakdown structure is the instrument by which diverse but related users, such as enterprise management, the project owner, contractors, and suppliers can communicate among themselves and with the people who are performing the work required to complete a portfolio, program, or project successfully. It is also used to communicate, when appropriate, with regulatory and government organizations.

The Project Management Institute (PMI®) publishes *The Practice Standard for Work Breakdown Structures*. The first two editions were limited to establishing a work breakdown structure for a single project. For the needs of project business management, the concept of the work breakdown structure must be expanded down through the enterprise so that it encompasses portfolios, and programs as well as projects. EWBS design, development, and implementation are critical skills in the project business management arena.

Senior management-directed development of an EWBS offers a controlled technical approach to address many of the challenges inherent in developing a robust (effective) project business management approach. It allows management integration of many processes, work phases, and organizations; it also ensures integration of business strategies, business objectives, scope, schedule, and cost. Management-based enterprise-wide work breakdown structuring affords a means for complying with business objectives that can accommodate ever-changing enterprise and work priorities. After the business objectives, portfolios, programs, and projects have been defined and the impact of constraints determined, the EWBS is developed within the business planning process. Associated statements of work (SOW) are then prepared by the EPMO and portfolio, program, and project management.

Enterprise-Wide Work Breakdown Structure

The authors define the enterprise-wide work breakdown structure (EWBS) as:

> *A deliverable-oriented hierarchical decomposition of the work to be executed to accomplish the enterprise's strategic business objectives, create the required deliverables, and obtain the resulting benefits. The EWBS is composed of one or more portfolio WBSs, program WBSs, project WBSs, and supplier WBSs.*

The definitions the authors use to describe the enterprise-wide work breakdown structure hierarchical components are as follows.

Portfolio Level WBS

The authors define the *portfolio work breakdown structure* (Portfolio WBS) as:

> *A deliverable-oriented hierarchical decomposition of the portfolio work to be executed by the portfolio team and required to accomplish the portfolio-related strategic business objectives and create the required deliverables. It organizes and defines the total scope of the portfolio down to the supporting programs and projects and down through the portfolio-associated nonproject work.*

Program Level WBS

The authors define the *program work breakdown structure* (Program WBS) as:

> *A deliverable-oriented hierarchical decomposition of the program work to be executed by the program team and required to accomplish program-related or other strategic business objectives and create the required deliverables. It organizes and defines the total scope of the program down to the supporting projects and down through the program-related nonproject work.*

Project WBS

PMI® defines the concept of a project work breakdown structure (Project WBS) as:

> *A deliverable-oriented hierarchical decomposition of the work to be executed by the project team to accomplish the project objectives and create the required deliverables. It organizes and defines the total scope of the project. Each descending level represents an increasingly detailed definition of the project work. The WBS is decomposed into work packages. The deliverable orientation of the hierarchy includes both internal and external deliverables.*

Supplier WBS

The PMI® also defines the concept of a supplier contract work breakdown structure (Supplier WBS) as "a portion of the work breakdown structure for the project developed and maintained by a seller contracting to provide a subproject or project component."

EWBS as a Management Tool

Enterprises employing the EWBS as a key management tool will increase efficiency on their portfolios, programs, and projects so that they can gain a competitive edge. Developing the enterprise level WBS involves organizing a business strategy—and its related business objectives—by breaking down the work effort into portfolios, programs, and projects and further decomposing them into small, manageable segments, such as work packages and schedule activities.

This WBS technique as applied to project business management can best be described as the process of selecting the business objectives, establishing a predetermined course of action, and creating the structures necessary for achieving the objectives through projects within a defined environment. WBS development is a decision-making process because it involves choosing among alternatives. The work breakdown structure method can be used to organize the portfolio, program, and project objectives by defining all the activities that must be performed in the conception, design, development, fabrication, test, and delivery of the project products or services. The WBS is prepared at the earliest possible point in the portfolio, program, and project life cycle and, at the same time, formal change control procedures are established to ensure it remains current and accurate. This process eliminates the need to immediately comprehend and structure complex problem solutions involving interacting factors while in the strategic and tactical planning stages.

The WBS is a product- and goal-oriented work-task structure, as opposed to the more common uses of functional organization structures, production code of accounts, or similar breakdowns for scope and cost.

Business influences affect the development of an EWBS more than they affect any other area of program and project planning and control. Business factors that influence selecting and creating an EWBS include assigning responsibilities, measuring performance, defining the desired level of management visibility versus performer's needs, establishing the required degree of control, and requiring cost identification. Other influential factors include program and project life cycle phases, as well as the mixture of program and project types in a project business management portfolio. As various factors are added, the complexity of the methods used to develop a PBM EWBS increases.

The key to developing a robust (effective) project business management environment is building an EWBS that fulfills all the requirements for work definition and control, while accommodating the numerous business and organizational factors present in today's competitive global marketplace. To successfully develop an EWBS, executive and senior managers must understand why an EWBS is necessary, what benefits it provides, how and by whom it is developed, and how it can be used by project and functional management for effective work scope planning, performance measurement, and control of change.

The work breakdown structure technique is equally effective with any of the standard organizational management structures identified in the *PMBOK® Guide: Third Edition, Section 13.3: Organizational Structure* for projects: functional, pure project, or matrix. The technique is flexible and may be adjusted depending on the size, needs, and characteristics of the specific portfolios, programs, and projects, and the desires of management. If properly applied, the WBS techniques presented in the following subchapters will provide a powerful tool for communicating portfolio, program, and project information to all members of the organization.

14.2 Why Is an EWBS Prepared, and What Are the Benefits?

A business objective is defined by the enterprise's desired technical or operational objectives. It is a unique, complex, time- and resource-limited set of activities that may involve multiple programs and interrelated projects in a project business management portfolio. For a program or project to be manageable, planning documentation should describe the intent of the program or project and identify the actions necessary to accomplish the related business objectives. The degree of detail required for this documentation depends on the complexity of the portfolio, program, or project, and the level of management visibility chosen to ensure adequate control.

Therefore, the first step in planning any portfolio, program, or project must be to define the work to be accomplished and the deliverables to be completed and managed. Development of a realistic program or project management plan is not possible without an EWBS that is detailed enough to meaningfully identify all activities. The EWBS is a tool that functions throughout the life cycle of the portfolio, program, or project. It plans and tracks the work required to achieve the portfolio/program/project objectives.

Developing an effective WBS involves progressively subdividing the work into smaller and smaller increments until a manageable package of work for planning and control purposes is reached. The reason for this subdivision is simple; it organizes the work into manageable segments to facilitate better control. Control, therefore, becomes the purpose behind the integration of activities, where the portfolio, program, and project managers act as the integrators using the EWBS as the common framework.

Project business management requires effective and precise communication of information during all life cycle phases of portfolios, programs, and projects, and with all stakeholders. Providing timely information to stakeholders improves the project business management effort. This, in turn, leads to more successful projects. Effective and efficient distribution of information requires that all of the work be broken down into work packages that can be quantified and qualified with a defined scope and for which the cost and schedule can be accurately established.

The successful accommodation of both portfolio/program/project and enterprise objectives requires a structured plan with statements of work that define the entire effort and assign the responsibility for each component to a specific performing organizational element.

Because the work is broken down into smaller components, a greater probability exists that it will account for every major and minor activity. A high degree of confidence that the objective can be reached will almost always exist whenever work is structured, understood, easily identifiable, and within the capabilities of the enterprise's staff.

The EWBS provides the following benefits as a project business management tool:

Total work is structured as a summation of subdivided components by:

- Uniquely identifying and hierarchically relating the products, services, and material needed to accomplish business objectives.
- Describing detailed activities required for engineering, licensing, research, development, construction, installation, demonstration, operation, production, and so on, of the facility, unit, plant, major items, service, or product.
- Defining the relationship between the components.

Responsibility for all work is established by:

- Assigning responsibility for accomplishment of EWBS components to specific performing organizations and individuals.
- Identifying responsible organizations for each EWBS component and thereby preventing gaps in responsibility assignments.

Planning, budgeting, and scheduling is facilitated by:

- Providing, early in the portfolio, program, and project life cycles, a method for clear definition of the related scope.
- Linking objectives to resources in a logical manner and providing a basis for allocation of resources to perform the work.
- Interrelating scope, cost, schedule, and productivity on an EWBS basis, thereby enabling scope, cost, and schedule to be integrated.
- Helping identify work requiring special attention, such as replanning, when necessary, future additional work breakdown.

Performance measurements are obtainable by:

- Making the EWBS structure the basis for meaningful schedule and cost status reporting, monitoring, and coordination. This ensures that all work to be done can be compared to a well-defined baseline.
- Using the structure for the orderly summarization of work performance to selected levels of consolidation.

Communication and information reporting are facilitated by:

- Helping all participants, by means of the EWBS development process, clearly understand the objectives and related portfolio/program/project during the initiation stages.

- Using the EWBS as the basis for all communication between information systems and allowing written correspondence to be done with reference to a single applicable EWBS component.
- Using the EWBS everywhere that project information is collected or issued to ensure that all information has a common meaning, regardless of its source.
- Establishing an effective basis on which to establish communication systems policies and procedures.

A properly selected, designed, and developed EWBS, with its codes and statements of work, supplies the common basis for all scope, cost, schedule, and productivity information and forms the foundation of quality project business management for any portfolio, program, or project. It provides the common communication link, the common language, and the common device whereby diverse users can communicate from the inception of the portfolio or the program to each project's deliverable final completion.

14.3 What Makes a Successful Enterprise-Wide Work Breakdown Structure?

What project and business management factors have supported successful EWBS development endeavors and provided the benefits expected from an EWBS?

A review of the project management literature and lessons learned by the authors provide the answer to this question. The most common factors leading to success can be divided into business management and project management factors.

Business Management Factors

- Business objectives were clear and well defined by senior management.
- Practical assessments of realistic requirements and constraints were prepared.
- Personnel with training, practice, or experience in work structuring were used to develop the EWBS.
- EWBS component descriptions were required, thereby providing the structure components with work scope definition.
- Structure was fully prepared in advance of beginning work.
- Work product end-item orientation of the EWBS was *not* confused by the introduction of company functions, organizations, or

financial accounts (e.g., mechanical engineering may be an important function and/or organization, but it is not product-oriented in the same sense as a major mechanical assembly or mechanical engineering work).
- EWBS development was not constrained or driven by the finance and accounting systems.

Project Management Factors

- Project objectives were clarified and/or refined.
- EWBS development was by a team composed of people who would manage and perform the work.
- Adequate time was taken and allowed for EWBS development.
- EWBS component coding was well conceived.
- Developers were concerned with overall structure and provided for necessary and sufficient levels of breakdown.
- EWBS change control was adequate and did not mix old and new scope in the same element.

Or, simply put, to be successful the EWBS must be planned and developed in a managed, structured, and systematic way.

14.4 How to Design and Develop a WBS

The EWBS methodology can structure work so that the enterprise can reach such diverse objectives as lowering costs, reducing absenteeism, improving morale, eliminating work jurisdictional disputes, and lowering scrap factors. Building an EWBS is an art rather than a science that requires experience and techniques, as well as an understanding of the enterprise's needs. The process uses cascading analysis to subdivide a business objective into its components. The objective is broken down level by level into portfolios, programs, projects, subprojects, and finally into packages of work. A work package is a single, identifiable job with clearly defined start and finish times and a unique scope description called a statement of work. Care must be taken to ensure that the ESWBS represents the needs of the various functions involved with project business management (i.e., EPMO, operations, construction, procurement, engineering, project control, design, research, marketing, quality, etc.). The EWBS structure needs to be simple, clear, and meaningful.

The work structuring process produces a multilevel, deliverables-oriented, structure-defining, organizing, and graphically displayed work designed to meet the commitments and deliverables of the business objective. Each level becomes progressively more specific about the work to be accomplished. The basic requirement for the configuration of the structure is that it be in a hierarchal format (i.e., lower level elements must relate to and logically add up to one, and only one, next higher element. An objective's deliverables may be products (facilities, computers, drugs, etc.), services (facility operation, test and evaluation, project management, etc.), data (technical reports, engineering data, management data, etc.), or other quantified items. Work definition and structuring is the unifying theme between these elements and the business objective. It reflects ordering of the detailed products and the work to be accomplished, relates these elements to each other and to the business objective, and provides the conceptual framework for planning and controlling the associated work.

The preparation of the EWBS is the responsibility of the portfolio, program, and project managers, with EPMO management providing assistance in accordance with senior management directives. EPMO management is responsible for developing the complete structure and component definition for all portfolio-/program-/project-related work. To prepare the master EWBS, EPMO management first develops a summary EWBS based on the business objectives and appropriate summary EWBS components. Participating business units and other enterprise performing organizations supporting specific portfolios, programs, or projects need to develop, coordinate, and submit individual EWBS elements for their work. Finally, the EPMO integrates the individual performing organizations' EWBS components with the summary EWBS to develop the total EWBS. The process of breaking down the work forces the portfolio/program/project managers and all involved to think through all aspects of each portfolio, program, and project.

The overall design of the EWBS is the key to an effective monitoring and control system and process. Therefore, the EWBS must be studied carefully from both information input and output points of view. For a successful EWBS, the design and development must:

- Be based on the most likely way the portfolios, programs, and projects will be worked, managed, and controlled.
- Progressively and logically subdivide the work into manageable activities down to the levels at which work will be monitored, controlled (a monitoring element), performed, and status reported (a work package).
- Have each control account and work package as a unique, definable, goal-oriented segment of the project.
- Have each EWBS element serve as a meaningful group of related work that can be connected to other related WBS elements and, in a logical manner, to the WBS element above it, thereby providing de-

fined scope, schedule, and cost parameters for all elements of the EWBS.

- Have each summary level element be meaningful from monitoring and control viewpoints.
- Have work packages small enough to permit realistic estimates, but not so small as to result in excess control costs.
- Include in the EWBS those level-of-effort activities that also result in some form of deliverable.
- Have critical products or services, which are to be subcontracted, identified, and treated as individual elements.
- Provide an element or series of elements applicable to support work, such as test equipment, spare and repair parts, transportation, training, and project management.
- Subdivide the work to a level at which activities are assignable, identifiable, and manageable by the business units performing the work.
- Not have duplicate work between EWBS elements nor omit any required work.
- Have the statement of work for each element explicitly itemize the work that is *not* included as well as work that is included in cases where confusion is possible. The statement should reference the work statement where other similar work is included.
- Test structure and account codes applied to the EWBS elements to ensure that relationships are meaningful and summarizing is possible.

For the EWBS to serve as a communications tool, it must be defined with regard to all the elements that make it a working entity. The base elements are objectives and constraints, structure, coding, and reporting. Before integrating these elements, each must be analyzed separately. Then, their relationship to each other must be studied. The design of the structure, the code, and the reports should contain as much input as possible from the performing and responsible organizations that will be using it, given whatever time, cost, or system constraints are applied.

14.5 How to Prepare a WBS

Essentially, the preparation of an EWBS involves proceeding from objectives to portfolios to programs to projects to products and services. This is achieved by subdividing the work until a level is reached that provides the required effective technical performance, schedule, and cost control for a specific project activity and the associated performing organization. The number of subdivisions in the EWBS varies according to the complexity of the work. The level of detail should be clearly defined so that no duplication of effort occurs within or between performing organizations.

An EWBS is traditionally prepared using a top down approach that ensures that all work is planned and all derivative plans and associated work contribute directly to the desired end. The top level of the structure is defined as the total work scope for the enterprise as it relates to project-based portfolios and programs. This level is then subdivided into finer and finer sublevels. As the levels become more detailed, the scope, complexity, and cost of each component (portfolio, program, and project) becomes smaller. Eventually, a level is reached at which the elements represent manageable units for visibility, planning, and control, and scheduled activities can be accomplished. The lowest levels of the EWBS identifies the individual work packages, which is the smallest element in an integrated cost and schedule EWBS. When fully developed, a work package is a single, definable, monitorable, and controllable segment of work. It is the point at which cost and schedule are integrated and responsible and performing organizations can be assigned.

The development of the EWBS must take into account the fact that the creation of work definition, cost, and schedule information is evolutionary—activities further out in time mature or become more detailed and precise as the work progresses. All work must eventually be planned and controlled through fully developed detailed packages of work. However, it is not usually practical or possible to produce such detailed planning at the inception of the portfolio, program, or project. The rolling wave work planning concept acknowledges that a person or organization has a sufficient depth of information to plan in detail today's work (the near term), but lacks that depth of information about tomorrow (the future). It makes sense, then, to plan and schedule those future activities at a more summary level, starting with planning packages. A planning package is a logical aggregation of work within a higher level EWBS element. Usually, the far-term effort can be identified in finite, but sizeable, pieces early in the planning, but it must be further defined and broken down to the work package level as a better definition becomes available. As the project progresses and information matures, more detailed scope, schedule, and cost estimates are developed, and the summary activities are broken down into work packages and lower level activities.

The early versions of the EWBS are usually summary in nature, with further detail being added as the definition of the portfolios occur and progressively finer divisions of effort in the form of programs, projects, and work packages are developed. By defining the subdivisions, greater understanding and, hopefully, clarity of action is added for those individuals who will be required to complete the projects, programs, and portfolios.

The sequence for performing this preparation is:

1. Determine/Define Portfolio, Program, and Project Objectives
2. Review External Constraints
3. Develop Summary EWBS
4. Develop Portfolio Level WBS
5. Develop Program Level WBS
6. Develop Project Level WBS
7. Develop Supplier/Contractor/Performer Level WBS
8. Develop EWBS Coding
9. Issue and Control the EWBS

The preceding sequence may become iterative as planning evolves and contracts are awarded. EWBS revisions may also result from expansion or contraction of the project/contract scope and the movement of a project through its various phases (e.g., research, design, development, construction, testing, demonstration, and operation). The approved EWBS is maintained and revised to incorporate changes throughout the life of each portfolio, program, and project to ensure traceability of the work efforts. When major changes in the business objectives, portfolio content, program approach, or project scope or resource levels occur after the initial EWBS has been defined, a formal change process is used to update the structure. Without such procedures, visibility of status information that changed the original EWBS are lost in the transition to the revised EWBS.

CHAPTER 15

Project Business Management System

15.1 What Is a PBMS?

Enterprise project business management is a business management concept that combines project management processes, skills, and methodologies with more traditional business management processes and methodologies to manage the enterprise in meeting its business objectives. This combination requires integrating project management information with traditional business information to produce more current and relevant information with only the level of accuracy needed to support decision making. This integration of information is used to eliminate the organizational stovepipes or islands of information typically associated with either a single project or a business unit managed portfolio. Enterprise project business management also emphasizes collaboration, workflow processes, enterprise-wide change management, and enterprise-wide information management.

However, one common and frustrating problem that can plague an enterprise's control of its resources, facilities, portfolios, programs, and projects is the lack of a formal processes and procedures system with timely integrated information that will support safe, prudent, and cost-effective business practices.

The Project Management Institute (PMI®) defines a *system* as:

An integrated set of regularly interacting or interdependent components created to accomplish a defined objective, with defined and maintained relationships among its components, and the whole producing or operating better than the simple sum of its components. Systems may be either physically process based or management process based, or more commonly a combination of both. Systems for project management are composed of project management processes, techniques, methodologies, and tools operated by the project management team.

174

The Project Management Institute (PMI®) then defines a *project management system* (PMS) as:

> *The aggregation of the processes, tools, techniques, methodologies, resources, and procedures to manage a project. The system is documented in the project management plan and its content will vary depending upon the application area, organizational influence, complexity of the project, and the availability of existing systems. A project management system, which can be formal or informal, aids a project manager in effectively guiding a project to completion. A project management system is a set of processes and the related monitoring and control functions that are consolidated and combined into a functioning, unified whole.*

The most common automated tools employed in a project management system are *project management software*, which the Project Management Institute (PMI®) defines as:

> *A class of computer software applications specifically designed to aid the project management team with planning, monitoring, and controlling the project, including: cost estimating, scheduling, communications, collaboration, configuration management, document control, records management, and risk analysis.*

Although the definitions above are only project oriented, they can be extrapolated for project business management (PBM) to portfolios and programs, as well as projects. Viewing a PMS from a PBM perspective requires three major components: the enterprise project management office (EPMO); the project business management methodology (PBMM); and a project business management information system (PBMIS). This creates a Project Business Management System (PBMS) as shown in Figure 15-1.

Based on the above, the authors define a *project business management system* (PBMS) as the aggregation and unification of the enterprise project management office resources, the project business management methodology including policies, processes, procedures, tools, and techniques, that are determined by the enterprise to be both necessary and sufficient to manage a combination of portfolios, programs, and projects. The PBMS is a formal system that includes a project business management information system (PBMIS) that provides the requisite information to support decision making, as well as the monitoring and controlling of every portfolio, program, and project.

Any project business management system provided by a supplier under contract is in reality first for the benefit of the supplier; it may only in-

Figure 15-1. PBMS Structure and Components

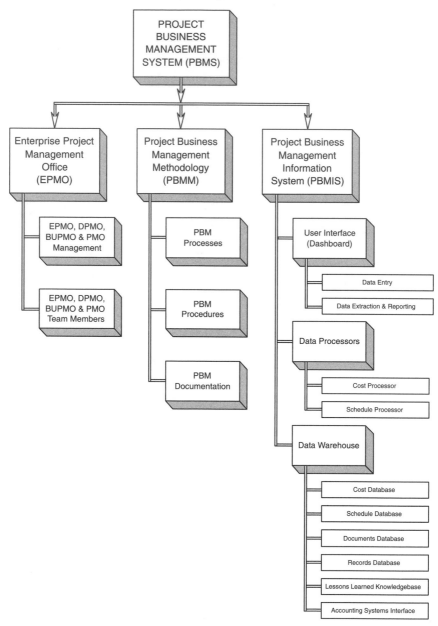

directly benefit the enterprise owning that project or projects. The enterprise owning the project has no way of assessing the maturity or applicability of each supplier's project business management methodology or processes or if those processes will provide cost effective results. In addition, if more than one supplier works on a project, the overall cost of project management will be higher than if the project management were driven by the owning enterprise using an integrated PBMIS provided by the project owner.

A variety of project management information systems (PMIS) are currently used. Most PMISs were developed for a particular project, program, and portfolio or business unit and differ because they were based on particular sets of requirements. Many of these systems are based on software vendors' systems and tools, some are totally home grown, and others are adaptations of capabilities supplied with accounting systems coupled with pieces of project management software.

Sections 2, 3, and 5 of this book provide an understanding of the first two components of the PBMS model. Section 2 discusses the establishment, staffing, and use of the enterprise project management office (EPMO). Section 3 discusses the development and standardization of the project business management methodology (PBMM), while Section 5 discusses the execution of the PBMM. The following subchapters outline the better attributes of a standard integrated Project Business Management Information System (PBMIS), which is the third major component of the PBMS.

15.2 What Are the Purposes and Benefits of the PBMIS?

The PBMIS is a budget, cost, and schedule data and information management and reporting system that employs an earned value technique to support project business management in monitoring and controlling portfolios, programs, and projects. The PBMIS is a decision support system that aids the EPMO and other business units in effectively guiding a portfolio, program, or project to completion. The PBMIS stores budgeted costs, estimated costs, accrued costs, actual costs, schedule, forecast, progress, and related information within one or more databases.

The project business management processes use the PBMIS to provide a single, flexible, current, integrated, and responsive data source that allows effective decision making. It is the combination of skilled and trained personnel, mature project business management processes, and implemented project control processes in combination with the PBMIS tool that generates the benefits. Simply put, the key benefits sought are cost elimination, cost minimization, and return on investment.

The following specific business management benefits can be received from the implementation of the PBMIS and its associated standardized project business management methodology processes:

- Various shadow systems used in the business units by various project managers are eliminated. This results in the elimination of minimally productive labor hours (saved) and better quality and more timely data.
- All business units and suppliers use the common PBMIS system for planning and controlling work. Only one system and one common set of processes needs to be applied by management, enterprise wide.
- It does not matter where a particular portfolio manager, program manager, project manager, or project staff individual is located, because they can all communicate through a common web-enabled PBMIS, which can also reduce meeting time and travel costs.
- PBMIS is owner (enterprise) operated, thereby providing clear visibility to the enterprise of all the costs associated with all project, program, and portfolio in all business units and suppliers.
- PBMIS is owner (enterprise) controlled, thereby assuring uniform application at the appropriate level of rigor to all projects within the enterprise's programs and portfolios.
- Investments in the PBMIS and the associated processes and advancements in project business management capability and maturity accrue to the benefit of the enterprise, thereby increasing the enterprises return on investment in project business management.
- An enterprise business unit operated common PBMIS and processes minimize overall operational costs, while maximizing project control data quality and usability. Only one tool and one set of processes needs to be used and understood by all involved parties, whether they be enterprise or supplier personnel.
- An enterprise level PBMIS and standardized project business management processes can be operated and maintained by a minimum number of trained personnel, thereby optimizing the required skill levels and minimizing the number of personnel and associated costs.

The PBMIS is of direct value, benefit, and use to portfolio, program, and project managers because it:

- Supports the project business management methodology (PMMM) for project planning and control within the enterprise work break-down structure (EWBS) for every portfolio, program, and project.
- Provides a single integrated source for budgets, actual costs, accrued costs, estimates at completion, and schedules that are available via web access to all participants.
- Reduces inconsistencies in management data obtained from different programs and projects.
- Provides early warning about possible issues so management action can be taken before more funds are spent.
- Can generate reports tailored to each manager's needs.
- Saves management time by providing and leveraging existing actual cost data.
- Shifts management labor away from routine data collection and compiling data for reports to providing in-depth analysis.
- Provides improved project planning and cost and schedule estimating to support decisions review and analysis at transition points.
- Enables on-line drill down capability for budgets, actual costs, commitments, forecast, and schedules with data that can be accessed from anywhere on the Internet.
- Improves the consistent planning, controlling, and executing of programs and projects with single point entry of the data for many PBMM processes.
- Simplifies generation and documentation of budget input.
- Automatically generates and enables visibility at the portfolio, program, and project levels of earned value performance measurement data (performance metrics) based upon budget, schedule, forecast, and progress data.
- Provides for resource leveling and allocation of critical resources.
- Accrues incurred costs for work performed by suppliers, but not yet reported or invoiced to the enterprise, to maintain reliable data that can be 30 to 60 days ahead of the enterprise's accounting system. This provides near real time-related cost data.
- Tracks reported actual cost and schedule progress.
- Manipulates actual and forecast data for cost and schedule analysis.
- Supports total project duration reporting as well as current year reporting.
- Provides critical-path scheduling of planned EWBS components.
- Documents the execution of planned decisions via actual cost and schedule reporting and performance measurement reports.

The PBMIS is neither an accounting system nor an accounting support system and has no direct or implied financial functions or cost accounting functions. However, the actual costs in the PBMIS are reconciled on at least a calendar quarterly basis with the enterprise's accounting books of record. If those actual costs reconcile within plus or minus an acceptable predefined amount, such as three percent by project, then the PBMIS can be considered sufficiently accurate for use in making project management-related decisions. Its purpose is to support the enterprise's project business management operations and be used by the enterprises EPMO staff, portfolio, program, and project managers, preferred suppliers, project staff, enterprise management, and enterprise finance and accounting personnel.

The data components of a PBMS are relatively simple and straightforward in concept and include:

- EWBS Structure
- WBS Elements
- Work Packages
- Resources
- Cost Elements
- Estimated Cost
- Estimated Cost Changes
- Estimated Cost to Complete
- Estimated Cost at Completion
- Budgeted Cost
- Budgeted Cost Changes
- Actual Cost
- Accrued Cost
- Milestones
- Schedule Activities
- Schedule Activity Start and Finish Dates
- Estimated Dates
- Forecasted Dates
- Actual Dates

Although the data elements are fairly simply, the data relationships are integral and complex. This requires sophisticated data storage, computation, and reporting.

The PBMIS has powerful capabilities for both EPMO and business unit management reporting to virtually any level of detail, across any time frame and context: financial period or project period, for project, program, or portfolio-wide data. Managers and staff can drill down to various levels of detail to resolve issues. With the application of basic EPMO competency, high-quality current project status information and forecasts are produced to support decisions. PBMIS affords the enterprise's management the ability to independently and directly monitor and control project execution and prevent the scope changes and cost growth commonly experienced in projects.

The most effective PBMIS is a state-of-the-art, web-based, mature, completely documented, and fully deployed system that affords real-time access for enterprise and supplier personnel. To be of use, the system is made available remotely to users with PBMIS access rights and is available twenty-four hours a day, seven days per week. A defined and announced window of downtime is established for scheduled system maintenance.

The PBMIS provides at least 95% uptime (438 hours maximum downtime annually) on equipment components and applications. Data recovery methods and processes are established and implemented so that, at a maximum, only one workshift of data could be lost and the system could be restored back to the exact point of failure, if technically possible.

15.3 User Interface?

The PBMIS main user interface provides a brief overview of each portfolio, program, and project and allows the user to easily navigate the overall system. The user interface (some call it a dashboard) is composed of a main screen, related web screens, and associated data entry and data display screens. Budget, commitment, accrual, schedule, forecast, and progress data are entered manually. The user has the capability to filter (select) the data using specific components of the EWBS and to sort the data alphanumerically. The system also provides for the manual entry of cost accrual data through the dashboard. From the perspective of work planning, authorization, and actual and accrual costs, the term supplier encompasses the enterprise and its suppliers and vendors.

To support data entry into PMIS and as part of the EWBS development, each EWBS element is assigned an identification code for the life of the portfolio, program, and project. Coding is the process of identifying data by a short, unique symbol or set of symbols. The design of the coding is the key to establishing the EWBS as the device to be used by the PBMIS and enterprise accounting.

Work is planned and budgeted directly within PBMIS and entered down through the work package level of detail. Budgeting at this level is for both the enterprise business unit budgets and supplier budgets. Work is then authorized to the appropriate business unit or supplier and the associated work authorization values by EWBS work package are captured within PBMIS. EWBS changes, budget revisions, schedule data, percentage of work completed, manual cost accruals, and estimate to complete are all directly entered online in real-time by any authorized manager or project staff from anywhere in the world that has high speed Internet access.

Using the same Internet access, they can also access various reports with user selectable data. These reports use consistent and integrated data to provide insights into the status of all projects, programs, and portfolios. The reports allow management to drill down to any level of detail within the EWBS to identify trends and issues.

The PBMIS uses either the standard twelve or thirteen annual planning and reporting periods. These periods are based on the enterprise's fiscal year using the specific day of the month set by the enterprise's accounting procedures as the end of one period and the start of another. The PBMIS uses these periods for all planning and reporting processes, including, but not limited to, budgeting, scheduling, actual cost reporting, accruing costs, providing progress status data, and calculating/reporting earned value parameters.

Data Entry

Typical data input screens provide the following options:

- EWBS Data Entry
- Estimated Cost
  Data Entry
- Schedule Data Entry
- Budget Data Entry
- Progress Data Entry
- Commitments
  Data Entry
- Actual Cost Data Entry

- Accrual Data Entry
- Forecast Data Entry
- Percent Complete
  Data Entry
- Change Control Data Entry
- Planned Capital Expenditures
  Data Entry
- Work Authorization
  Data Entry

Data Extraction and Reporting

Standard project control, schedule, and cost reports are provided. Report customization includes the ability to change the content of certain columns to different data elements or predefined calculations on report templates. The use of the EWBS structure provides functionality that allows the user to expand and collapse levels of the EWBS. For the various roll up levels of the EWBS, the data is a summary of all levels of the EWBS below the level displayed. Therefore, all data contained in any one level EWBS within the PMIS can be progressively collapsed into higher levels until all data is moved through the portfolio scope level to the enterprise level.

At any level of the EWBS, control accounts may be identified in the PMIS. These are elements of the structure chosen to monitor and control a specific portion of the work at or above the work package level, such as a subproject or a set of nonproject related work packages. It is a management control point at or below which actual costs and schedule status can be accumulated. Within a single project, it represents the work assigned to one responsible organizational element.

The use of the EWBS code for entering and extracting all information into the PBMIS ensures that all data collected can be measured against a baseline. Actual progress, resource usages, forecasts, productivity information, and anticipated problem data can be communicated in a meaningful manner through the use of the EWBS, because all references to the information are made through a uniform and consistent code referencing method. This also allows creation of effective reports based on which logical management decisions can be made.

The PBMIS may also include an off-the-shelf project management software report writer application to produce user-defined reports with minimal support from the enterprise's information systems function. Information display includes screen views and hard-copy report formats generated by the PBMIS. Examples of these reports include, but are not limited to:

- Project Controls Reports
- Earned Value Charts
- Earned Value Reports
- Earned Value Metrics Reports
- Estimate Change Reports
- Budget Change Reports
- Budget versus Commitment Reports
- EWBS Structure Reports
- Schedule Reports
- Milestone Reports
- Capital Expenditures Reports

These reports provide the user with the capability to view the current status of any EWBS level, individual EWBS elements, and individual work packages down through the schedule activities and cost elements on an enterprise-wide basis. Users are also able to view data based on the current year, incurred-to-date, and specific period "from" and "through" dates.

15.4 Data Processors

The system includes the functions of a budget and cost processor and the functions of a schedule and resource processor.

Budget and Cost Processor

This processor may be a commercially available project management software application, a custom-built application, or a defined portion of the enterprise's accounting system. Budget and cost information is identified and stored by EWBS element, by cost element, and by a supplier-identifier. Actual costs and accrued costs will be identified by and stored by work package identifier, cost element, period of performance, and supplier-identifier. The system needs to accommodate between five and fifteen cost elements.

Budget and budget change information is also identified and stored by budget status (pending, approved, or cancelled) and an effective date for the budget or change. Budget changes are further categorized as scope additions, scope deletions, scope deferrals, cost savings, or budget revisions. Out year budgets and changes are entered against a specific level of the EWBS and are not further categorized. The processor is able to show budget changes from the original budget value to the current year budget value for any revised budget year.

Supplier work is usually authorized by issuing an approved contract, change order, work order, service order, task order, and so on covering a scope of work. This release to perform work contractually commits the supplier to the associated budgeted cost for the identified EWBS elements (scope of work) and thereby reduces the amount of approved budget available for other work. For PBMIS, a commitment is considered to have been made if a work authorization document has been issued. Based on each budget year's commitments versus that selected year's budget, the system also tracks the available remaining uncommitted budget.

Schedule and Resource Processor

This processor may be a commercially available project management software application or a defined portion of the enterprise's larger accounting and management systems. Schedule work planning is done on a daily or weekly basis. Each supplier has the ability to enter schedule activity, forecast, and progress data into the schedule processor from the dashboard. This data is then transferred from the processor into the PBMIS database on a periodic basis through an electronic interface controlled through the dashboard.

For projects deemed too small to warrant the technical complexity of a schedule and resource processor, the user is able to enter schedule and progress data directly into the schedule database directly through the dashboard.

15.5 Data Warehouse

The data warehouse can be composed of one fully integrated database or a set of related databases. PBMIS data storage structure and functionality is based on the enterprise's predefined EWBS structure. It accommodates an EWBS with multiple legs and supports a minimum of ten levels. Each level is different and is composed of one or more EWBS elements. The lowest level, which is the work package, is the level at which scope, cost, and schedule are integrated within the PBMIS for planning, monitoring, and reporting purposes. The common thread in the data warehouse is that each WBS element at all levels in the EWBS has an EWBS identifier that is unique within the EWBS. It could be composed of the concatenation of all the identification codes for each EWBS element down to and including the EWBS element being identified. Each EWBS element also has a descriptive title and can be associated with (designated/identified/flagged) a number of different user-defined codes. This enables the user to select (filter), edit, sort, sum, and display information based on these various identifications.

Schedule Database

Each planning and work package can be scheduled through one or more schedule activities. This is done either through direct data entry using the dashboard or by entering into and uploading data from the standalone schedule and resource processor. A schedule activity is a scheduled element of work that will be performed during the course of a project. In the system, such an activity will usually have definite schedule and cost requirements. Each schedule activity identifier is an extension of the EWBS element identifier (code) with which it is associated.

Cost Database

Each planning package, control account, and work package can be estimated and budgeted either through direct data entry using the dashboard or by entering into and uploading data from the standalone budget and cost processor. The cost database portion of the data warehouse stores each individual budget, estimate, actual, and accrual cost and related changes by EWBS element, supplier-identifier, and time frame.

Documents Database

A document is defined by the Project Management Institute (PMI®) as:

> A medium and the information recorded thereon, that generally has permanence and can be read by a person or a machine. Exam-

ples include project management plans, specifications, procedures, studies, and manuals.

Those documents related to identification, selection, initiation, authorization, planning, monitoring, controlling, execution, and closing of each portfolio, program, and project are included in the documents database. The stored PBMIS-related electronic documentation includes the PBMIS user manuals, technical support manuals, and training manuals.

Records Database

The PBMIS also stores records that are specific formal documents generated in performance of a plan or procedure and that show compliance with those plans and procedures.

Lessons Learned Knowledgebase

Lessons are learned during the execution of the processes supporting the implementation of a portfolio, program, or project. Those lessons may be identified at any point in a program or project life cycle. This is a store of historical information about the outcomes of the identification, selection, initiation, authorization, planning, monitoring, controlling, execution, and closing of projects, the related decisions made, and specific performance.

15.6 Actual Costs and Accounting Systems Interfaces

The data source for all actual costs will usually be the enterprise's accounting system. Actual costs include, but are not limited to, labor, materials, equipment, travel, and other direct costs (ODCs). Accruing costs in PBMIS is the process of entering costs incurred but not yet invoiced or entering costs that have been incurred by a supplier and invoiced but not yet entered into an enterprise's accounting system. The system interface provides for a user-initiated electronic upload from the supplier's systems of data invoice files as cost accrual data. The inbound data from the supplier is stored by supplier-identifier, work package, cost element, and period of performance. The accrued costs are reversed within PBMIS when the related actual costs are loaded from the enterprise's accounting system.

Enterprise Accounting System's Data Interface(s)

Actual costs are electronically transferred from the enterprise's accounting system to the PBMIS on a periodic basis. The electronic transfer of invoiced costs needs to occur at least once a month, but, if possible, it should occur weekly. The actual cost data from the enterprise's accounting system are supplied by EWBS element, cost element, and period of performance. It is also associated with and stored by the supplier-identifier.

Supplier Accounting Systems' Data Interface(s)

The supplier's accounting system sends actual cost data to PBMIS in the electronic data interface invoice format defined by the enterprise. These data are supplied by EWBS element, by cost element, by period of performance and is associated with and stored by the supplier-identifier.

CHAPTER 16

Earned Value and
Real Project Cost Accounting

The subject of earned value as a management methodology has generated and will continue to generate considerable discussion in executive management circles, particularly among senior managers. The main discussion involves cost, schedule, and, most important, technical progress toward attaining project objectives. Maintaining schedule and budget is, alone, not significant, if the management teams are not demonstrating related progress in developing the desired deliverables that are the reason for the existence of the project.

The Project Management Institute (PMI®) defines *earned value management* (EVM) as:

> *A management methodology for integrating scope, schedule, and resources, and for objectively measuring project performance and progress. Performance is measured by determining the budgeted cost of work performed (i.e., earned value) and comparing it to the actual cost of work performed (i.e., actual cost). Progress is measured by comparing the earned value to the planned value.*

Earned value is a methodology for managing all aspects of a project or program. It belongs in the general area of business management as it supports both project management and business operations. Each project business management process contributes to project and program progress and has input to EVM. To be successful, EVM requires cooperation between the EPMO and the enterprise's accounting organization and support from the enterprise's accounting system. The three main processes key to successfully employing EVM are:

- Defining, planning, scheduling, and budgeting the work in a structured way and at the level of detail where the work can be performed, managed, and controlled.

- Collecting actual cost and accrued cost information at the same level of detail at which the work was budgeted for control and work authorization purposes.
- Monitoring and reporting the actual work progress and performance of the work at the level of detail at which it was planned for control purposes.

16.1 Earned Value Measurements

Mature project business management and controls for large multiproject operations require the ability to plan and document the work, estimated costs, budgets, and schedules. This requires a common enterprise work breakdown structure (EWBS) for planning the work in detail for the near term and at summary levels for long-range work plans. The most successful PBMISs are those that can routinely integrate budgets, estimates, actual costs, physical progress, and schedule progress within a single system and generate integrated budget/cost/schedule reports and earned value performance metrics.

In the earned value methodology, the EWBS is the structure around which the work is planned, with the lowest level being the work package. At that level, the work is planned in detail, schedule activities are developed and logically related, resources are assigned, costs are estimated, budgets are applied, and the schedule is developed.

EVM uses the earned value technique (EVT), which is defined by the Project Management Institute (PMI®) as:

> *A technique for measuring the performance of work, and used to establish the performance measurement baseline (PMB).*

Senior management has a key role in defining the performance measurement baseline for the enterprise and each portfolio, program, and project. Management must also decide the level of EWBS at which performance will be measured and reported. They have three choices: (1) each schedule activity within the work package, (2) the work package itself, or (3) a management-defined control account at a specified level within the EWBS.

The planning and reporting of costs at the schedule activity level is conceptually possible based on the structure of the PBMIS. However, it is not very feasible. The enormous amount of cost-related planning data that would need to be prepared and generated would glut the accounting system.

In addition, some organizations use an activity-based costing practice called "ABC." It produces a cost/benefit analysis by measuring the cost of work performed in each business unit function, as well as the loss in profits when that work is not performed effectively. However, ABC uses an accounting activity that bears no resemblance to either a PBM schedule activity, work package, or control account, and the accounting activity is generally used for functional organizational operations or production operations business planning, not project management planning.

Therefore, the first logical point in the EWBS structure is the work package which is designed to provide the integrated EVT data relationships discussed above. The next is the use of the control account, which has some benefits to the enterprise with respect to actual cost reporting, progress reporting, and performance measurement. There are types of work where it is not necessary to track actual costs and progress at the more detailed work package level. In these instances, the use of the control account, which is a roll-up of those related work packages, reduces the administrative cost for both the enterprise and performing organization of progress reporting, actual cost collecting, and performance analysis and reporting.

Monitoring and controlling using the EV technique is built on the concept of integrating scope, performing organization, schedule, and cost to manage and control a project and to obtain performance measuremenet evaluations by assimilating all information on a common basis. Each element must interface with the organization responsible for accomplishing that element. Flexibility must be provided to establish these interfaces at meaningful and appropriate levels. Whatever type of planning and control technique is used, all the important interfaces and interface events must be identified. Five major interfaces to the EWBS are established during its design to properly integrate data to support EVM. These are:

- EWBS versus Organization relationship
- EWBS versus Schedule relationship
- EWBS versus Estimated Cost relationship
- EWBS versus Cost versus Schedule interrelationships
- EWBS Component versus Actual Cost (Project cost accounting charge number) relationship

For a PBMIS implementation to effectively provide earned value technique cost reports, the enterprise's accounting system must be able to prepare timely and detailed project EWBS-oriented actual cost collection and project cost accounting.

16.2 Project Cost Accounting Methodology

Accounting for costs and revenue is a standard part of the business operations of all enterprises, whether they are private entities or public agencies. In the public sector the key requirement is to not incur more costs than the funds allocated by a legislative body. In the private sector, it is to ensure that revenues as a minimum cover costs incurred.

To support financial cost accounting, the accounting system is set up to generate balance sheets and income statements. The general ledger and supporting code of accounts are then established to the requisite level of detail. In addition, most enterprises also require revenue and cost reports for the various business units and supporting functional organizations. To produce these managerial reports, the accounting system needs to identify cost and revenue by business unit and functional organization. Therefore, the code of accounts should be detailed enough to support more finite incurred cost collection and budgeting and an organizational structure coding should be added to support the business unit accounting reports.

Most enterprises, other than those engaged solely in product manufacturing, have some projects that require specific accounting of incurred costs. If the project is being performed for others, then accounting for the associated revenues is necessary. Most systems can be manipulated to provide this minimum level of project cost accounting. However, an accounting system that just compares budget to actual cost at some summary level is not a project cost accounting system. Rather, it is a cost reporting system that is of limited use in performing project cost control because it lacks the requisite detail for planned work, progress, and schedule data.

To effectively support portfolios, programs, and multiple projects, project cost accounting requires the following four key functions:

- The collection of actual and accrued costs at the enterprise WBS work package level and the summarization of the costs at project, program, portfolio, and enterprise levels. Thus, the accounting system must be able to manipulate costs on an EWBS structure basis that is distinct from the enterprise's organizational structure.
- The collection of actual and accrued costs by the performing organization, whether an internal business unit or a contracted external supplier. Thus, the accounting system must be able to explicitly identify and distinguish between internal organizations and external supplier performing work through some form of supplier identifier that can also be used by the enterprise's procurement system.
- The collection of actual and accrued labor hours by the performing organization, whether an internal business unit or a contracted external supplier. Thus, the accounting system must be able to explicitly identify and distinguish between an internal organization and an external supplier performing work.
- The collection of actual and accrued costs by cost element by supplier (performing organization) by period of performance. Thus, the accounting system must be able to summarize selected codes of ac-

count within the enterprise's accounting system up into predefined cost elements used for project cost estimating, budgeting, and incurred cost summary cost reporting. Thus, the accounting system must be able to collect and store costs incurred data by contracted external suppliers at those summary cost element levels.

A cost element is a unique code assigned to a particular type of cost (e.g., equipment) and used within the finance and accounting systems, budget processors, cost processors, and project cost accounting applications, such as PBMIS, to categorize specific types of costs. They are also known as general ledger (G/L) summary account codes in finance and accounting systems. Examples of six PBMIS cost element types and one quantity reporting element for an enterprise engaged in work with a large volume of labor costs as compared to equipment and material costs, such as a consulting enterprise, are:

- *Labor Quantity:* The total of all directly charged person hours expended and recorded by a single supplier. This could include all person hours directly charged to work regardless of labor category or discipline.
- *Labor Cost Element:* The total cost of all directly charged person hours expended and recorded by a single supplier in performing work. This summary cost element could include labor hours at pay rate with fringe benefit costs plus overhead, general and administrative expenses, and profit as applicable per the supplier's accounting procedures and contracts.
- *Equipment Cost Element:* The total cost of all supplier-owned equipment utilized and recorded in performing work, such as trucks, mobile generators, instruments, sensors, communications equipment, and computing equipment and their associated maintenance and repair.
- *Permanent Material Cost Element:* The total cost of all equipment and material supplied and installed in the project deliverables, such as pumps, electric motors, concrete, roofing, and instrumentation.
- *Material Cost Element:* The total cost of all items provided, consumed, and recorded by a single supplier, such as disposable personal clothing and equipment, sample bottles, packing material, and fuel and lubricants for equipment.
- *Travel Cost Element:* The total cost of all travel expenses incurred and recorded, such as airfare, car rental and fuel, private auto mileage, parking, lodging, meals, per diem, relocation expenses, taxis, and tolls.
- *Other Direct Cost (ODC) Element:* The total cost of all directly charged nonequipment, nonmaterial, nontravel items utilized, such as office

supplies, reprographics, communications, computer rental/lease, permit or license fees, insurance, other taxes, shipping charges, courier services, and so on.

If the enterprise's accounting system is used to directly provide the full set of cost-related parameters needed to support the earned value technique calculations, then the system needs the ability to maintain budgets and budget changes at the work package or control account level by cost element for both internal business units and contracted external suppliers. It also needs the ability to document work authorization commitments made to external suppliers at the work package or control account level.

Thus, for an enterprise's accounting system to provide real project cost accounting and supply the project cost accounting parameters that are needed to support the earned value technique, it must:

- Provide for the structuring and reporting of costs by the EWBS.
- Provide for structuring and summarizing the enterprise's code of accounts up to a predetermined set of cost elements used for project cost planning and reporting.
- Accommodate the actual costs, actual labor hours, accrued costs, and accrued labor hours collection and storage for external suppliers at the work package and cost element level.
- Provide the ability to assign budgets and budget changes at the work package or control account levels.
- Provide the ability to store the work authorization commitments made to external suppliers at the work package or control account levels.
- Provide the ability to relate actual and accrued cost and labor hours to the period when they were incurred and not just when they were entered into the accounting system.
- Collect and record incurred cost within ten business days or less of the close of the period of performance. Monthly at a minimum, preferably bimonthly or weekly.
- Utilize accounting charge numbers that are either the EWBS identifier for the work package or can be directly related on a one-to-one basis.

Table 16-1 gives a general overview of the key PBMS control functions and how well they can be accommodated by the standard PBMIS and a common enterprise accounting system. Although some of the functions might be better implemented by an enterprise resource planning (ERP) software package, most the of the ERP packages focus on produc-

Table 16-1.   PBMS Control Functions–Enterprise Accounting System versus PBMIS

Project Business Management Systems Control Function	Accounting System		PBMIS		Implementation
	Yes	No	Yes	No	
1. Plan and Structure the Work	P		F		• Requires uniform structured planning process by EWBS. Standard for PBMIS. Enterprise's accounting system would need to support planning by EWBS and EWBS work packages.
2. Prepare, Maintain, and Control Budget by Project by Work Package	P		F		• Standard for PBMIS. Requires adding budgets at the work package level in enterprise's accounting system.
3. Prepare, Maintain, and Control Project Schedules		N	F		• Schedule processor is integrated within PBMIS. Enterprise accounting system has no scheduling capabilities but an ERP or MPP system might.
4. Prepare, Maintain, and Control Supplier Budgets by Project by EWBS work package or control account		N	F		Supplier budgets are standard capability within PBMIS. Requires modifying use of the enterprise's accounting system to support external supplier budgeting.
5. Manage and Control Changes to Budgets	P		F		PBMIS provides for tracking of each individual change. Requires modifying enterprise's accounting system to support tracking budget changes at work package and control account levels.
6. Prepare, Maintain, and Control Commitments to Suppliers		N	F		PBMIS includes capability. Most enterprise accounting systems could track commitments if properly entered at sufficient level of detail.

(continued)

Table 16-1.   *(Continued)*

Project Business Management Systems Control Function	Accounting System		PBMIS		Implementation
	Yes	*No*	*Yes*	*No*	
7. Collect, Process, and Control Incurred Cost Information.	P		F		PBMIS includes capability. Enterprise accounting could do a partial effort if enterprise procurement can require project staff to supply data and shorten time needed to manually accrue and re-accrue missing cost information each period in enterprise's accounting system.
8. Obtain or Develop, Maintain, and Control Project Progress and Forecast Information		N	F		PBMIS includes capability. Most enterprise accounting systems neither provide progress status tracking nor cost forecast projections. However an ERP or MPP might.
9. Develop and Issue Project Progress, Status, Exception, and Variance Reports		N	F		PBMIS includes capability. Enterprise accounting systems could provide variance at some EWBS level between actual cost and budget, but provide no indication of work progress or schedule status. Enterprise accounting systems lack sufficient information to provide earned value metrics. However, an ERP or MPP might.
10. Develop and Issue Portfolio Progress, Status, Exception, and Variance Reports		N	F		PBMIS includes capability. Enterprise accounting system could provide variance at some WBS level between actual cost and budget, but provide no indication of work progress or schedule status.

(continued)

Table 16-1. *(Continued)*

Project Business Management Systems Control Function	Accounting System		PBMIS		Implementation
	Yes	*No*	*Yes*	*No*	
11. Develop, Maintain, Control, and Report Cost Contingency by EWBS Level		N	F		PBMIS includes capability. PBMIS can also compare to current updated forecast. Could be added as a feature to some enterprise accounting systems.
12. Integrate with Other Enterprise Work Processes		N	F		PBMIS methodology already integrates with the budget and business planning processes, and it uses electronic actual cost extracts from enterprise's accounting system. Enterprise accounting systems lack the capability to integrate schedule and progress data, but an ERP or MPP system might.
13. Integrated Planning, Scheduling, Cost, Budget, Progress, Metric, and Forecast Data Is Available to All Affected Parties		N	F		PBMIS data is available anywhere through the Internet. Enterprise accounting system is normally proprietary to the enterprise and lacks the other identified parameter. However, an ERP or MPP might provide these capabilities.
14. Actual Cost Charging to the EWBS Identifier for the Work Package	P		F		PBMIS includes capability. Some enterprise accounting systems may have ability but may use an accounting charge number related to the EWBS identifier for actual cost extraction.

Legend: *P = Partially addresses the requirement; F = Fully addresses the requirement; N = Does not address the requirement*

tion and sales and not projects or actual resource management. A number of project portfolio management (PPM) packages are also available or are being developed that might be employed to develop a PBMIS. However the majority of these PPMs focus on information technologies (IT) type project work and enterprises with heavy involvement in IT portfolios and projects.

CHAPTER 17

Communications and Risk Management

17.1 Communications Management

Why should enterprise management establish PBM communications on an enterprise-wide basis?

Establishing enterprise-wide project management (EWPM) practices, the project business management (PBM) methodology, and the project business management systems (PBMS) can significantly improve the way management teams communicate and work together. This enhanced communication is also directly supported by the technological capabilities of the project business management information systems (PBMIS) and the competency of trained managers. Portfolio, program, and project managers coordinate and control all communications to satisfy executive management, the business objective sponsor, and customer expectations. Those managers, supported by various business functions, are responsible for meeting these expectations.

The management of projects, programs, and portfolios requires timely, tangible, and accurate information about such items as scope, schedule, cost, changes, working conditions, risks, and resources. For PBM to be successful, this quality and type of information must be provided on a routine basis. Delivering the right information to the right people at the right time is essential to support any decision-making processes affecting the production of deliverables and benefits. A failure to communicate what needs to be accomplished can be just as detrimental to the successful completion of a component of work as inadequately performing the work itself. Both situations lead to an unacceptable result. The lack of timely or adequate information can also result in the failure to stop unnecessary project work in a timely manner, which is a waste of funds and resources.

For example, mission critical work may need to proceed using the best information available before final specifications or requirements are completed. Quality and timely communications with the customer can define the impacts at a particular point in time of proceeding, or not proceeding, with incomplete information. Effective communication can provide portfolio, program, and project managers, as well as the customer, the opportunity to properly assess the risks involved. Proceeding without this critical communication and resulting agreements or authorizations can potentially expose the enterprise to unacceptable risks.

How can communications be planned to support an enterprise-wide PBM methodology?

Managing information and communication issues requires an enterprise-wide methodology that effectively provides the data needed by project, program, and portfolio managers and their team members. Identifying the information and communications needs of all the project stakeholders requires an understanding of their information requirements, their influence, when information is required, and how information will be planned, managed, gathered, stored, and disseminated.

Communications planning information needs to be assembled into structured communications management plans from the EPMO down through each portfolio, program, and project. These communications management plans identify the PBMS, PBMIS, and other enterprise systems that will be used to manage information, as well as identification of any security requirements related to the dissemination of sensitive information. Enterprise level planning can maximize communications while minimizing the associated administrative costs.

The communication planning and execution processes discussed above are summarized in Figure 17-1. The primary output of the process steps shown are the communication management plans. Internal and external technical coordination should be also addressed in the communication plans and include items such as:

- Identifying regularly scheduled reporting, reviews, and meetings.
- Defining the data flow.
- Specifying channels of communication.
- Establishing communication responsibilities for the customer and other external stakeholders.
- Identifying intergroup commitments and subsequent changes.
- Establishing the frequency of regularly scheduled communications.
- Establishing information management and archiving.
- Setting rules for managing proprietary, secure, controlled, and classified information.
- Defining access requirements to store and retrieve printed and electronic files.
- Defining the chain for escalation of issues that cannot be resolved at the core management team level.

Figure 17-1.   Communications Management Processes

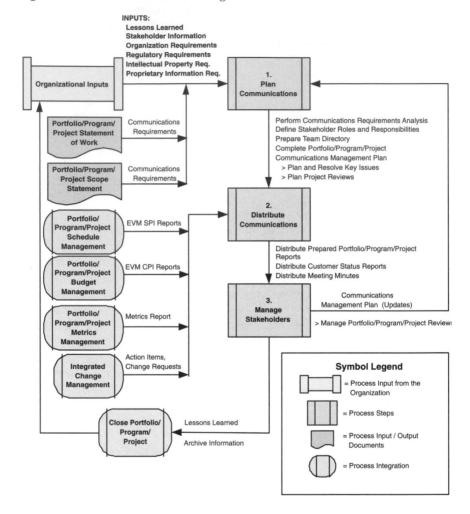

- Defining the process for updating each Communications Management Plan.

Additional topics to consider including in the plans are:

- Holding and documenting status/progress reporting/reviews.
- Handling and reporting performance metrics.
- Documenting and communicating risk status.
- Resolving issues and problems.
- Reporting earned-value/performance/trend analysis.

- Managing technical, specification, and requirements documentation and updates.
- Documenting contracted and purchased items.
- Managing records and artifacts.

A key component in portfolio/program/project communication is the identification, documentation, and sharing of information on threats (negative risks) and opportunities (positive risks). This requires an enterprise-wide plan for managing risks.

17.2 Risk Management

How can risk management be viewed from a business perspective?

Managing risks is a fundamental aspect of any business. Most managers understand that market threats and opportunities (read as risks) can drive enterprise business strategies. From a business perspective, risk is an uncertain event or condition that, if it occurs, has a positive or negative effect on specific planned or in-process strategic initiatives and their supporting objectives. The consequence of these changes can have technical, schedule, or cost impacts; often, risk affects all three.

Many managers view risks as having negative consequences, but potential changes can also present positive opportunities, such as additional customer funding, (i.e., positive consequences). The positive potentials of risk must be thoughtfully considered, documented, and reported. The purposes of risk management are to increase the probability and impact of positive events and decrease the probability and impact of events adverse to business objectives. Risk management includes risk management planning, identification, analysis, and responses, as well as monitoring and control of a strategic initiative, objective, portfolio, program, or project.

Why should enterprise management establish risk management on an enterprise-wide basis in support of PBM?

Formal enterprise-wide EPMO management of risks results in proactive risk identification, allowing potential problems and opportunities to be addressed early on. A formal risk management approach also includes documentation of risks to better allow all levels of management to participate in threat reduction and opportunity capture activities.

A portfolio/program/project team can, with properly implemented risk management, quickly develop answers to questions such as:

- How much time and money should be allocated based on identified risks?

- How to measure the overall project performance with respect to each risk?
- How much help will be needed from the customer or other disciplines within the enterprise?

Answering these questions can feed the risk response strategies into other portfolio, program, and project processes, such as budgeting and scheduling. The management of risks is crucial to ensure that the effort expended on a risk is related to the level, type, and visibility of the risk and is commensurate with both the risk and importance of the strategic initiative, business objective, portfolio, program or project that will be affected.

How can risk management be developed and implemented to support an enterprise-wide PBM methodology?

To develop and implement an enterprise-wide PBM risk management methodology, an EPMO risk management plan must be prepared. The plan should describe in detail how the EPMO would administer the PBM risk program and should address each of the basic risk management techniques: Avoidance, Transference, Mitigation, Acceptance, and Combination(s) of the others. Figure 17-2 illustrates the steps of the Risk Management process. These processes and their interaction are well documented in the Project Management Institute's (PMI®) *PMBOK® Guide*.

The EPMO PBM methodology risk management plan would include the following:

- *Risk model:* Defines the methods, tools, and data sources that can be used to manage project risks.
- *Roles and responsibilities:* Identify the risk owners, support methods, and reporting responsibilities for managing project risks. Assignment of responsibilities for collecting, processing, and maintaining data.
- *Timing:* Establishes the frequency monitoring and controlling activities that will be performed throughout the project life cycle. These include the risk management activities in the project schedule.
- *Reporting formats:* Describes the content and format of the risk, as well as any other risk reports required. Defines how the outcomes of the risk management processes will be documented, analyzed, and communicated.
- *Tracking:* Documents how all facets of risk activities will be recorded for the benefit of the current project, future needs, and lessons learned. Documents whether and how risk management processes will be audited.
- *Checklists:* A checklist/questionnaire based on historical information and knowledge used as a tool to identify project risk and issues that

Figure 17-2. Risk Management Processes

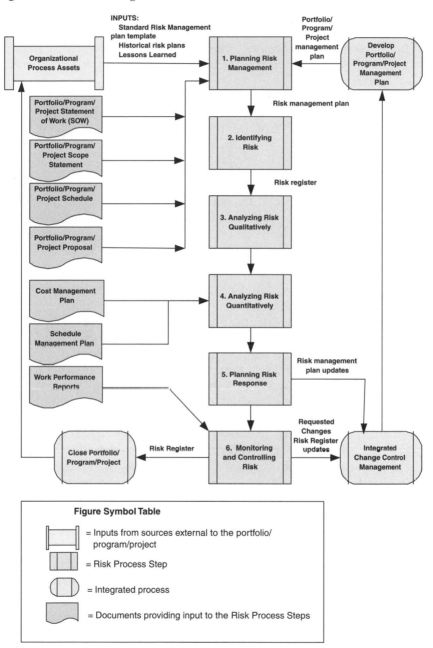

have proven to be factors in managing risks (A sample checklist is available at www.amacombooks.org/go/EnterpriseWidePM).

- *Guidelines:* Specific information on how to:

  - Prepare risk analysis sheets to identify risks, probability, impact, mitigation, and response plan (see, for example, Risk Analysis in Appendix A).
  - Approach and conduct the risk management activities.
  - Manage risks in a structured way during the business life cycle.
  - Monitor and control risk, including identifying, analyzing, and planning for newly arising risks and tracking identified risks and those on the watch list.

- *Risk register:* Repository, preferably computerized, that contains all of the data relating to the identification, qualification, quantification, and planned responses to risks. It contains the outcomes of risk analyses, prioritization and responses after other risk management processes are conducted, and has the following:

  - *List of identified risks:* Root causes and uncertain project assumptions are included as risks are identified.
  - *List of responses:* Potential and planned responses and mitigation plans (available at www.amacombooks.org/go/EnterpriseWidePM) for those risks and contingency plans for risks that have become actualized (i.e. 100% probable).
  - *Root causes of risk:* Fundamental conditions or events often help identify risks. Their root causes may create more than one risk, which is important to understand when developing effective risk responses.
  - *Updated risk categories:* Identifying risks often results in the identification of new risk categories, which should be added to the risk register.
  - *Risk impact magnitude:* Risks typically impact more than just one dimension. In quantifying risks, the cost, schedule, and technical impacts must be considered. The overall impact magnitude of the risk is set to the highest of all three areas. Each risk is ranked in five levels (see Risk Impact Magnitude definitions in Appendix A) to determine a relative magnitude, with cost and schedule impact expressed in dollars and magnitude set relative to the scope of the business objective.

SECTION 5

Execution

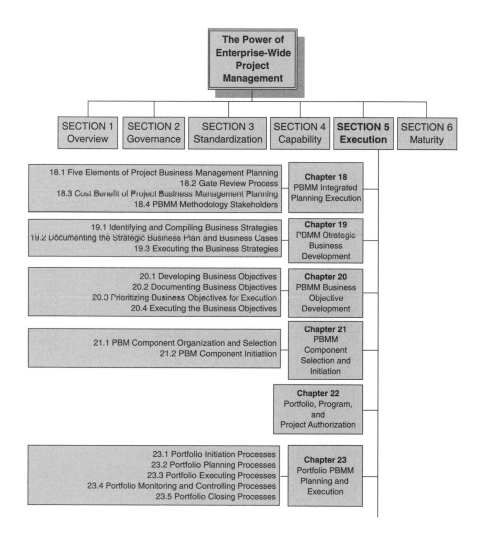

The Power of
Enterprise-Wide
Project
Management

| SECTION 1 Overview | SECTION 2 Governance | SECTION 3 Standardization | SECTION 4 Capability | **SECTION 5 Execution** | SECTION 6 Maturity |

18.1 Five Elements of Project Business Management Planning
18.2 Gate Review Process
18.3 Cost Benefit of Project Business Management Planning
18.4 PBMM Methodology Stakeholders

Chapter 18
PBMM Integrated
Planning Execution

19.1 Identifying and Compiling Business Strategies
19.2 Documenting the Strategic Business Plan and Business Cases
19.3 Executing the Business Strategies

Chapter 19
PBMM Strategic
Business
Development

20.1 Developing Business Objectives
20.2 Documenting Business Objectives
20.3 Prioritizing Business Objectives for Execution
20.4 Executing the Business Objectives

Chapter 20
PBMM Business
Objective
Development

21.1 PBM Component Organization and Selection
21.2 PBM Component Initiatiion

Chapter 21
PBMM
Component
Selection and
Initiation

Chapter 22
Portfolio, Program,
and
Project Authorization

23.1 Portfolio Initiation Processes
23.2 Portfolio Planning Processes
23.3 Portfolio Executing Processes
23.4 Portfolio Monitoring and Controlling Processes
23.5 Portfolio Closing Processes

Chapter 23
Portfolio PBMM
Planning and
Execution

24.1 Program Initiation Processes 24.2 Program Planning Processes 24.3 Program Executing Processes 24.4 Program Monitoring and Controlling Processes 24.5 Program Closing Processes	**Chapter 24** Program PBMM Planning and Execution
25.1 Project Initiation Processes 25.2 Project Planning Processes 25.3 Project Executing Processes 25.4 Project Monitoring and Controlling Processes 25.5 Project Closing Processes	**Chapter 25** Project PBMM Planning and Execution

CHAPTER 18

PBMM Integrated Planning & Execution

From a business perspective, PBM execution is concerned with controlling the resources and funds of the enterprise, as well as monitoring and controlling the deliverables from projects and the benefits derived from programs. Execution is the final and fourth major pillar of the enterprise-wide project management house of excellence. It applies the Project Business Management Methodology (PBMM) Model developed in Chapter 10.

The PBMM model provides an elementary top-down hierarchically integrated blend of strategic, tactical, portfolio, program, and project planning and execution processes. The model also provides the set of integrated processes to identify, define, evaluate, categorize, organize, prioritize, select and optimize (balance), initiate, authorize, and execute or terminate portfolios, programs, and projects within the enterprise's defined business planning cycles. The PBMM model is implemented, monitored, and controlled by the enterprise project management office (EPMO) governance, with its organizational structures and positions as developed in Section 2. The EPMO employs the capabilities of the EPMO staff and the project business management system (PBMS) developed in Section 4 to execute the enterprise's portfolios, programs, and projects. Execution begins with conceiving the business strategy that leads to the project and ends with the physical execution of the project's work and submittal of its deliverables.

Enterprises execute projects, programs, and portfolios to accomplish nonoperationally-based business strategies and related objectives. To perform portfolio, program, and project planning, project business management cannot be a part-time activity that is added on to the enterprise's processes and organizational structure. To effectively execute projects, programs, and portfolios, the enterprise as a whole must understand the need for project business management and commit the funding, personnel, processes, systems, and tools to make it successful.

When executing the PBMM model, the EPMO management and staff is concerned with business cycle development and management of the enterprise's *projects* (temporary endeavors undertaken to create a unique deliverable), *programs* (a group of related projects and other work managed in a coordinated way to obtain benefits and control not available from managing the projects separately), and *portfolios* (a collection of projects or programs and other work that are grouped together to facilitate effective management of that work to meet strategic business objectives). *Other work* is any specifically defined work related to and explicitly necessary to complete a project, program, or portfolio. In executing the PBMM model processes, the EPMO must take into account operational issues, processes, and results throughout the business cycle.

18.1 Five Elements of Project Business Management Planning

PBMM has five components for which process models for planning and execution were developed in Chapter 10: strategy, objective, portfolio, program, and project. The first two are enhanced business operations related to strategy development and business objective identification and selection and into which project business management content and activities have been integrated. Their implementation will add minimal administrative cost to normal business planning operations, as shown below:

1. *Business strategy development:* Involves establishing a business plan of prioritized strategies that is supported by business cases.
2. *Business objective (tactical) development:* Produces documented business objectives with stated accomplishment criteria and defined benefits that fully support the business strategies. They are arranged according to the final priority rank that defines the order in which they should be performed and completed. They are separated into two sets of objectives:

   - Nonproject business objectives and action items that could be directly performed by the respective business units.
   - Business objectives that need to be performed as projects.

   Objectives to be performed as projects are separated from normal business unit objectives that will be handled by the next phase of the enterprise's normal business cycle. Project-based business objectives are gathered into portfolios with programs and/or projects, programs with projects, and standalone projects. After initiation and authorization activities are performed, the portfolio, program, or project is formally recognized and authorized by the issuance of an approved charter.
3. *Portfolio Management:* Implementation planning and execution are performed according to the PBMM model portfolio established by the EPMO during the standardized PBMM model development.

4. *Program Management:* Implementation planning and execution are performed according to the PBMM model program established by the EPMO during the standardized PBMM model development.
5. *Project Management:* Implementation planning and execution are performed according to the PBMM model project program established by the EPMO during the standardized PBMM model development.

The additional administrative cost of implementing and operating the portfolio, program, and project management PBMM model processes depends on the enterprise's PBM maturity (see Section 6), the operational status of the EPMO, and the enterprise's business unit's acceptance of PBM as a business function. However, publicly traded corporations based in the United States can integrate much of the related PMIS and project cost accounting requirements into compliance with the Sarbanes-Oxley (Sar-Box) Law requirements related to management process control, data collection, and information analysis and reporting. This can minimize the direct and administrative costs of a PBMM implementation and help the enterprise recover some of the Sar-Box compliance costs.

18.2 Gate Review Process

Portfolios, programs, and projects should be routinely reviewed to determine if they should be replanned, stopped, or terminated. Although this can be part of the monitoring and controlling processes, it is prudent to establish points, such as gate reviews, in the execution schedule for additional reviews. These gate reviews, which are built into the PBMM model, should be performed following completion of the initiating, planning, and execution processes to ensure that the project, program, or portfolio is on track and ready to move to the next step. The appropriate level of management approval is required before proceeding to the subsequent processes.

Which gate review is most important depends on the perspective. From a business perspective, it is when an executive decision is made to continue executing the planned action at the end of the planning process. For strategic business development, it is when an executive decision is to develop further planning to support business objectives. For business objective development, the first gate is when management begins to plan the portfolios, programs, and projects that support the business objectives, and the second is when a charter is issued to authorize funds for this work. For portfolio management, the major gate is when a charter is issued to authorize the funds for the work on a supporting program or project. For program management, it is when a charter is issued to authorize the funds

Figure 18-1. Process Gate Reviews

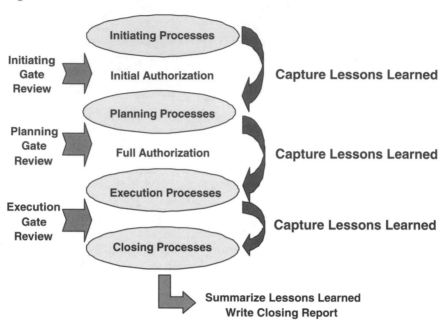

for the work on a supporting project. In project management, the most important gate is when the physical work is authorized. Figure 18-1 is a graphical illustration of these gates. The execution gate review is the last review and triggers the closing processes.

18.3 Cost Benefit of Project Business Management Planning

The benefits of effective, mature, standardized project business management planning increase with the complexity, size, and number of portfolios, programs, and projects, and with the establishment of an executive level enterprise project management office (EPMO). Mature project business management processes create significant benefits at a low cost through documented and implemented structured portfolio, program, and project planning and execution methodologies.

An empirical rule of thumb in project business management says that 80 percent of the value and potential benefit is accomplished in the planning phase and 20 percent is captured through managed and controlled execution of the plan. The factors that drive this outcome include:

- The application of the majority of the *enterprise environmental factors* and many *organizational process assets* in selecting the enterprise's strategies and supporting objectives occur as part of executive and senior management business operations' strategy development processes.
- Many MBA business management courses limit their focus to the impact of organizational culture and structure, infrastructure, and market conditions. This misplaced focus can lead to a poor selection of strategic initiatives and supporting business objectives.
- In addition to MBA factors, enterprise environmental factors include laws, regulations, and standards over which the enterprise has no control but with which it must comply. A wide range of these types of enterprise environmental factors have a significant impact on an enterprise's selection of strategies to implement its vision/ mission.
- The selection of business objectives and supporting portfolios, programs, and projects is completed during business objective development, which is before any portfolios, programs, or projects are authorized.

The application of the majority of enterprise environmental factors and organizational process assets used in selecting the business strategies occur during the PBMM model business strategy and business objective development processes. The application of those environmental factors can have a positive or negative impact on the desired outcome of the business objectives in advance of the initiation of any portfolio, program, or project, which is the timeline point when project management oriented processes are employed.

To be of value, a fully mature project business management implementation needs to address all the applicable enterprise environmental factors noted during the PBMM model strategic and tactical planning processes. It is not enough to only understand what benefits or value may be achieved if the work on the business objective is actually initiated.

As Figure 18-2 indicates, the greatest value is created in the strategic development and objective selection and planning stages. The figure also shows that substantial value can be lost through poor project execution.

A PBMM model of integrated and standardized practices, processes, and procedures can ensure that effective project business management is used throughout the enterprise's business operations. However, it is only through the uniform and consistent application of institutionalized project business management processes that greater benefits and value can be obtained during execution.

Plan the work and then work that plan is a project management expression used when discussing the first step to success. The iterative point is that if

Figure 18-2. Value of Project Business Management Planning & Execution

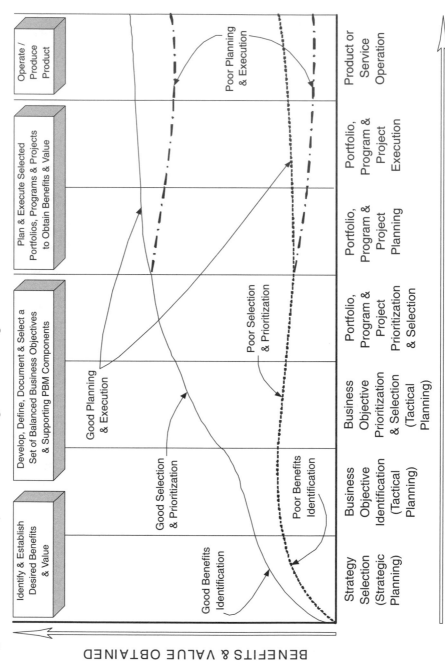

PROJECT BUSINESS MANAGEMENT METHODOLOGY PROCESSES FLOW

BENEFITS & VALUE OBTAINED

Identify & Establish Desired Benefits & Value

Develop, Define, Document & Select a Set of Balanced Business Objectives & Supporting PBM Components

Plan & Execute Selected Portfolios, Programs & Projects to Obtain Benefits & Value

Operate / Produce Product

Good Benefits Identification

Good Selection & Prioritization

Good Planning & Execution

Poor Benefits Identification

Poor Selection & Prioritization

Poor Planning & Execution

Strategy Selection (Strategic Planning)

Business Objective Identification (Tactical Planning)

Business Objective Prioritization & Selection (Tactical Planning)

Portfolio, Program & Project Prioritization & Selection

Portfolio, Program & Project Planning

Portfolio, Program & Project Execution

Product or Service Operation

a plan can not be totally implemented as-is (which is usually the case), then revise the plan and then work the revised plan. Another well worn adage is "an enterprise does not plan to fail—it just fails to plan" or, in many instances, just fails to follow the plan. These adages are an accepted part of business and project management literature. In addition, the Pareto Principle 80/20 rule, which is that 20 percent of the physical work can consume 80 percent of the total time and resources required to perform a complex task, might also be applicable to the execution of portfolios, programs, and projects when there is a lack of adequate planning or plan implementation.

The downside risk of poor project execution shown in Figure 18-1 could be 20 percent of the total costs. This means that as a result proper execution of a plan, an enterprise can gain 20 percent of the economic value and benefits of the related business objective that might otherwise be left on the table. It also illustrates that having good strategic and tactical planning positions the enterprise to obtain serious value and benefit from selected business objectives, but this requires dependable portfolio, program, and project management planning and execution processes.

A supporting qualitative point is that many project management experts indicate that between 30 and 50 percent of total project time should be spent in planning to ensure successful completion of the planned work. Therefore, lack of sufficient planning time is one of the primary reasons for project and program failures.

The preceding paragraphs call attention to the reasons why this book focuses so heavily on the initiation and planning processes. Those initiating processes and supporting planning processes can establish up to 80 percent of the value and benefit of the desired outcome. During these initiating and authorizing processes, executive and senior managements' involvement and decision making will have its maximum impact.

18.4 PBM Methodology Stakeholders

Many *stakeholders* are involved in planning and executing enterprises strategic initiatives and supporting business objectives. PMI® defines *stakeholders* as the persons and organizations, such as customers, sponsors, performing organizations and the public, that are actively involved in the portfolio, program, or project, or whose interests may be positively or negatively affected by execution or completion of the portfolio, program, or project. They may also exert influence over the portfolio, program, or project and the enterprise's desired benefits and deliverables.

A key stakeholder with respect to the enterprise's funds is the *sponsor*. PMI® defines a sponsor as the person or group that provides the financial resources, in cash or in kind, for the portfolio, program, or project. Each

Table 18-1. PBM Methodology Model Key Stakeholder Roles and Responsibilities

Line Number	Legend: O = Oversight S = Supports R = Responsibility I = Informed A = Approves C = Consults PROJECT BUSINESS MANAGEMENT METHODOLOGY PROCESSES	Chief Exec. Officer	Chief Proj. Mgmt. Officer	Business Unit Manager	Manager Division PMO	Manager Bus. Unit PMO	PMO Staff	Portfolio Manager	Program Manager	Project Manager	Program/Project Team	Customers
1	**BUSINESS STRATEGY DEVELOPMENT**											
A	Initiation Processes	A	R	S	S	S	S	S	I	I		
B	Planning Processes	A	R	S	S	S	S	S	I	I		
C	Executing Processes	A	R	S	S	S	S	S	I	I		
D	Monitoring and Controlling Processes	A	R	S	S	S	S	S	I	I		
E	Closing Processes	A	R	S	S	S	S	S	I	I		
2	**BUSINESS OBJECTIVE DEVELOPMENT**											
A	Initiation Processes	A	R	S	S	S	S	S	I	I		
B	Planning Processes	A	R	S	S	S	S	S	I	I		
C	Executing Processes	A	R	S	S	S	S	S	I	I		
D	Monitoring and Controlling Processes	A	R	S	S	S	S	S	I	I		
E	Closing Processes	A	R	S	S	S	S	S	I	I		
3	**PORTFOLIO MANAGEMENT**											
A	Initiation Processes	O	O	O	O	A	S	R	S	I		I
B	Planning Processes	I	I	I	O	A	S	R	S	I		I
C	Executing Processes	I	I	I	O	A	S	R	S	I		I
D	Monitoring and Controlling Processes	I	I	I	O	A	S	R	S	I		I
E	Closing Process	I	I	I	O	A	S	R	S	I		I
4	**PROGRAM MANAGEMENT**											
A	Program Initiation Processes	I	I	I	O	A	S	R	S	I		I
B	Program Planning Processes	O	O	O	O	A	S	S	R	I	R	I
C	Program Executing Processes	I	I	I	O	A	S	S	R	I	R	I
D	Program Monitoring and Controlling Processes	I	I	I	O	A	S	S	R	I	R	I
E	Program Closing Process	I	I	I	O	A	S	S	R	I	R	I
5	**PROJECT MANAGEMENT**											
A	Project Initiation Processes	I	I	I	O	A	S	R	S	I		I
B	Project Planning Processes	I	I	I	O	A	S	S	R	I	R	I
C	Project Executing Processes	I	I	I	O	A	S	S	R	I	R	I
D	Project Monitoring and Controlling Processes	I	I	I	O	A	S	S	R	I	R	I
E	Project Closing Process	I	I	I	O	A	S	S	R	I	R	I

Legend Details:

O = Oversight – Provides governance oversight establishes policy, procedures, and ultimate approval if escalated to executives for resolution of issues.

R = Responsibility – Ensures the work is completed, may also contribute to the work.

A = Approves – Signs off on the work, concurs that the work meets requirements.

S = Supports – Supplies supporting resources, completes the work. If there is no 'S' for a line, the role with the 'R' does the work.

I = Informed – Role is informed of the actions taken and the results.

C = Consults – Supplies input and recommended solutions, consultation is mandatory.

strategic initiative and business objective will have an executive or senior management sponsor within the enterprise. This person will be involved in the authorization of the portfolio, program, or project they are "sponsoring."

The number of stakeholders and the level of stakeholder involvement in the PBMM model implementation and execution varies from one portfolio, program, or project to another. The EPMO itself is both a key stakeholder and an information source, particularly during the initiation and planning stages of each portfolio, program, and project. The EPMO is an organizational body composed of various members of the enterprise. It is responsible for and focuses on centralized and coordinated management, planning, prioritization, and execution of the portfolios, programs, projects and subprojects tied to the enterprise's overall business objectives. EPMO members have a responsibility to make recommendations, request changes in directions, or suggest stopping or terminating a portfolio, program, or project to achieve the enterprise's business objectives.

Table 18-1 tabulates the key enterprise management and EPMO positions that are stakeholders in implementing the PBM methodology, and it indicates the roles and responsibilities they may have for each process group within the five levels of the PBM methodology (PBMM) model. The complete tabulation down through each process defined in the PBMM model is provided in Appendix A.

CHAPTER 19

PBMM Strategic Business Development

A characteristic of most successful enterprises is enlightened self-interest. A successful enterprise produces products, provides services, and completes business strategy-related projects, programs, and portfolios to maximize accrued benefits. Enterprises address their need for growth and change by creating strategic business initiatives to modify the enterprise or create and modify its processes or products. The enterprise business strategy, which is determined at the executive management level, drives the development of the supporting strategic initiatives and objectives. Thus, executive management must be responsible for developing and planning business strategy initiatives and related business objectives. The enterprise project management office (EPMO) staff can support and assist executive management in this strategic planning, but it should not supplant nor subsume the proper roles of executive management in strategic planning.

The first component of the PBMM model is business strategy identification and selection. This includes developing and documenting a set of business strategies as the primary output of an upper-level, formal strategic business planning process, as shown in Figure 19-1.

An enterprise may create many business strategy initiatives. Some will be addressed by one or more business objectives that can simply be accomplished by one or more of the functional organizations within the enterprise. This has been a common way of doing business in many enterprises. Executive management establishes the strategy accomplishment metrics that measure success in achieving each strategic initiative. These metrics include financial contribution, asset maintenance and development, end-user satisfaction, stakeholder satisfaction, risk profile, return on investment, desired net present value, and enhanced resource capabilities.

When business strategies require complex or large-scale projects for completion, a business also needs to involve project business management during the business strategy development stage. Initiating and planning processes for business strategy development were developed and defined in Chapter 10; their relationships and interactions are shown in Figure

Figure 19-1. PBMM Business Strategy Development Data Flow

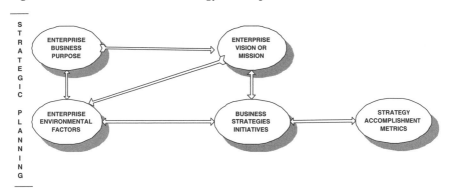

19-2. The significant PBM aspects of those processes are discussed in the following sections.

19.1 Identifying and Compiling Business Strategies

The first management action in the strategic planning process is executive development of a set of strategies that support the enterprise's vision/mission. The next step is to create a list of strategies that describes executive management's purpose and scope for each strategy. Table 19-1 provides the general steps for this process; the results are documented in Table 19-2. The final step, which many enterprises fail to perform, is to prioritize the business strategies (see examples in Table 19-2).

The success of a project often depends on whether management understands and has accounted for the necessary *enterprise environmental factors* (see Subchapter 4.2) in the operations of the enterprise and the planning of business objectives. For example, an apparently simple business strategy involves a commercially oriented business that decides to expand by acquiring government project contracts. Unless the business understands government regulations for contract accounting, it may fail to even be awarded a government project. Therefore, how well the business strategy is supported by the enterprise environmental factors related to that strategy will directly affect the enterprise's ability to have a successful project that supports that strategy.

The output from this strategic planning step should be similar to that shown in Table 19-3, with a planning item number column (Section 1), a strategy item name column (Section 2), a strategy purpose and scope de-

Figure 19-2. Business Strategy Development Initiating and Planning Processes

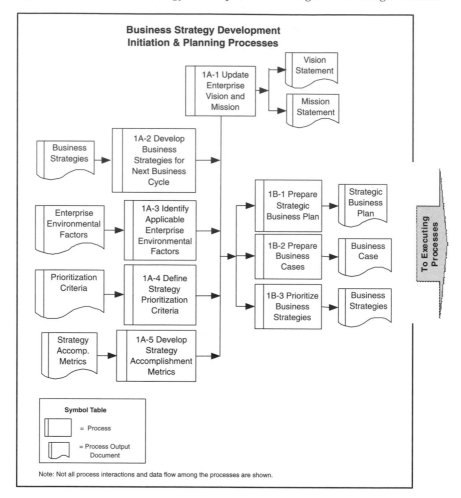

scription column (Section 3), and a column for each criterion (see Table 19-2) that reflects the rank assigned to that criterion for that strategy (Section 5).

19.2 Documenting the Strategic Business Plan and Business Cases

The final step in business strategy development planning, and a key factor in the successful planning, development, and implementation of strategic initiatives, is developing and documenting the strategic business plan and

Table 19-1. Business Strategies Planning Process Steps

Step	Step Definition	Roles	Activity Description
1	Identify Enterprise Business Strategy	Executive Management Team	Table Section 2 is filled in by identifying the enterprise business strategy item name for the next business cycle to create a template for the business units to use for their part in the tactical planning process.
2	Establish Purpose And Scope For Business Strategy	Executive Management Team	Table Section 3 is filled in by identifying the purpose and scope for the enterprise business strategy. This includes identifying the enterprise's related business case study.
3	Assign Enterprise Business Strategy Sponsors	Executive Management Team	Table Section 4 is completed by listing a sponsor for each of the corresponding business strategies in Section 2.
4	Assign Business Strategy Criterion And Rank	Executive Management Team	Table Section 5 is completed by assigning the applicable business strategy criterion and its rank to each of the corresponding business strategies in Section 2.

business cases that support those strategies. This prudent step captures the value of the management effort expended in developing that plan and supporting initiatives.

What is a simple, realistic strategic business plan?

The strategic business plan is a high-level business document that describes the enterprise's purpose and vision/mission. It also identifies the strategic

Table 19-2. Example Business Strategy Initiative Prioritization Criteria

Criterion #	Rank(s)	Criterion Description
1	1 thru 10	How well strategy supports the enterprise's vision or mission
2	11 thru 15	How positively do the Enterprise Environmental Factors (see Section 1, Subchapter 4.2) support the business strategy
3	16 thru 20	How much risk is associated with the strategy
4	21 thru 25	How much business growth potential is associated with the strategy
5	26 thru 30	How much financial investment is associated with the strategy
6	31 thru 35	How much impact to headcount is associated with the strategy

Table 19-3. Business Strategies Tabulation

Sec 1	Section 2	Section 3	Section 4	Section 5			Section 6			
Item	Item Name - Strategic Initiative/Business Objective/Business Unit (BU) Objective & Action	Description (Purpose & Scope)	Sponsor	Strategy Criterion & Rank			Objective Criterion & Rank			RANK
				1	2	m	1	2	n	
1.0	Name 1–Strategic Initiative	*Strategic Initiative* to have benefit & capability of item Name 1	CFO							
2.0	Name 2–Strategic Initiative	*Strategic Initiative* to have benefit & capability of item Name 2	CTO							
3.0	PBM as Core Competency	*Strategic Initiative* to have EWPM capability	CEO							

initiatives that will be adopted to achieve the vision/mission during the business cycle covered by the document. It may include, where practicable, the business objectives and related benefits to be achieved. The strategic initiatives define the enterprise's intended achievements in terms of cultural outcomes and business benefits within a specified time. It is usually associated with specific accomplishment or performance metrics.

What is the purpose and content of a simple business case document?

Business case documents significantly increase the probability of accomplishing the enterprise's business strategies by documenting each strategy in one or more cases. A *business case* articulates the intent and desired benefits of a specific strategy in a feasibility study format. Each business case provides the bases for authorizing further PBM planning activities, so that an adequate definition of the intent of each strategy initiative and supporting objectives can be developed.

The purposes of the business case are to:

- Be the official document by which the results of the business analysis of a proposed business opportunity or identified threat are communicated within the enterprise.
- Document the market, technical, operational, and financial analyses for the initiative.
- Serve as an initial basis for prioritization of the initiative, including its funding and the allocation of other resources.

- Provide the parameters for measuring how well the initiative was accomplished.
- Set the milestones by which the initiative will be tracked.
- Establish accountability and documentation for the benefits being proposed.

The business case answers the following business-related questions:

- How did the initiative come about?
- What is the opportunity/threat/issue/improvement being addressed?
- Why, in clear and concise terms, is the initiative necessary?
- What is the desired product, service, or result?
- What is the nature of any improvement?
- What are the benefits to the enterprise and its customers?
- What are the qualitative benefits, such as customer satisfaction, strategic value, cycle time improvements?
- What are the linkages to the enterprise's vision, mission, and value drivers (that is, market, quality, efficiency).
- Why will the initiative succeed?
- What must be invested to get the desired product, service, result, or benefit?
- What are the expected incremental production or operational costs for the new or modified product, service, or production process?
- What are the proposed spending reductions, revenue improvements, or profit improvements related to just the initiative?
- What is the enterprise's capacity to successfully implement the initiative while meeting financial objectives?
- What other factors materially impact the potential success of the initiative, such as additional services, required efficiencies, minimum or maximum quantities, required product quality, and deployment objectives?
- What are the concerns, issues, and risks?
- What are the parameters and criteria used for prioritizing the initiative with respect to other business strategic initiatives?
- What is the exit strategy if the strategic initiative is not delivering the desired return on investment?

The business case document provides a common basis and format for supplying information required for both business and project business management planning. The basic information includes the strategic initiative's identification and description. The initial business case submissions should be able to adequately substantiate the request for any initial or incremental funding to further develop the initiative by establishing the:

- Need for incremental funding.
- Communication of resource allocation as it relates to incremental funding.
- Benefits to be derived.
- Corporation's ability to execute the initiative.
- Initiative's ability to provide adequate financial return.

A business case document is usually divided into sections that reflect the type of business case being created. For example, it could be in the form of an internal proposal for market or technical trial funding. Another example is a service enterprise with a business strategy to acquire larger competitive contracts that would have more than one project. This would begin as a marketing document that identifies opportunities far enough into the future for the enterprise to position itself to be competitive. Each opportunity would then be incorporated into a bid or no-bid decision document. Each opportunity with a positive bid decision would then be articulated in a comprehensive business case document that would include a draft proposal.

Each business strategy initiative and its associated business case document flow down from the strategic planning phase into the tactical planning phase. This information aids in developing supporting business objectives, as well as the business objective prioritization and selection processes.

19.3 Executing the Business Strategies

Once initiation and planning of the strategic initiatives are completed, the execution of each strategy begins with the first step in the implementation of the initiative in the PBMM model, which is executive management's authorization of business objective development planning.

The PBMM executing, monitoring and controlling, and closing processes for business strategy development that were developed and defined in the PBMM model in Chapter 10 and their relationships and interactions are shown in Figure 19-3. Strategic initiative execution is finished when work on the business strategy is either terminated or completed and the strategy is closed.

Figure 19-3. Business Strategy Development Executing, Monitoring, and Closing Processes

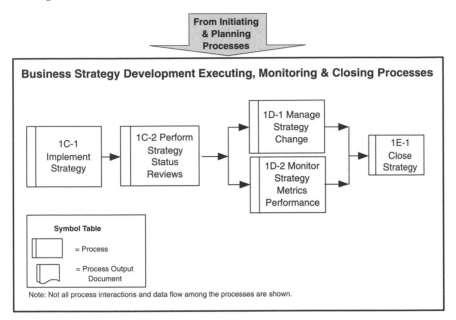

Note: Not all process interactions and data flow among the processes are shown.

CHAPTER 20

PBMM Business Objective Development

The finalization of business plan strategies leads the executive and senior management to develop a set of supporting business objectives. Whether the identified objectives can be accomplished depends on other *enterprise environmental factors*, such as existing resources, including material, equipment and available funds. Accomplishment also depends on whether certain *organizational process assets* (see Subchapter 4.3) are owned or have been developed by the enterprise, such as a standardized project business management methodology, appropriate contracting procedures, and required accounting procedures.

A major focus of project business management in tactical business planning is bringing value and benefits to the enterprise through the integration of general business management, operations management, and project/program/ portfolio management. This requires that the enterprise select and implement only those objectives that best meet its defined business strategies, so that the resulting portfolios, programs, projects, and other work will produce the desired deliverables, values, and benefits.

The PBMM model includes the formal processes for developing business objectives (see Figure 20-1) that address and support various strategic initiatives developed during the planning process. Those business objectives are the primary output of the enterprise's tactical planning process.

Once the business objectives are defined and prioritized, documentation should justify their inclusion as a part of the organization's objectives for the business cycle. A subset of those objectives are then selected for execution; the selection is limited by resource availability and which of the required *organizational process assets* are operational and can be made available.

The enterprise's executive management establishes the objective accomplishment metrics, which sets the desired values to be attained and the benefits to be realized from the objectives. Management also specifies the desired progress toward established targets, such as cost and milestone achievements and the fulfillment of deliverables.

Initiating and planning processes for business objective development are defined in the PBMM model in Chapter 10; their relationships and in-

Figure 20-1. PBMM Business Objective Development (Tactical Planning) Data Flow

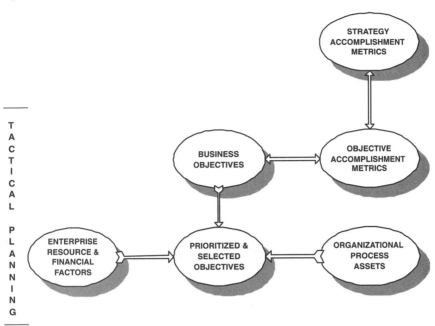

teractions are shown below in Figure 20-2. The significant PBM aspects of those processes are discussed in the following subchapters.

20.1 Developing Business Objectives

Establishing objectives is a forecasting activity that requires significant planning and training to achieve the intended results. Defining business objectives starts at the top and cascades down through the organizational structure to the individual business unit manager. The objectives at each level of the organization should support the enterprise's business strategies as well as the business objectives of the supporting units. The resulting business objectives must be quantified and qualified, so they can be prioritized, ranked, and measured in terms of performance.

Although identifying and developing business objectives seems an obvious requirement of doing business, many enterprises do not set objectives or do not set them properly. Many positive actions can be taken to perform this important development effort effectively, including:

Figure 20-2.   Business Objective Development Initiating & Planning Processes

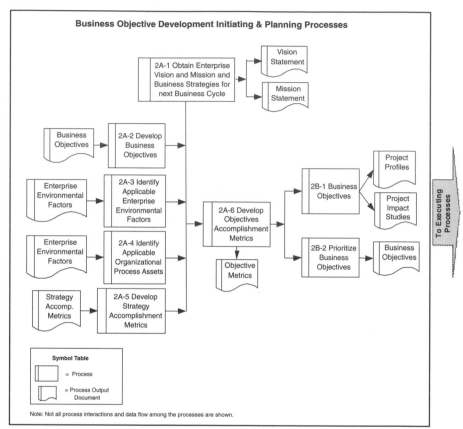

- Establishing a formal process to define business strategic goals and associated business objectives.
- Ensuring stated business strategic goals and business objectives are quantifiable.
- Preparing procedures on how to develop business objectives and the associated roles and responsibilities required to meet them.
- Providing training on how to properly develop objectives at all levels of the enterprise.
- Involving middle management in developing business objectives; do not stop with the top management of the enterprise.
- Establishing a formal measurement process and accomplishment metrics to validate the status of business objectives.
- Establishing accountability to achieve business objectives.

- Ensuring there is personal or organizational reward for achieving business objectives and a penalty for failing to achieve them.
- Ensuring that accomplished business objectives actually produce the desired results.
- Minimizing the organization's need to constantly address unexpected near-term issues (firefighting) that divert attention from long-range planning.

The following is a generalized discussion of a tactical planning process similar to Management by Objectives (MBO) or Management by Planning (MBP), which are techniques of cascading business analysis. MBP is based on the Japanese system known as *hoshin kanri,* which owes a debt of gratitude to Shewhart and Deming. The following information about the origins of *hoshin kanri* was extracted from the third edition of the *Hoshin Handbook* written by Pete Babich, President, Total Quality Engineering, Inc.:

> Understanding the origin of the words can provide insight into *hoshin* concepts. The term *"hoshin"* is short for *hoshin kanri.* The word *hoshin* can be broken into two parts. The literal translation of ho is "direction." The literal translation of shin is "needle," so the word *hoshin* could translate into "direction needle" or the English equivalent of "compass." The word *kanri* can also be broken into two parts. The first part, *kan,* translates into control or channeling. The second part, *ri,* translates into reason or logic. Taken altogether, *hoshin kanri* means management and control of the company's direction needle or focus.

方針   *hoshin* = a course, a policy, a plan, an aim

管理   *kanri* = administration, management, control, charge of, care for

The most popular English translation for *hoshin* is "Policy Deployment." Most books by American authors use Policy Deployment as the name for *hoshin.* No matter what you call it, however, *hoshin* is effective and helps organizations become more competitive (available at http://www.tqe.com; reprinted with permission).

An enterprise's operating philosophy is usually based on sets of relationships among five major stakeholders: customers, owners, employees, suppliers, and the communities in which they operate. These planning processes are also designed to identify business objectives that support improvements defined during the strategic planning efforts for any of these stakeholders

Most business managers are familiar with some form of business object planning. However, our tactical planning process goes heavily into the objective documentation and prioritization processes that are necessary to effectively support business objective selection and to clearly differentiate between those business objectives that can be accomplished simply and directly by the affected business units of the enterprise and those that need to be performed as projects. Our process is simple but effective and can be used by organizations of all sizes. It is illustrated in Figure 20-3 with the step activities described in Table 20-1. The discussion shows how business objectives can be developed and selected; the process is just as effective for an enterprise that has primarily ongoing operations.

Once the initial stage of this process has been competed, the action items are consolidated and listed in the tabulation for all business units of the organization. Table 20-2 shows a format for summarizing the list of developed business objectives (some may become programs or projects) and action items (some may become subprojects). The list is organized by the enterprise strategies listed and prioritized in Table 19-3. The output from this tactical planning process should be similar to that shown in Table 20-2,

Figure 20-3.   Business Objective Planning Process

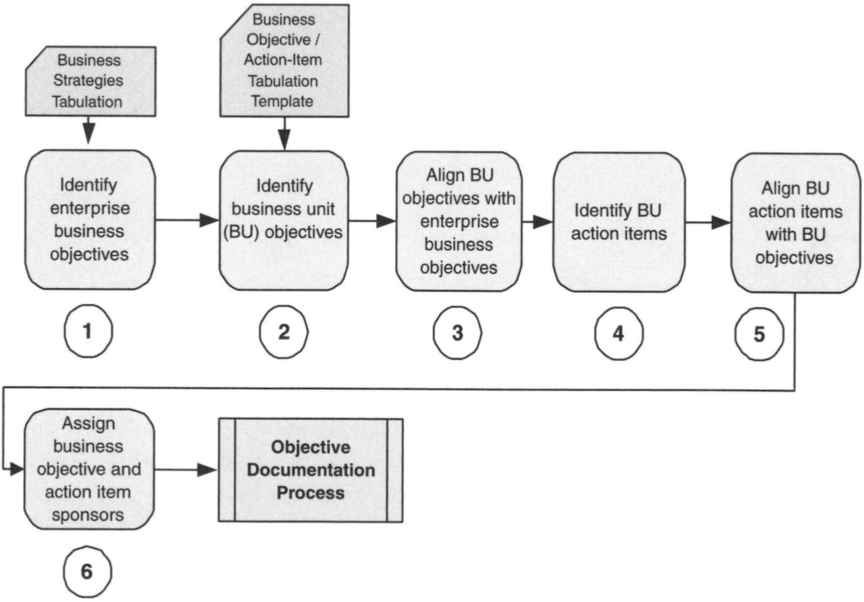

Table 20-1. Business Objectives Planning Process Steps

Step	Step Definition	Roles	Activity Description
1	Identify Enterprise Business Objectives	Executive Management Team	Table Section 2 is filled in by identifying the enterprise business objects' item names for the next business cycle to create a template for the business units to use in their part of the planning process.
2	Identify Business Unit (BU) Objectives	Business Unit Team	Table Section 2 is populated with the BU team objectives' item names that are required to satisfy one or more enterprise business objectives listed in Section 2.
3	Align BU Objectives With Enterprise Business Objectives	Business Unit Team	Table Section 1 is completed by aligning each BU objective with one or more of the enterprise business objectives.
4	Identify BU Action Items	Business Unit Team	Table Section 2 is further completed by listing BU action items that will be required to complete one or more of the BU objectives listed in Section 2.
5	Align BU Action Items With BU Objectives	Business Unit Team	Table Section 1 is completed by aligning one or more BU action items with one or more of the BU objectives.
6	Assign BU Objective And Action Item Sponsors	Business Unit Team	Table Section 4 is completed by listing a sponsor for each of the business unit objectives and action items in Section 2.

with a planning item number column (Section 1), a strategy/objective/action-item name column (Section 2), a strategy purpose and scope description column (Section 3), and one column for each criterion that reflects the rank assigned to that criterion for that strategy (Section 5).

It is not unusual to find the same or similar business objectives or action item listed in more than one business unit. One of the values of this process is identifying and reducing any potential duplication of effort among multiple organizations. Apparent duplications need to be investigated to validate there is an actual connection between the same or similar objectives supporting the same enterprise strategy. In many cases, it makes sense to combine action items into one composite objective assigned to just one of the organizations involved. Elimination of duplicate business objectives and unit actions in the final tabulation supports effective man-

Table 20-2. Business Objective/Action-Item Tabulation

Sec 1	Section 2	Section 3	Section 4	Section 5			Section 6			RANK
				Strategy Criterion & Rank			Objective Criterion & Rank			
Item	Item Name - Strategic Initiative/Business Objective/Business Unit (BU) Objective & Action	Description (Purpose & Scope)	Sponsor	1	2	m	1	2	n	
1.0	Name 1–Strategic Initiative	Strategic Initiative to have benefit & capability of item Name 1	CFO							
1.1	Business Objective 1A		CAO							
1.1.1	BU Objective 1B		CAO							
1.1.1.1	BU Objective 1C		CAO							
1.1.1.1.1	BU Action 1C1		CAO							
1.1.1.1.2	BU Action 1C2		CAO							
1.1.1.2	BU Objective 1A3		CAO							
1.2	Business Objective 1D		Accntng Mgr							
1.2.1	BU Objective 1D1		Accntng Mgr							
1.2.2	BU Objective 1D2		Accntng Mgr							
1.3	Business Objective 1E		AP Mgr							
1.3.1	BU Objective 1E		AP Mgr							
1.3.1.1	BU Objective 1F		AP Mgr							
1.3.1.1.1	BU Action 1Fa		AP Mgr							
1.3.1.1.2	BU Action 1Fb		AP Mgr							
1.3.1.1.3	BU Action 1Fc		AP Mgr							
2.0	Name 2 – Strategic Initiative	Strategic Initiative to have benefit & capability of item Name 2	CTO							
2.1	Business Objective 2A		System Mgr							
2.1.1	BU Action Item 2A1		System Mgr							
2.1.2	BU Action Item 2A2		System Mgr							
2.2	Business Objective 2B		WAN Mgr							
2.2.1	BU Objective 2B		WAN Mgr							
2.2.1.1	BU Action Item 2B1		WAN Mgr							
2.2.1.2	BU Action Item 2B2		WAN Mgr							
2.3	Business Objective 2C		LAN Mgr							
2.3.1	BU Objective 2C		LAN Mgr							

(continued)

Table 20-2. (*Continued*)

Sec 1	Section 2	Section 3	Section 4	Section 5			Section 6			RANK
	Item Name - Strategic Initiative/Business Objective/Business Unit (BU) Objective			Strategy Criterion & Rank			Objective Criterion & Rank			
Item	& Action	Description (Purpose & Scope)	Sponsor	1	2	m	1	2	n	
2.3.1.1	BU Action Item 2C		LAN Mgr							
3.0	*Strategic Initiative #3*	PBM as Core Competency	CEO							
3.1	Business Objective 3A	Implement EWPM	CEO							
3.1.1	BU Action Item 3A1	Prepare and Issue PM Policy	CEO							
3.1.2	BU Objective 3B	Develop PBM Capability	Chief PM Officer (CPMO)							
3.1.2.1	BU Action Item 3C	Develop PBM Methodology	CPMO							
3.1.2.2	BU Action Item 3D	Implement PBM Methodology	CPMO							
3.1.2.3	BU Objective 3F	Develop PBM System (PBMS)	CPMO/CIO							
3.1.2.3.1	BU Action Item 3F1	Develop & Implement PBMS	CPMO							
3.1.2.3.2	BU Action Item 3F2	Design & Implement PBMIS	CIO							
3.1.2.4	BU Objective 3G	Train Personnel in PBM	CPMO							
3.1.2.4.1	BU Action Item 3H	Develop Training Materials	CPMO							
3.1.2.4.2	BU Action Item 3I	Provide Personnel Training	CPMO							
3.1.3	Business Objective 3J	Establish an EPMO	CEO/COO							
3.1.3.1	BU Action Item 3J1	Prepare and Issue EPMO Charter	CEO/COO							
3.1.3.2	BU Objective 3J2	Establish EPMO	CPMO							
3.1.3.3	BU Objective 3J3	Establish DPMO	CPMO							
3.1.3.4	BU Objective 3J4	Establish BUPMO	Manager DPMO							
3.1.3.5	BU Objective 3J5	Establish PMO	Manager BUPMO							

Figure 20-4. Business Objective/Project Profile Tool

Objective/Project ID		Name	

General Information

Business Unit		Completed By:	
Manager:		Target Start Date:	

Objective/Project Description

Objective/Project Rationale

Corporate Goal

Objective/Project Risk(s) if Not Implemented

Rough Order of Magnitude - Estimated duration of objective/project

Level	Effort - Hrs	Est. Accuracy H-M-L	Comments

Business Units and Systems Impacted

Business Unit	Associated Impacts	H-M-L

Skills Required

Skill Required	Number of Resources

Equipment/Hardware & Software/Facilities Required

Equipment/Hardware & Software/Facilities Description	Quantity	Est. Cost

Estimated Objective/Project Budget

Cost Description	Estimated Cost

Estimated Savings

Savings Description	Est. Savings

agement of the organization's resources, reduces operating cost, may improve profits, and allows business objectives to be more clearly and effectively documented and prioritized.

20.2 Documenting Business Objectives

To continue with the planning process example in Subchapter 20.1, the business objectives and action items identified by the business unit teams are then further defined. To accomplish this, the sponsor assigned to each objective and business unit action item prepares or oversees the preparation of an objective/project profile (see Figure 20-4) and a potential impact study (see Figure 20-5). Copies of the Business Objective/Project Profile Tool and Potential Impact Study Tool can be found in Appendix A.

The objective/project profiles and potential impact studies provide information that the management team, supported by the EPMO, can use to prioritize and select business objectives for the next business cycle.

Figure 20-6 shows a planning process that can be followed to further document the business objectives and business unit action items. The process steps are described in Table 20-3.

To further illustrate the old adage, "an enterprise does not plan to fail, it just fails to plan," the success of a project may well depend on whether appropriate, necessary, and sufficient objective accomplishment metrics have been established and are understood by management. In the case of a simple business objective, where a commercially oriented business decides to acquire a specific government project contract, the business needs to understand what the government buyer (the customer) considers successful project performance. Otherwise, the business may lose money in performing the work.

20.3 Prioritizing Business Objectives for Execution

To continue with the process planning example in Subchapters 20.1 and 20.2, the business objectives and action items identified and documented by the business-unit teams are now prioritized. Many enterprises fail to perform this step, but this prioritizing before selecting any specific business objective for implementation requires that management develop a list of business objective prioritization criteria (see key examples in Table 20-4).

The next step in the further evaluation of each potential business objective is to enter the prioritization and selection criteria into an Objec-

Figure 20-5. Potential Impact Study Tool

Objective/Project ID		Name	

Objective/Project Benefits

Benefit Description	Measurement to Validate Level of Achievement

Objective/Project Deliverables

Deliverable Description	Review and Approval Requirements

Objective/Project Critical Success Factors (CFS)

CSF Description	CSF Owner(s)

Objective/Project Cost Benefit Analysis

Estimated Budget	
Estimated Project Savings	
Return On Investment	
Net present value	

Objective/Project Integration

Business Unit/Functions Impacted	Skills Required	Quantity

Objective/Project Risks

Risk Description	Probability (H-M-L)	Impact (H-M-L)

tive/Project Selection Form template (see Figure 20-7). A Business Objective/Project Selection Form is available at www.amacombooks.org/go/EnterpriseWidePM.

Next the Objective/Project Selection Form is used to rate each business objective using the information gathered and documented in the profile document and the associated potential impact study. During the objective/project selection process, management decides whether a business objective is simple enough to be accomplished by a few business-unit action items assigned to one or two functional organizations. If yes, then each spe-

Figure 20-6. Business Objective Documentation Process

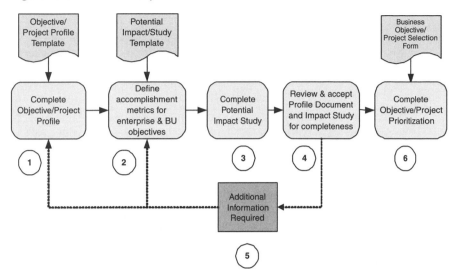

cific action item would be performed independently by the associated business unit as part of its functionally managed and controlled work.

The objective/project selection process is also when management decides if a business objective is complex enough, significant enough in size, or has sufficiently large and interdependent business-unit action items that it needs to be handled as a project, program, or portfolio (see Chapter 1). The management team, supported by the EPMO, enters the ranking for each objective criterion (Table 20-4) on the objective/project selection form.

To further illustrate the old adage, "an enterprise does not plan to fail, they just fail to plan," the success of these future projects may depend on whether the necessary "enterprise environmental factors" (see Subchapters 4.2 and 4.3) and the "organizational process assets" (see Subchapter 4.3) are well understood by management and accounted for in the business objective development processes.

Return to the the business strategy in which a commercially oriented business decides to acquire government project contracts. If one of the related business objectives is a specific project contract that is actually won, the business needs to have an accounting system compliant with government regulations or they will eventually receive a stop work order for that project. If the business lacks the funds or time necessary to make the accounting system compliant, the contract will be cancelled. Therefore, how well the business objective is supported by the enterprise environmental factors and organizational process assets related to that objective will di-

Table 20-3. Business Objective Documentation Process Steps

Step	Step Definition	Roles	Activity Description
1	Complete Objective/Project Profile	Business Objective Sponsor	Complete profile document for assigned objectives and action items that expands upon the purpose and basic scope stated in the objectives tabulation.
2	Define accomplishment metrics for enterprise business objectives and business unit objectives	Business Objective Sponsor	Complete the "objective accomplishment metrics" section of the profile to establish the metrics that will be used to judge successful completion of the objective.
3	Complete Potential Impact Study	Business Unit Sponsor	Prepare an impact study document for assigned business objectives and action items.
4	Review & Accept Profile Document and Impact Study for completeness	EPMO Project Management	Assure the documents are completed and contain sufficiently detailed information to define each objective.
5	Additional Information Required	Business Unit Sponsor	Provide additional information to support project profile and impact study documents.
6	Complete Objective Prioritization	EPMO Project Management	Complete the prioritization of business objectives or projects using the Prioritization/Selection Criteria check list tool.

rectly affect the ability to have a successful project that supports that objective. Figure 20-8 shows the prioritization and selection process and Table 20-5 provides all the associated steps for this phase of the tactical planning process.

The final product should be in a form similar to Table 20-6, with a planning item number column, a strategy/objective/action-item name column, an item purpose and scope description column, a sponsor column, one column for each strategic criterion (see Table 20-2, Section 5) that reflects the rank you assigned to that strategic criterion for that objective, one column for each objective criterion (Table 20-4) that reflects the rank assigned to that objective criterion (Table 20-6, Section 6), and a last column with the final composite business priority rank for each business objective. The list is organized by the enterprise business objectives listed in Table 20-2.

Table 20-4. Example Business Objective Prioritization & Selection Criteria

Criterion #	Rank(s)	Criterion Description
1	1 thru 5	How well does business objective support the related business strategy
2	1 thru 5	Can the financial factors (such as budget, cash, and funding) of the Enterprise Environmental Factors (see Section 1, Subchapter 4.3) support the business objective
3	1 thru 5	Are the required organizational process assets (see Section 1, Subchapter 4.3) available and operational to support the business objective
4	1 thru 5	Are the required resources available to meet selected business objectives
5	1 thru 5	Non-project action items that can be directly performed by the respective business unit(s)
6	1 thru 5	Non-project action item that can be directly performed by the respective business unit
7	1 thru 5	The business objective can only be accomplished by being managed as a project, program, or portfolio

The tabulation is completed by entering into the form the final rank of each business objective or unit action item based on the enterprise's prioritization and selection criterion. The overall priority rank (last column of tabulation in Table 20-6) is created by using a formula called a scoring model, which is developed by the management team. The team then applies a weighting (multiplication factor used to convey the relative importance of each criteria used in the scoring model) to each individual criterion and then sums up the weighted criteria for that business objective to create its "rank."

In making ranking decisions, the scoring model may be driven by a variety of constraints and dynamics, such as the short-term and long-term interest and influence of stakeholders, perceived value, or limited available resources, while still maintaining an alignment with the business objective and related strategic initiative.

Every enterprise has limited resources (people and funds type criteria). Therefore, most enterprises share the challenge of distributing those resources effectively to achieve the highest return on their investment. This may require that resource criterion, for funds or budget as an example, not be included in the weighted composite final ranking number. Instead, the cumulative value of the funds or budget for all business objectives could be used to establish a criterion in the scoring model. This criterion would establish the budget/funds level above which a business objective would

Figure 20-7.   Business Objective/Project Selection Form

| Objective/Project ID | | Name | |

Instructions: Use the information contained in the project profile and impact documents to complete this form. Place an "X" below the rating you feel to be most accurate for this project. Rating: 1 = A Lot > 5 =

Objective/Project Description

Objective/Project Selection Criteria

Criteria	1	2	3	4	5	?
1. Business objectives support the related business strategy.	1 Lots	2	3	4	5 No	?
2. Financial factors (such as budget, cash, and funding) of the Enterprise Environmental Factors (see Section 1, Subchapter 4.3) do support the business objective.	1 Easy	2	3	4	5 Hard	?
3. Required Organizational Process Assets (see Section 1, Subchapter 4.3) are available and operational to support the business objectives?	1 Easy	2	3	4	5 Hard	?
4. Required resources are available to meet selected business objectives.	1 Lots	2	3	4	5 Hard	?
5. Non-project action items can be directly performed by the respective business units.	1 Easy	2	3	4	5 Hard	?
6. The business objectives can only be accomplished by being managed as a project, program, or portfolio.	1 Easy	2	3	4	5 Hard	?
7. The strategic objectives of the business objectives have been clearly defined.	1 Yes	2	3	4	5 No	?
8. The objective/project benefits and validation measures have been clearly identified.	1 Easy	2	3	4	5 Hard	?

have to be located to be included in the next business cycle. This also means both business unit and operations management teams need to understand that at least a portion of those business strategies related to the lower ranked business objective may neither be begun nor completed in the next business cycle.

Figure 20-8. Business Objective/Project Prioritization and Selection Process

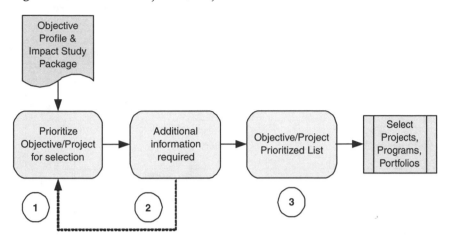

The completed final tabulation (Table 20-6) contains two different sets of business objectives that could be executed during the next business cycle based on the final priority "rank" in which they should be performed and completed:

- Nonproject business objectives and action items that could be directly performed by the respective business units
- The enterprise's business objectives that need to be performed as projects

Table 20-5. Business Objective/Project Prioritization & Selection Process Steps

Step	Step Definition	Roles	Activity Description
1	Prioritize Objective/Project for Selection	Business Unit Sponsors & EPMO Project Management	Complete a project selection document for each proposed and identified objective/project.
2	Additional Information Required	Business Unit Sponsors	Provide additional information to support project profile and impact study documents.
3	Prioritized Objective/ Project List	EPMO	Prepare and manage objective/project prioritization list.

Table 20-6. Business Objective/Project Prioritization Tabulation

Sec 1 Item	Section 2 Item Name - Strategic Initiative/Business Objective/Business Unit (BU) Objective & Action	Section 3 Description (Purpose & Scope)	Section 4 Sponsor	Section 5 Strategy Criterion & Rank			Section 6 Objective Criterion & Rank			RANK
				1	2	m	1	2	n	
1.0	Name 1–Strategic Initiative	Strategic Initiative to have benefit & capability of item Name 1	CFO	1	3	5				5
1.1	Business Objective 1A	Business Objective 1A	CAO				2	2	3	
1.1.1	Portfolio 1B	BU Objective 1B	CAO							
1.1.1.1	Program 1C	BU Objective 1C	CAO							
1.1.1.1.1	Project 1C 1	BU Action 1C1	CAO							
1.1.1.1.2	Project 1C 2	BU Action 1C2	CAO							
1.1.1.2	Project 1A 3	BU Objective 1A3	CAO							
1.2	Business Objective 1D	Business Objective 1D	Accntng Mgr				3	3	2	
1.2.1	BU Objective 1D1	BU Objective 1D1	Accntng Mgr							
1.2.2	BU Objective 1D2	BU Objective 1D2	Accntng Mgr							
1.3	Business Objective 1E	Business Objective 1E	AP Mgr				1	4	3	
1.3.1	Portfolio 1E	BU Objective 1E	AP Mgr							
1.3.1.1	Program 1F	BU Objective 1F	AP Mgr							
1.3.1.1.1	Project 1Fa	BU Action 1Fa	AP Mgr							
1.3.1.1.2	Project 1Fb	BU Action 1Fb	AP Mgr							
1.3.1.1.3	Project 1Fc	BU Action 1Fc	AP Mgr							
2.0	Name 2–Strategic Initiative	Strategic Initiative to have benefit & capability of item Name 2	CTO	2	5					4
2.1	Business Objective 2A	Business Objective 2A	System Mgr				2	3	1	
2.1.1	BU Action Item 2A1	BU Action Item 2A1	System Mgr							
2.1.2	BU Action Item 2A2	BU Action Item 2A2	System Mgr							
2.2	Business Objective 2B	Business Objective 2B	WAN Mgr				1	3	4	
2.2.1	Program 2B	BU Objective 2B	WAN Mgr							
2.2.1.1	Project 2B1	BU Action Item 2B1	WAN Mgr							
2.2.1.2	Project 2B2	BU Action Item 2B2	WAN Mgr							

(continued)

Table 20-6. (*Continued*)

Sec 1	Section 2	Section 3	Section 4	Section 5			Section 6			
				Strategy Criterion & Rank			Objective Criterion & Rank			RANK
Item	Item Name - Strategic Initiative/Business Objective/Business Unit (BU) Objective & Action	Description (Purpose & Scope)	Sponsor	1	2	m	1	2	n	
2.3	Business Objective 2C	Business Objective 2C	LAN Mgr				2	5	3	
2.3.1	Project 2C	BU Objective 2C	LAN Mgr							
2.3.1.1	BU Action Item 2C	BU Action Item 2C	LAN Mgr							
3.0	PBM as Core Competency	*Strategic Initiative* to have EWPM capability	CEO	1	1	1				1
3.1	*Business Objective* 3A Implement EWPM	*Business Objective* 3A to develop & implement EWPM	CEO				1	2	1	1
3.1.1	*BU Action Item* 3A1- Prepare and Issue PM Policy	*BU Action Item* 3A1 to prepare & issue policy statement	CEO							2
3.1.2	*Portfolio* 3B - Develop PBM Capability	*BU Objective* 3B to infuse PBM enterprise-wide	Chief PM Officer (CPMO)							3
3.1.2.1	*Project* 3C - Develop PBM Methodology	*BU Action Item* 3C to create standardized PBM processes and procedures	CPMO							4
3.1.2.2	*Project* 3D - Implement PBM Methodology	*BU Action Item* 3D to apply PBM method- ology processes enterprise-wide	CPMO							4
3.1.2.3	*Program* 3F - Develop PBM System (PBMS)	*BU Objective* 3F to prepare and implement the PBMS	CPMO/CIO							5
3.1.2.3.1	*Project* 3F1 - Develop & Implement PBMS	*BU Action Item* 3F1 to define, develop, document & imple- ment a PBMS	CPMO							5
3.1.2.3.2	*Project* 3F2 - Design & Implement PBMIS	*BU Action Item* 3F2 to design, program, document & imple- ment a PBMIS	CIO							6

(*continued*)

Table 20-6. *(Continued)*

Item	Item Name - Strategic Initiative/Business Objective/Business Unit (BU) Objective & Action	Description (Purpose & Scope)	Sponsor	Strategy Criterion & Rank			Objective Criterion & Rank			RANK
Sec 1	Section 2	Section 3	Section 4	Section 5			Section 6			
				1	2	m	1	2	n	
3.1.2.4	Program 3G - Train Personnel in PBM	BU Objective 3G for PBM training development & implementation	CPMO							7
3.1.2.4.1	Project 3H - Develop Training Materials	BU Action Item 3H for training materials design & development	CPMO							7
3.1.2.4.2	Project 3I - Provide Personnel Training	BU Action Item 3I to train staff in PBM methodology	CPMO							7
3.1.3	Portfolio 3J - Establish an EPMO	Business Objective 3J to set up PBM organizational governance in the form of the EPMO and supporting organizational structures	CEO/COO				1	2	1	3
3.1.3.1	BU Action 3J1 - Prepare and Issue EPMO Charter	BU Action Item 3J1 to prepare & issue charter for EPMO	CEO/COO							2
3.1.3.2	Project 3J2 - Establish EPMO	BU Objective 3J2 to design, develop, and implement Enterprise PMO business unit	CPMO							4
3.1.3.3	Project 3J3 - Establish DPMO	BU Objective 3J3 to design, develop, and implement Division level PMOs	CPMO							4
3.1.3.4	Project 3J4 - Establish BUPMO	BU Objective 3J4 to design, develop, and implement Business Unit PMOs	Manager DPMO							4
3.1.3.5	Project 3J5 - Establish PMO	BU Objective 3J5 to design, develop, and implement single project PMOs	Manager BUPMO							4

Business objectives that become a reality are then developed into portfolios, programs, and projects, which require that strategic initiative alignment continue to be addressed.

20.4 Executing the Business Objectives

Once the initiation and planning (Figure 20-2) of the business objectives are completed, each objective is executed. The first step is to perform the objective implementation process (Chapter 21), which includes portfolio, program, and project organization and selection and preliminary scope definition. This is followed by the charter issuing process (Chapter 22), which authorizes funds for work to begin.

The PBMM executing, monitoring, controlling, and closing processes for business objective development were developed and defined in the PBMM model of Chapter 10; their relationships and interactions are shown in Figure 20-9. Business Objective execution is finished when work on the business objective is either terminated or completed and the objective is closed.

Figure 20-9. Business Objective Development Executing, Monitoring, and Closing Processes

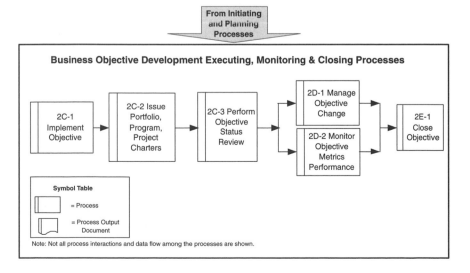

CHAPTER 21

PBMM Component Selection and Initiation

The first stage of business objective implementation/execution (see Figure 21-1) involves formally organizing and selecting those project-based business objectives that were prioritized for execution. This is a coordinated planning effort performed by the enterprise management team and the EPMO staff. This portion of the PBMM approach to achieving the enterprise's business objectives maintains alignment of the portfolios, programs, and projects of the objectives with its related strategic initiatives.

21.1 PBM Component Organization and Selection

After business objectives have been prioritized, the PBM objective implementation begins by separating the business objectives to be performed through the use of projects from the normal business unit objectives. The Business Objective/Project Prioritization Tabulation (Table 20-6) produced during the business objective development planning processes (Subchapter 20.4) is modified to include only project-related business objectives and strategies as shown in Table 21-1.

PBM Component Identification and Organization

Table 21-1, with just the project-related business objectives, is used in conjunction with the business strategy case studies, the completed objective/project profile documents, associated potential impact studies, and the objective/project selection form developed to categorize and organize the business objectives. This identification and organization is performed

Figure 21-1. PBMM Portfolio/Program/Project Data Flow

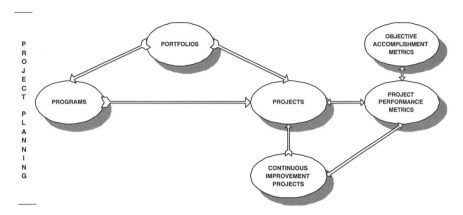

to assemble the selected business objectives into three groups of identified manageable PBM components to facilitate further decision making:

1. Standalone portfolios with programs and projects and supporting subportfolios.
2. Standalone programs with projects and supporting subprograms.
3. Standalone projects and supporting subprojects.

The resulting PBM components will include existing and potential portfolios, programs, projects, and related other work. A key purpose of the identification and organization processes is to assemble the prioritized PBMM planned components into a mix of enterprise investments that has the best potential to collectively achieve the intent of the supported strategic initiatives.

Assembling the Standalone Portfolios with Programs and Projects

The Business Objective/Project Prioritization Tabulation (see Table 21-1) produced during business objective development planning processes (Subchapter 20.3) is further modified to reflect the desired set of portfolios and their associated subsidiary programs and projects.

By definition, a portfolio is a standalone planning component. In the context of integrating business management with project portfolio manage-

Table 21-1.   Portfolio, Program, and Project Ranked Tabulation

Sec 1	Section 2	Section 3	Section 4	Section 5			Section 6			RANK
	Item Name - Strategic Initiative/Business Objective/Business Unit (BU) Objective	Description		Strategy Criterion & Rank			Objective Criterion & Rank			
Item	& Action	(Purpose & Scope)	Sponsor	1	2	m	1	2	n	
1.0	Name 1–Strategic Initiative	*Strategic Initiative* to have benefit & capability of item Name 1	CFO	1	3	5				5
1.1	Business Objective 1A	Business Objective 1A	CAO				2	2	3	
1.1.1	Portfolio 1B	BU Objective 1B	CAO							
1.1.1.1	Program 1C	BU Objective 1C	CAO							
1.1.1.1.1	Project 1C 1	BU Action 1C1	CAO							
1.1.1.1.2	Project 1C 2	BU Action 1C2	CAO							
1.1.1.2	Project 1A 3	BU Objective 1A3	CAO							
1.2	Business Objective 1D	Business Objective 1D	Accntng Mgr				3	3	2	
1.2.1	BU Objective 1D1	BU Objective 1D1	Accntng Mgr							
1.2.2	BU Objective 1D2	BU Objective 1D2	Accntng Mgr							
1.3	Business Objective 1E	Business Objective 1E	AP Mgr				1	4	3	
1.3.1	Portfolio 1E	BU Objective 1E	AP Mgr							
1.3.1.1	Program 1F	BU Objective 1F	AP Mgr							
1.3.1.1.1	Project 1Fa	BU Action 1Fa	AP Mgr							
1.3.1.1.2	Project 1Fb	BU Action 1Fb	AP Mgr							
1.3.1.1.3	Project 1Fc	BU Action 1Fc	AP Mgr							
2.0	Name 2–Strategic Initiative	*Strategic Initiative* to have benefit & capability of item Name 2	CTO	2	5					4
2.1	Business Objective 2B	Business Objective 2B	WAN Mgr				1	3	4	
2.1.1	Program 2B	BU Objective 2B	WAN Mgr							
2.1.1.1	Project 2B1	BU Action Item 2B1	WAN Mgr							
2.1.1.2	Project 2B2	BU Action Item 2B2	WAN Mgr							
2.2	Business Objective 2C	Business Objective 2C	LAN Mgr				2	5	3	
2.2.1	Project 2C	BU Objective 2C	LAN Mgr							
2.2.1.1	BU Action Item 2C	BU Action Item 2C	LAN Mgr							

(*continued*)

Table 21-1. *(Continued)*

Sec 1 Item	Section 2 Item Name - Strategic Initiative/Business Objective/Business Unit (BU) Objective & Action	Section 3 Description (Purpose & Scope)	Section 4 Sponsor	Section 5 Strategy Criterion & Rank			Section 6 Objective Criterion & Rank			RANK
				1	2	m	1	2	n	
3.0	PBM as Core Competency	*Strategic Initiative* to have EWPM capability	CEO	1	1	1				1
3.1	*Business Objective* 3A Implement EWPM	*Business Objective* 3A to develop & implement EWPM	CEO				1	2	1	1
3.1.2	*Portfolio* 3B-Develop PBM Capability	*BU Objective* 3B to infuse PBM enterprise-wide	Chief PM Officer (CPMO)							3
3.1.2.1	*Project* 3C-Develop PBM Methodology	*BU Action Item* 3C to create standardized PBM processes and procedures	CPMO							4
3.1.2.2	*Project* 3D-Implement PBM Methodology	*BU Action Item* 3D to apply PBM methodology processes enterprise-wide	CPMO							4
3.1.2.3	*Program* 3F-Develop PBM System (PBMS)	*BU Objective* 3F to prepare and implement the PBMS	CPMO/CIO							5
3.1.2.3.1	*Project* 3F1-Develop & Implement PBMS	*BU Action Item* 3F1 to define, develop, document & implement a PBMS	CPMO							5
3.1.2.3.2	*Project* 3F2-Design & Implement PBMIS	*BU Action Item* 3F2 to design, program, document & implement a PBMIS	CIO							6
3.1.2.4	*Program* 3G-Train Personnel in PBM	*BU Objective* 3G for PBM training development & implementation	CPMO							7
3.1.2.4.1	*Project* 3H-Develop Training Materials	*BU Action Item* 3H for training materials design & development	CPMO							7

(continued)

Table 21-1.   *(Continued)*

Sec 1	Section 2	Section 3	Section 4	Section 5			Section 6			RANK
Item	Item Name - Strategic Initiative/Business Objective/Business Unit (BU) Objective & Action	Description (Purpose & Scope)	Sponsor	Strategy Criterion & Rank			Objective Criterion & Rank			
				1	2	m	1	2	n	
3.1.2.4.2	Project 3I - Provide Personnel Training	BU Action Item 3I to train staff in PBM methodology	CPMO							7
3.1.3	Portfolio 3J - Establish an EPMO	Business Objective 3J to set up PBM organizational governance in the form of the EPMO and supporting organizational structures	CEO/COO				1	2	1	3
3.1.3.1	Project 3J2 - Establish EPMO	BU Objective 3J2 to design, develop, and implement Enterprise PMO business unit	CPMO							4
3.1.3.2	Project 3J3 - Establish DPMO	BU Objective 3J3 to design, develop, and implement Division level PMOs	CPMO							4
3.1.3.3	Project 3J4 - Establish BUPMO	BU Objective 3J4 to design, develop, and implement Business Unit PMOs	Manager DPMO							4
3.1.3.4	Project 3J5 - Establish PMO	BU Objective 3J5 to design, develop, and implement single project PMOs	Manager BUPMO							4

ment, a portfolio is a group of projects and programs identified as necessary to accomplish defined business objectives that support specific strategies.

The PBM components (programs, projects, and other related work) of a portfolio have distinguishing features and attributes that permit the enterprise to group them for efficient and effective management. The projects and programs within a portfolio generally share general resources for programs and specific resources for projects. If a program was part of a business strategy that had one or more projects or other programs, then that set of projects and programs would be formed into a portfolio. In addition, a set of projects could be assembled into a portfolio of "standalone" projects, if those projects had some common attribute that would warrant managing them as a group.

The content of each portfolio is based on such business criteria as strategic business alignment, organizational impact, and cost/benefit results. In addition, as with a common business management portfolio, a project portfolio may include other nonproject work needed to accomplish the goal of the portfolio. In assembling the components of each portfolio, management must consider the risk to accomplishing the related business objective that could result from the mix of programs and projects in the portfolio at any one time. Previously selected components may need to be deferred when the risk of adding one or more of them to the current portfolio would unreasonably upset the balance of the portfolio and exceed the risk tolerances of the enterprise.

A structured portfolio represents the enterprise's strategic intent and reflects its decisions and willingness to make investments and allocate resources to deliver business objectives. Each portfolio represents the sum of its selected components and can directly affect the strategic initiatives of the enterprise.

Assembling the Standalone Programs

In addition to identifying portfolios, the results of the PBMM business strategy and business objective development efforts may define some programs that are not part of a portfolio. Also, some enterprises may not use the portfolio as a top-level planning component; the program may be the PBM planning component at the top of their hierarchy of projects.

The Business Objective/Project Prioritization Tabulation (see Table 21-1) which has been updated to reflect each portfolio's required programs and associated subsidiary projects is modified to establish any programs not associated with a defined portfolio. The tabulation is used in conjunction with the business strategy case studies, the completed business objective/project profile documents, associated potential impact studies, and the business objective/project selection form to further organize the remaining projects into standalone programs and standalone projects.

Programs, whether standalone or part of a portfolio, are established to deliver a strategically defined set of benefits to the enterprise. In the context of integrating business management with program business management, a program is a group of related objectives to be accomplished through projects whose objectives were selected on the basis of specific criteria. In addition, the program can include nonproject work that supports or compliments the completion of the projects in the program.

Multiple related projects are often assembled into a program to optimize the management of those projects and the desired benefits. The projects for a program can be considered related or interdependent on the basis of related scopes or efforts; integrated, dependent, sequenced, or otherwise related deliverables; delivery of incremental or collective benefits; sharing a common attribute, such as a client, customer, seller, specific technology, or major or unique resource; and optimization of staffing—all in the context of the program's business objectives.

In a business context, a program is the highest level at which related work planning and execution will be directed across multiple business units and operations, although a specific program could support a single business operation or business unit of the enterprise.

Assembling the Standalone Projects

The Portfolio, Program, and Project Tabulation (see Table 21-1) also reflects any remaining standalone projects. In the business context of integrating business management with project business management, a single project associated with a single business object would be handled as a standalone project. These standalone projects are selected for implementation if they produce deliverables, incremental benefits, or value to fulfill a specific and selected business objective. The desired deliverables may include processes or products that result in ongoing work that is required for the organization to realize other desired benefits or that the enterprise can use to sustain, enhance, and deliver other nonproject related objectives.

Selecting the PBM Components
to Initiate and Authorize

The second major step within the business objective implementation process (Figure 20-9) is the selection of the standalone PBM components that need to be accomplished during the next business cycle. Selection is the process of deciding which identified, assembled, and prioritized PBM components (portfolios, programs, and projects) to implement based on their ranked evaluation scores. A selected PBM component also reflects the investments potentially to be made by the enterprise. A key purpose of the selection process is to optimize the overall contribution (value and benefits) of the PBM components to the enterprise. If any PBM component cannot be or is not aligned with a specific business objective or if there are funds or resource limitations that can preclude accomplishing the PBM component, then it should not be selected for initiation.

21.2 PBM Component Initiation

The third major step in the business objective implementation process (Figure 20-9) is the initiation of each standalone PBM component selected to be accomplished during the next business cycle. A PBM component must be initiated and then authorized before work can begin on that portfolio/program/project. The PBM component initiation documentation can be viewed as similar to, but more extensive than, an action item plan in a business management planning process. The basic initiation documentation for each standalone PBM component includes the:

Portfolio: Statement of work, enterprise business management plan with related business case(s), identified applicable enterprise environmental factors, and organizational process assets, and accomplishment metrics.

Program: Statement of work, preliminary scope statement, identified applicable enterprise environmental factors and organizational process assets, and desired benefits metrics.

Project: Statement of work, preliminary scope statement, identified applicable enterprise environmental factors and organizational process assets, and project performance metrics.

The objective/project profile document, potential impact study, objective/project selection form, and any related business case study for the PBM component that provides the information necessary to develop those documents used to initiate a PBM component. Once the initiation documentation has been produced and approved, these portfolios, programs, and projects are authorized (Chapter 22). The work required to accomplish the portfolios, programs, projects, and related nonproject work are eventually planned in detail and then executed (Chapters 23, 24, and 25).

Figure 21-2 shows the typical PBM component initiation documentation development flow diagram. Table 21-2 gives the process step descriptions, roles, and responsibilities. The templates used to complete this process and facilitate the development of the related documentation are found in Appendix A.

Figure 21-2. Standalone PBM Component Initiation Documentation Development Steps

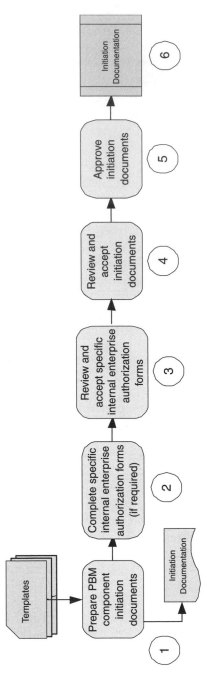

Table 21-2. PBM Component Initiation Documentation Development Steps

Step	Step Definition	Role(s)	Activity Definition
1A	Begin Work on Initiation Documents	Chief PM Officer	Authorizes the start of preparation for the portfolio initiation documents.
1B	Prepare Initiation Documents	EPMO Staff, PBM Component Manager	Identify and prepare requisite initiation documentation.
2	Complete Specific Internal Enterprise Authorization Forms (if required)	EPMO Staff with Sponsor support	Develop, if required, specific forms within the enterprise, such as a request for capital funds. Finance and accounting assists in the proper completion any special forms.
3	Review and Approve Specific Internal Enterprise Authorization Forms (if required)	Authorized Enterprise Executive, Financial Controls	The Sponsor may need to provide the initial approval of these forms. The Sponsor submits for approval the specific internal authorization forms for the PBC component.
4	Review and Accept Initiation Documentation	EPMO Staff, Sponsor, Financial Controls	The EPMO staff submits the completed initiation documents to the Sponsor and Financial Controls for review and comment. Once these two reviews are completed the documents are submitted to the portfolio manager for review and comment. They may request clarification and modifications to the initiation documents before they are approved.
5	Approve Initiation Documents	Authorized Enterprise Executive, Internal Customer	

CHAPTER 22

Portfolio, Program, and Project Authorization

The second process in the business objective execution group (see Figure 20-9) is the formal authorizing of those PBM components (portfolios, programs, and projects) that were prioritized and selected for execution. These were provided as the primary output of the enterprise's objective selection process (Table 21-1). Authorizing is the process of writing the charter for a PBM component and communicating the PBM initiating documentation and charter to the appropriate PBM component manager.

The charter is the document that formally authorizes the existence of the PBM component and provides the PBM component manager with the authority to apply the enterprise's resources to the PBM component activities. The authority thereby granted, as defined by PMI®, is the right to apply resources, expend funds, make decisions, and give approvals. Charters are issued during the execution processes in:

- *Business objective development* to authorize the work during the next business cycle for each portfolio and for each program and project that are not part of a portfolio.
- *Portfolio management* to authorize the work during the next business cycle for each program and standalone project that is part of the portfolio and any major subportfolio (if required).
- *Program management* to authorize the work during the next business cycle for each project that is part of the program and any major subprogram (if required).
- *Project management* to authorize work during the next business cycle for each subproject (if required).

A PBM component charter is the final step of the PBM component authorization process. Once a PBM component is authorized, the PBM component management is responsible for applying the correct management processes to ensure the work is done effectively and efficiently.

Table 22-1. Portfolio/Program/Project Authorization Process Steps: Authorizing New PBM Components at Start of Business Cycle

Step	Step Definition	Roles	Activity Description
1	Portfolio, Program or Project	Business Unit Sponsors & EPMO Management	Select the next scheduled program or project to be started and evaluate for potential updates prior to authorization.
2	Evaluate Profile for Updates	Business Unit Sponsors & EPMO Management	Evaluate the profile completed during the objective planning process to determine if the information is still valid and update with current information if needed.
3	Evaluate Impact Study for Updates	EPMO Staff	Evaluate the impact study completed during the objective planning process to determine if the information is still valid and update with current information if needed.
4	Evaluate Portfolio, Program, Project Prioritization for Updates	EPMO Staff	Evaluate the portfolio/program/ project selection prioritization checklist completed during the objective planning process to determine if the information is still valid and update with current information as needed.
5	Issue Charter	Sponsors & EPMO Management	Select next portfolio/program/ project on the prioritized PBM component list. Develop and approve the charter, which provides formal recognition and authorization of the PBM component. Issue the charter to authorize the start of the Initiation Processes.

The charter document needed to efficiently authorize each PBM component can be prepared using a set of simple form templates contained in Appendix A. The PBM component (portfolio/program/project) authorization process begins with the start of the new business cycle or fiscal year by selecting the desired portfolios, programs, and projects from the prioritized PBM component list.

Table 22-2. Business Cycle- Additional Portfolio/Program/Project Authorization Process Steps

Step	Step Definition	Roles	Activity Description
1	New PBM Component Request	Business Objective Sponsor	New portfolio, program, or project opportunity submitted for review and approval to be added to the business plan.
2	Complete PBM Component Profile	Business Objective Sponsor	Complete the "objective accomplishment metrics" section of the profile to establish the metrics that will be used to judge successful completion of the business objective.
3	Complete Potential Impact Study	Business Unit Sponsor	Prepare an impact study document for assigned business objectives and PBM components.
4	Complete PBM Component Prioritization	EPMO Management	Complete the prioritization of business objectives and supporting PBM components using the Prioritization/Selection Criteria check list tool. Add PBM component priority tabulation and reprioritize the list.
5	Issue Charter	PBM Component Manager	Select the next scheduled portfolio, program, or project and issue a charter to authorize the start of initiation.

We recommend the authorization process start at least 4 to 6 weeks before the planned start of the portfolio, program, or project. This lead time is necessary to allow completion of the evaluation steps described in Table 22-1 and illustrated in Figure 22-1 and also to notify the portfolio, program, or project manager that they have been selected to lead the program or project.

To successfully and cost effectively execute a PBM component, the initiation and authorization to begin work should be provided by senior management. Management has the responsibility and authority to oversee that component's execution and the activities of the associated PBM component manager. This may seem intuitively obvious, but the opposite happens all too frequently. Allowing the business unit manager who wants to see a particular PBM component executed or allowing the PBM component manager to do a self-authorization destroys any checks and balances the enterprise may have and allows self-serving managers to assume control

Figure 22-1. Portfolio/Program/Project Authorization Process

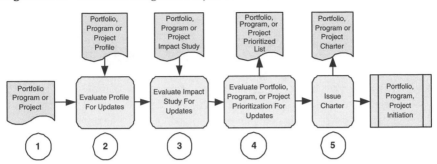

of funds and resources that would be better spent on other strategic initiatives and business objectives that could create a greater return in value and benefits to the enterprise.

Once the new business cycle begins, it is not unusual for new opportunities to arise and require an evaluation to determine if they should be added to the current business objectives and implemented through a PBM component. Changes in industry regulations, laws, or rules, or new strategic objectives require the enterprise to evaluate the need for new portfolios, programs, or projects to meet these requirements. The steps necessary to complete the evaluations and ultimately issue a charter to authorize these new portfolios, programs, or projects are described in Table 22-2 and illustrated in Figure 22-2.

Sometimes, when authoring a sensitive or complex project the following additional activities may need to be performed and the resulting doc-

Figure 22-2. Business Cycle - Additional Portfolio/Program/Project Request Authorization Process

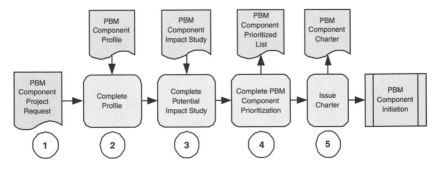

umentation added to the set of initiation documents before the enterprise executive will approve the project charter:

- Update estimated project budget.
- Investigate alternative solutions with the project customer.
- Define project skills requirements.
- Prepare a preliminary project management plan.
- Prepare a preliminary communication plan.
- Prepare a project milestone list.

CHAPTER 23

Portfolio PBMM Planning and Execution

The Project Business Management Methodology (PBMM) Model developed in Chapter 10 defines the basic processes to be followed in planning and executing the portfolio work. The PBMM is a contiguous framework of processes, each relying on the proper application of the others, while at the same time it is a set of separate, definable processes that can standalone. The process procedures developed in Chapter 10 for portfolio management should be used in the planning and execution of portfolios. In implementing portfolio management, one needs to consider its effect on the enterprise's operations, what features of project business management need to be employed, and the impact on the ongoing operations that use recurrent activities and ongoing operations management processes. Portfolio management must assure that the portfolio and its supporting programs and projects are being effectively managed to obtain optimal results using an optimum set of resources.

23.1 Portfolio Initiation Processes

Portfolio initiation consists of the processes required to formally recognize the authorization of the new portfolio or the updating of any ongoing portfolio. This includes receipt and review of the portfolio charter issued by the sponsor, who is outside of the portfolio, the accompanying scope of work documents, and the business needs and requirements. Figure 23-1 illustrates the integration of the processes contained within the portfolio management processes.

23.2 Portfolio Planning Processes

Portfolio planning defines and matures the portfolio scope, develops the management plan, and identifies and schedules the activities. Good plan-

Figure 23-1. Portfolio Initiation Process Integration

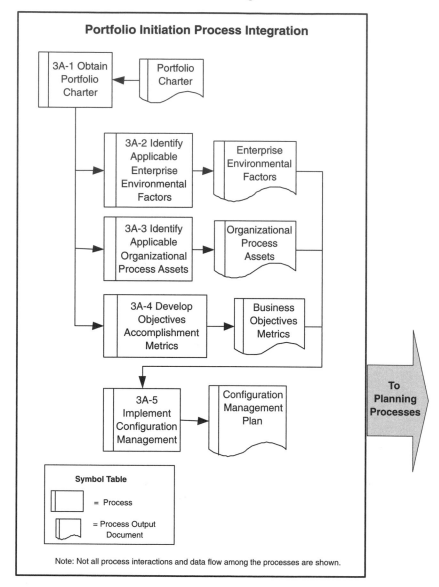

ning helps the portfolio manager supported by the EPMO, to manage the portfolio successfully. The planning processes gather information from many sources and establish the course of action required for attaining the related business objectives. Figure 23-2 defines the integration of the processes contained within the project management planning processes.

23.3 Portfolio Executing Processes

Portfolio management requires executing the activities needed to complete the work defined in the portfolio management plan. This involves coordinating any other related work performed by the enterprise and the EPMO, as well as integrating and performing the activities in accordance with the plan. These processes also address the scope defined in the portfolio scope statement and implement approved changes. Portfolio execution requires updates from the strategic planning processes to ensure programs or projects no longer related to the current strategic initiatives or business objectives are stopped or terminated.

Figure 23-2. Portfolio Planning Process Integration

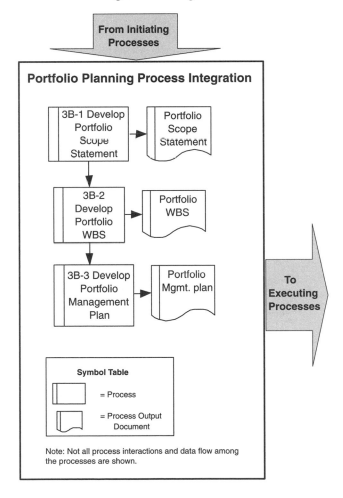

The PBMM portfolio executing process group covers the "aligning processes" described in the PMI® *Standard for Portfolio Management.* These steps include the identification of specific portfolio components, categorizing and evaluating those components, selecting the components to perform, prioritizing the components for execution, and balancing the value and benefits that will be provided versus available time and resources. This is accomplished by applying the same processes described in Chapter 21, but focusing them on the potential components within just one specific portfolio. From a business management perspective, the development of the statements of work for the supporting programs and standalone projects is also a key step in the further definition of the work needed to accomplish the supported business objective.

The next major step in committing the enterprise's resources and funds for the portfolio's supporting programs and standalone projects

Figure 23-3. Portfolio Execution Processes Integration

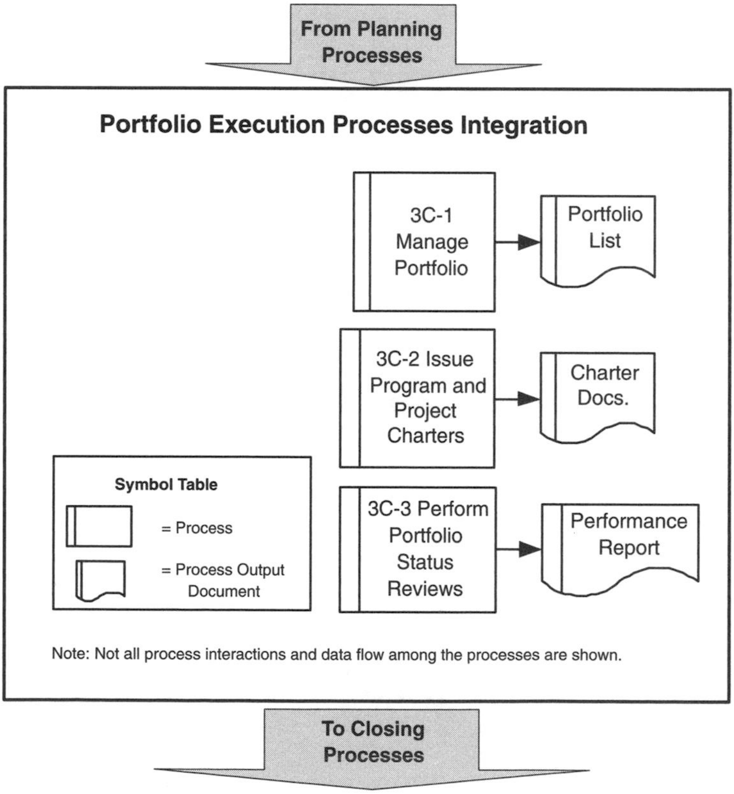

is the preparation and issuance of the program and project charters to authorize the work. Authorization is also part of the PMI® portfolio "aligning processes" group, and chartering is performed as described in Chapter 22.

Execution focuses on assuring that programs and projects are initiated in the order required to support execution of the portfolio; this may be driven by the allocation of resources. Figure 23-3 illustrates the integration of the processes contained within the portfolio management executing processes.

23.4 Portfolio Monitoring and Controlling Processes

Monitoring and controlling processes are used to measure and monitor progress to identify variances from the baseline documentation so that corrective action can be taken to meet portfolio objectives. The processes contained in this group are developed and implemented at the start of the portfolio initiation processes, but they are defined in this process because they are applied from start to finish of the project.

Monitoring and controlling consists of those processes performed to observe portfolio execution, so that issues, risks, and potential problems may be identified in a timely manner and corrective action can be taken. The key benefit of these processes is that portfolio performance is observed and measured regularly so that reports of progress and planned recovery from identified variances are routinely provided to executive management.

Continuous portfolio monitoring provides the enterprise executives insight into the health of the portfolio and highlights any areas that require attention from senior management. For example, these processes not only monitor and control the work being done within a portfolio process, but also the efforts of the supporting programs and projects. They provide feedback to the planning and executing processes of the portfolio so that corrective or preventive actions can be implemented to bring the portfolio into compliance with the portfolio management plan. When variances jeopardize portfolio objectives, appropriate management processes are revisited. This review can result in recommended updates to the portfolio management plan. For example, a program may not be able to deliver the expected benefits. This may require that portfolio management seek direction from executive management on how to redefine the scope of the portfolio. Figure 23-4 indicates the process interactions that are essential to monitoring and controlling the portfolio.

Figure 23-4. Portfolio Monitoring and Controlling Process Integration

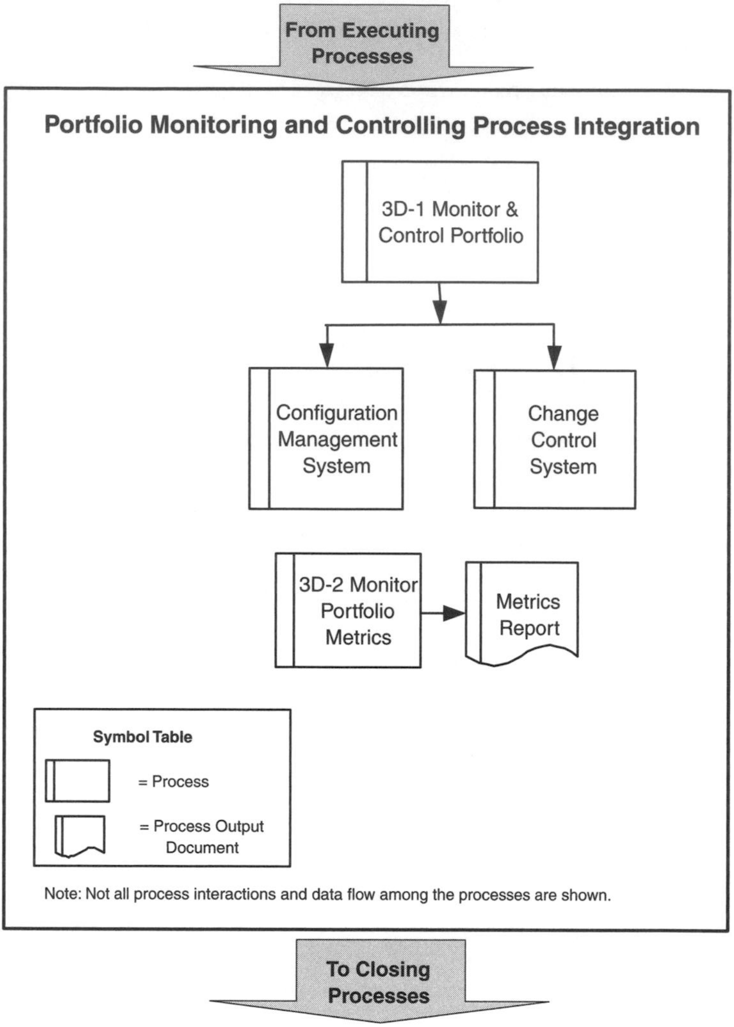

23.5 Portfolio Closing Processes

Portfolio closing formalizes acceptance of the products, services, or results and brings the portfolio to an orderly end. It includes termination of all activities and closure for the supported business objectives and strategic initiatives. When completed, this small group of processes confirms that the

Figure 23-5. Portfolio Closing Processes Integration

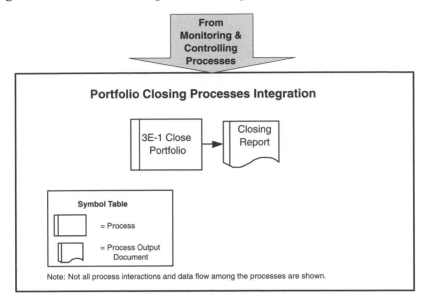

work defined in the portfolio procedures are completed across all portfolio management processes. If a project or program is prematurely terminated for any reason, the activities identified in the closing process must still be completed. Figure 23-5 defines the integration of the closing processes.

CHAPTER 24

Program PBMM Planning and Execution

The Project Business Management Methodology (PBMM) Model developed in Chapter 10 defines the basic processes to be followed in planning and executing a program. Programs that are part of a portfolio will have been chartered by the portfolio manager, while standalone programs will have been chartered by the enterprise's senior management (see Chapter 22).

24.1 Program Initiation Processes

Program initiating begins with the processes external to the program that are required to formally authorize and start a new program. For example, when beginning the initiating processes, all activities, business needs, and requirements are reviewed, the program initiation documentation is assembled, and a charter is obtained to perform the work. Figure 24-1 illustrates the integration of the processes contained within the program management initiating processes.

24.2 Program Planning Processes

Planning defines and matures the program scope, develops the program management plan, and identifies and schedules the program activities. Planning helps the EPMO direct and manage the program successfully. The planning processes gather information from many sources, including the portfolio's management team if the program supports a portfolio, with each source having varying levels of impact, completeness, and confidence.

The program management planning processes refine and address the program planning products listed in the program initiating processes. They also plan the course of action required for attaining the desired benefits and developing supporting projects. Figure 24-2 illustrates the inte-

Figure 24-1. Program Initiation Process Integration

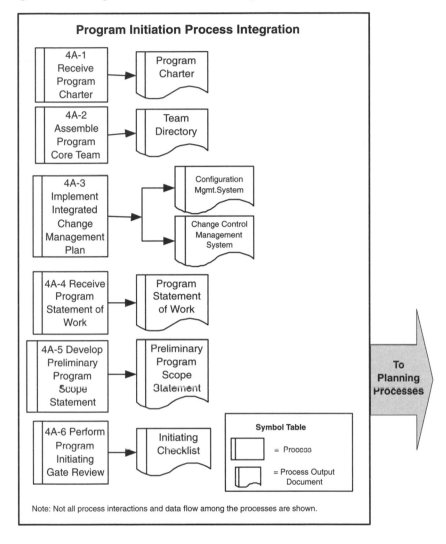

gration of the processes contained within the program management planning processes.

24.3 Program Executing Processes

Managing the execution of a program requires completion of those activities defined in the program management plan. This involves coordinating

Figure 24-2.   Program Planning Process Integration

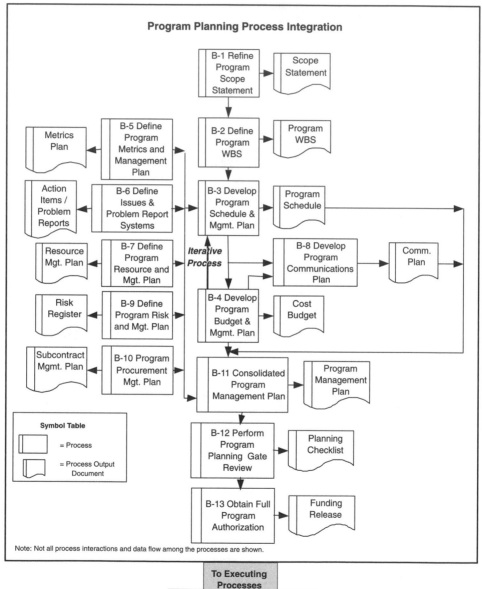

other related work performed by the business unit operations and the EPMO, as well as integrating and performing the activities of the planning phase in accordance with the program management plan. This also addresses the scope defined in the program scope statement and implements approved changes.

From a business management perspective, the development of the statements of work for the projects supporting the program is a key step in the further definition of the work necessary to accomplish the supported business objective. In addition, the preparation and issuance of the charters for those supporting projects is the next major program management step in committing the enterprise's resources and funds to the program's projects. The chartering of each project is performed as described in Chapter 22. Figure 24-3 illustrates the integration of the processes contained within the program management executing processes.

24.4 Program Monitoring and Controlling Processes

Monitoring and controlling regularly measures and evaluates progress to identify variances from the program baseline documentation and management plan, so that corrective action can be taken when necessary to assure delivery of the desired benefits. The processes contained in this group are developed and implemented at the start of the program and are applied from start to finish of the program.

Monitoring and controlling consist of those processes performed to observe program execution, so that potential problems with the supporting projects and related other work may be identified in a timely manner and corrective actions can be taken. The processes also include recommending actions to prevent possible issues or problems with the supporting projects and controlling changes to the program and other related work.

Continuous monitoring provides the program manager or an EPMO manager with insights into the health of the program and supporting projects; it also highlights any areas that require additional attention from the program manager. The monitoring and controlling processes provide feedback on planning and execution in order to implement corrective or preventive actions to bring the program into compliance with the program management plan. When variances jeopardize the program benefits, appropriate program management processes are revisited. This review can result in recommended updates to the program management plan. For example, a delayed project in the program can require adjustments to current staffing or tradeoffs between benefit and schedule objectives. Figure 24-4

Figure 24-3.   Program Execution Processes Integration

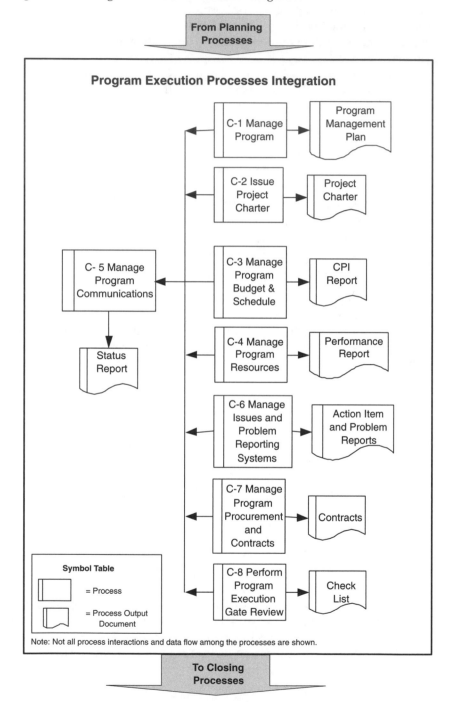

Figure 24-4. Program Monitoring and Controlling Process Integration

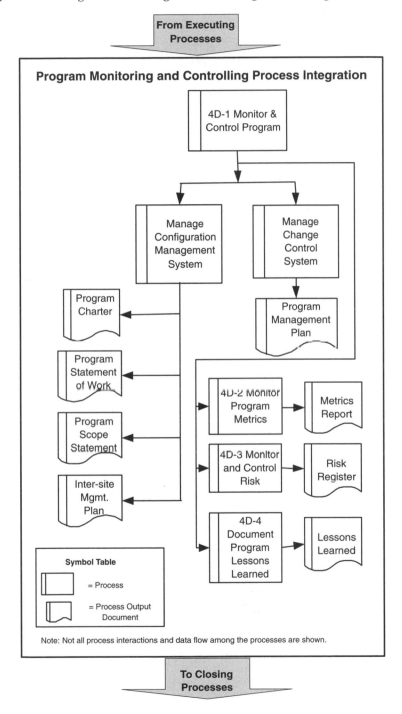

indicates the process interactions that are essential to the program monitoring and controlling processes.

24.5 Program Closing Processes

Program management closing formalizes acceptance of the products, services, or results of the supporting projects, assures the other related work has been completed, and brings the program to an orderly end. If a program is prematurely terminated for any reason, the closing processes implement the procedures required to formally terminate all program activities. This group of processes, when completed, requires that the defined procedures be completed across all the program management processes. Figure 24-5 illustrates the integration of the closing processes.

Figure 24-5.   Program Closing Processes Integration

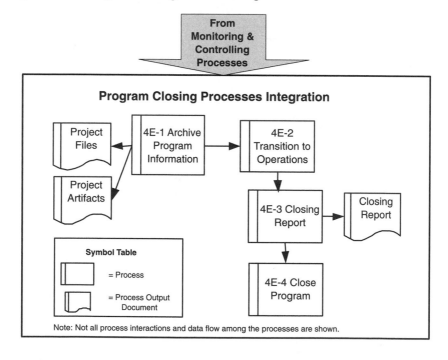

CHAPTER 25

Project PBMM Planning and Execution

A lmost all executives and managers understand the concept of a project in the form of developing a new product, implementing a reorganization plan, improving a production process, and so on. In the business context of integrating business management with project business management, a project is either all of, or a specific component of, a selected business objective. As with portfolios and programs, a project (specific business objective) is usually accomplished with limited resources, which can include time and funds. The goal of project business management is to produce the desired deliverables that will support the project's related business objective and program or portfolio.

The processes to be applied are selected from the enterprise's standardized PBMM model, developed in Chapter 10, that has been accepted within the organization for managing a single project. The implementing procedures will have been developed by the EPMO staff. In most business management processes and in all project business management processes, a project is usually managed or overseen by a single person designated as the project manager.

25.1 Project Initiation Processes

Project initiation consists of formally authorizing the start of planning for a new project. For example, when beginning the initiating activities, business needs and requirements are reviewed. The project is initialized with a charter issued by either the associated program manager or portfolio manager or, if it is a standalone project, by the project's sponsor (see Chapter 22). The charter contains a basic description of the project scope, deliverables, and duration, as well as a forecast of the resources needed. The charter authorizes the manager to expend the organization's resources. The core project team is identified and assembled just before the planning process begins to help develop the plan that will be used to execute and manage the project.

Figure 25-1.   Project Initiation Processes Integration

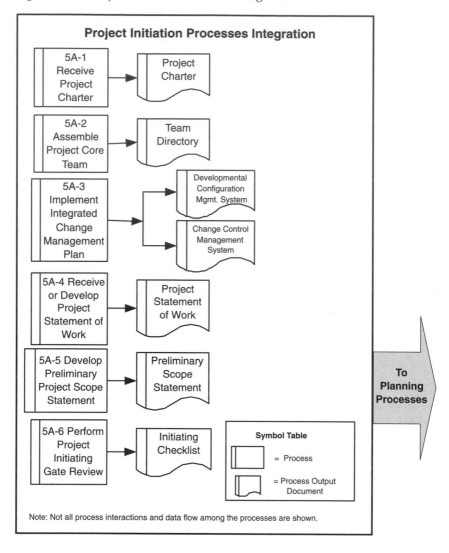

Figure 25-1 illustrates the integration of the processes contained within the project management initiating processes.

25.2 Project Planning Processes

Once the project charter has been approved and issued and the additional initial project planning documents have been completed and accepted, the project manger and team complete the project execution planning. This follows the project planning process activities set forth in the PBMM and is completed before proceeding with any physical work. Planning defines and matures the project scope, develops the project management plan, and identifies and schedules the project activities. Planning helps the core team select the processes and interactions that are needed to plan and manage the project successfully. Figure 25-2 illustrates the integration of the processes contained within the project management planning processes.

25.3 Project Executing Processes

The execution of a project consists of managing those activities needed to complete the work defined in the project management plan. This involves coordinating people and resources, as well as integrating and performing the activities of each project phase in accordance with the plan. This also addresses the scope defined in the project scope statement and implements approved changes. Project management execution coordinates the performing organizations and other resources to carry out the intent of the project management plan and produce the project deliverables. Figure 25-3 defines the integration of the processes contained within the project management executing processes.

25.4 Project Monitoring and Controlling Processes

Monitoring and controlling regularly measures and evaluates progress to assure completion of the project deliverables. The processes in this group are developed, implemented, and applied from the start of the project. Monitoring and controlling includes processes performed to observe project execution so that potential problems and issues may be identified in a timely manner and corrective or preventive actions can be taken. The processes might include:

- Regularly monitoring the ongoing project activities and comparing them to the project management plan and the project performance baseline to identify variances from the baseline.
- Controlling the scope, changes, and factors that could cause changes, so that only approved changes are implemented.

Continuous monitoring provides the project core team insight into the health of the project and highlights any areas that require additional at-

Figure 25-2.   Project Planning Processes Integration

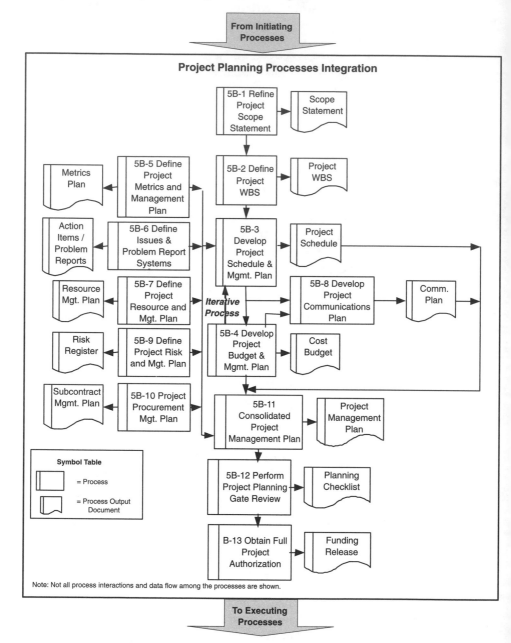

Figure 25-3. Project Execution Processes Integration

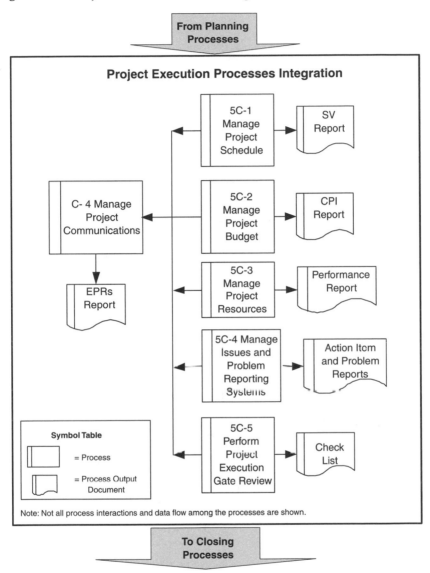

tention. These processes provide feedback so that corrective or preventive actions to bring the project into compliance with the project management plan can be implemented. When variances jeopardize the deliverables, appropriate project management processes are revisited. This review can result in recommended updates to the project management plan. For exam-

Figure 25-4.   Project Monitoring and Controlling Process Integration

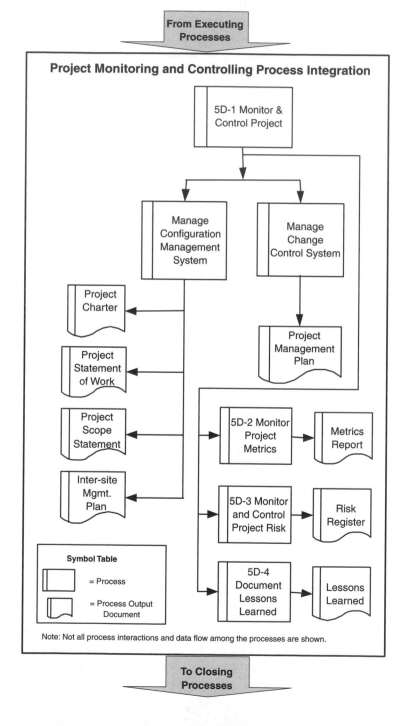

ple, a missed activity finish date can require adjustments to resource utilization, result in overtime, or necessitate tradeoffs between budget and schedule requirements. Figure 25-4 illustrates the process interactions that are essential to monitoring and controlling processes.

25.5 Project Closing Processes

Project management closing formalizes acceptance of the product, service, or result and brings the project to an orderly end. Closing includes the processes required to formally terminate all activities of a project and hand off the completed product to others or to close a cancelled project. This group of processes, when completed, requires that the defined procedures be completed across all the project management processes. If a project is prematurely terminated for any reason the activities identified in the closing process must still be completed. Figure 25-5 illustrates the integration of the project closing processes.

Figure 25-5. Project Closing Processes Integration

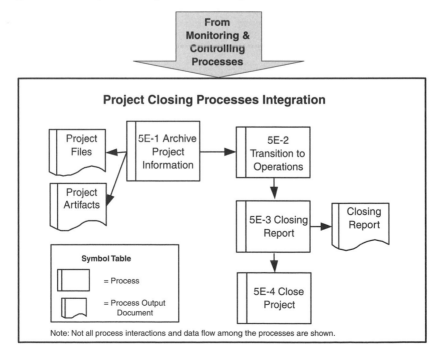

SECTION 6

Maturity

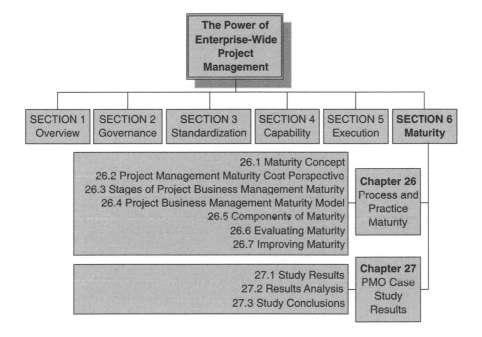

CHAPTER 26

Process and Practice Maturity

The value and benefits an enterprise will derive from implementing project business management is determined by the maturity of its policies, plans, procedures, organizational governance, management personnel, and Project Business Management (PBM) methodology and processes. These processes identify, plan, implement, control, accomplish, and communicate the enterprise's business strategic initiatives and related business objectives.

26.1 Maturity Concept

Four major factors sustain cost effective project business management:

- Integrated business management and project management disciplines.
- Integrated business management and project related processes.
- Maturity of the integrated project business management processes.
- Maturity and competency of the enterprise's management in applying those processes.

A significant body of literature in recent years has addressed project management practices in business. It indicates that successful business enterprises are increasingly dependent on the use of projects, thereby making project business management a needed core competency. However, for project business management to be a valuable core competency in an enterprise, program and project success cannot be an occasional outcome. Performance that is only good, on average, is not adequate. What is needed is repeatable successful performance on programs and projects. This should be accompanied by continuous improvements in the implementation of active project business management processes. The more uniformly and consistently project business management processes are applied by the enterprise and the more mature those processes are, the greater are the positive results and benefits obtained. In addition, the return on an enterprise's investment in project management will increase as the project business management processes become more mature.

If an enterprise has an active project, some form of project management—whether good or bad, mature or immature—is being applied to that project. Best-in-class project organizations are highly mature (well-developed and effective project business management competency) and are routinely on-budget and on-schedule. Enterprises with a low level of project business management maturity consistently jeopardize their likelihood of delivering successful projects. This lack of maturity can increase project costs, as a result of late project deliverables and ineffective implementation and execution of an adequate project management plan or implementation and execution of an inadequate project management plan.

When building a facility, the management of a construction firm will ensure the building site's soil is stable and capable of supporting the installation of standard foundation footings. The builder will then lay a firm foundation on which the structure will be erected. If the footings are undersized or the foundation is unstable, the facility will not be properly supported and may collapse. At the very least, it may require significant repairs. Therefore, it is prudent and beneficial for the facilities' management to ensure proven, integrated, and mature project business management processes are followed for designing, planning, managing, and executing the construction of the facility.

However, it is unusual for an enterprise—or its personnel—to achieve the mature capabilities derived from embracing project business management. Developing and sustaining mature project business management processes require management dedication, direction, and involvement.

The concept of developing mature business processes is not new nor is management's desire to employ them. The business literature is replete with discussions on business management maturity: what it is, what it means, and how to achieve it. In the field of information technology management and project management, there has been a steady attempt to better define project management maturity and how to qualitatively and quantitatively measure it.

A plethora of articles has appeared on the subject of management capability maturity models. The Project Management Institute (PMI®) developed the *Organizational Project Management Maturity Model* (OPM3®) Standard in 2003 to enable organizations to examine how to pursue strategic objectives by using best practices in organizational project management. OPM3 is comprised of three general elements: *Knowledge,* which presents the contents of the Standard; *Assessment,* which provides a method for comparison with the Standard; and *Improvement,* which sets the stage for possible organizational changes. OPM3® is not prescriptive; it does not tell an enterprise what improvements to make or how to make them. Rather, it offers a basis for an organization to develop project management training so that it can achieve the competency levels identified in its project management competency model.

The PMI® maturity assessment model, as well as those created by other enterprises, show a coninuum of steps from ad-hoc operations to fully defined and implemented mature processes. Those models are very good at determining the maturity of project management processes, but they do not provide executive management with any quantifiable results. Thus, management is not informed about the impact of project management practices on the return on its investment.

26.2 Project Management Maturity Cost Perspective

The literature also has anecdotal information about the value of project management and the effect of its maturity on project performance and costs. Although most of this information is qualitative, some is quantitative.

In the late 1970s, the construction industry business round table conducted a quantitative study. It showed that successful companies spent between 6 percent and 8 percent of total construction costs on construction project management. However, this study did not quantify the effects of the maturity of the project management processes on the cost of construction project management.

In the mid 1990s, the Project Management Institute (PMI®) began supporting research on the value of project management. The first phase evaluated the qualitative values of project management. One set of results were reported in *The Benefits of Project Management – Financial and Organizational Rewards to Corporations* by C.W. Ibbs and Young-Hoon Kwak of the University of California, Berkeley, which was published by PMI in 1997.

The second phase analyzed the quantitative values of the return on investment in project management processes in terms of the maturity of these processes and their capabilities on information technology projects. The results were reported in *Quantifying the Value of Project Management,* by C.W. Ibbs and Justin Reginato of the University of California, Berkeley, which was published by PMI in 2002 referred to here as the Berkeley study.

The quantitative Berkeley study, along with data from other project management literature, indicates that the cost of project management ranges between 6 percent and 12 percent of the total cost of the project, depending on the project's size and complexity. The literature also shows that costs can increase to 20 percent and can depend on the maturity of project management capabilities. The Berkeley study corroborates the qualitative analyses that show the importance of the "maturity level" of project management processes in determing the amount of project management costs and the associated results of the project management processes.

Further, the literature indicates that in addition to increased project direct costs, organizations with low project management maturity jeopardize their likelihood of delivering successful projects. Failure to apply mature project business management processes on a chartered project leaves management at risk to miss planned cost avoidances. To avoid this, mature project business management must be applied throughout the total project life cycle. In addition, the application of a mature project business management process can provide opportunities for cost reductions of 10 percent to 20 percent and completion of the planned project on schedule.

26.3 Stages of Project Business Management Maturity

Project business management should provide accurate, routine, consistent, and adequate information into the progress and status of every project, program, and portfolio, so that management can take effective action when performance deviates from the approved work plan. However, project business management, as with other management functions, can be viewed as having, or operating at, various levels of effectiveness, also called levels of project business management maturity, in performing its work. One aspect of applying project management processes is to work toward improving the usefulness of those processes in supporting the selection, planning, execution, and control of portfolios, programs, and projects. Therefore, the EPMO function needs to be consistently and incrementally working on improving its capabilities and needs to routinely assess the general maturity of its project business management operations.

Many defined and formalized maturity assessment models assess the advancement of maturity through five or ten stages or assesses the maturity of various process groups or other factors. Most senior executives and other business managers have difficulty applying the results of those maturity evaluations to their business operations because they cannot:

- Connect the maturity results to the bottom line (return on investment).
- Relate the maturity evaluation model stages to their business processes.
- Relate to the maturity evaluation results presented as they are aligned with PMI®'s project management process group processes.

- Understand how attaining specific project business management capabilities at a predefined maturity level relates to the cost of effectively operating the business.
- Determine when the processes defining a maturity level would finally be standardized and institutionalized.

An examination of current literature suggests that best-in-class project management organizations today are those with a highly mature, well-developed, and effective project business management (PBM) competency. Their projects are routinely on-budget and on-schedule, with lower total costs. In contrast, less mature PBM organizations may spend as much or more, but commonly experience cost overruns. As PBM improvements are sought, organizations usually go through a four-stage process. Initial spending on PBM may increase, but performance improvements are not yet realized. Therefore, cost and/or schedule overruns continue to be common.

Many managers have been involved with or read about large investments in project business management where the value, quality, and usefulness of PBM processes did not improve. Therefore, before embarking on a PBM improvement initiative, executives want to know that there will be an end to the investment required to formalize and implement PBM processes.

26.4 Project Business Management Maturity Model

The detailed assessment results from the various models need to satisfy the executive's desire for a quick and simple process that show where the enterprise is on the maturity continuum from a business-oriented perspective.

A simple four-stage process does exist for evaluating the progress of implementing project business management. This model can be used to give executive management a quick and simple indication of the enterprise's placement on the maturity continuum and what needs to be improved to reach the next stage. Figure 26-1 illustrates the process stages and Table 26-1 indicates the maturity level and general cost/performance associated with each stage.

The model reflects the realities of implementing any complex multi-process functional capability within any general business operation. This four-stage model recognizes that as process improvements are implemented, project business management-related spending will increase as a percentage of project costs.

The common sequence of events begins with establishing the enterprise's system/processes baseline. The maturity level begins to change as

Figure 26-1.   Project Business Management Maturity Model

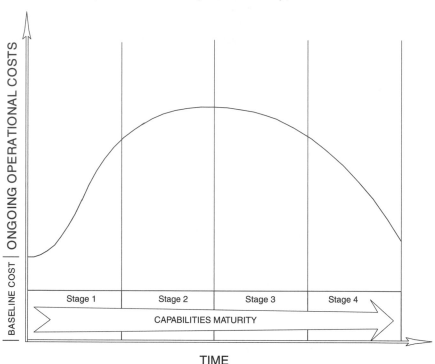

additional resources and budgeted funds are expended on the system/ processes (stage 1) to develop the modified system/processes to achieve stage 2. The newly developed processes must be fully documented and implemented to obtain the desired benefits of the next level (stage 3), which requires expenditure of additional resources and funds. Once the processes to achieve stage 3 have been implemented, personnel trained, and the new project business management processes become part of the day-to-day routine of the enterprise, then the level of resources required to sustain operations drops to a normal business operational level and the budgeted

Table 26-1.   The Four Stages of Maturity

Stage	Maturity Level	Cost/Performance
Stage 1	Standardized/Evolving	Low Cost/Low Return
Stage 2	Defined/Emerging	High Cost/Low Return
Stage 3	Managed/Controlling	High Cost/High Return
Stage 4	Optimized/Improving	Low Cost/High Return

cost returns to a lower operational level. A common example is implementing a new project cost accounting system and its associated processes and procedures.

This model indicates that the cost of project management increases as the implementation of project business management moves from maturity level one to the third level of maturity and then decreases as the PBM implementation moves through the third level of maturity to the fourth. In addition, the cost of project business management in the fourth stage could be less than when the enterprise had an immature project management process.

The more uniformly and consistently a mature project business management process is applied, the greater will be the results and benefits. In addition, the return on an enterprise's investment in project business management increases as the project management processes become more mature. Therefore, to receive the maximum benefits from the enterprise's selected project business management processes, the enterprise needs to drive its project management maturity through Stage 2, which is high cost with low return, and move quickly and steadily into Stage 4, which is low cost with high return on the investment. This minimizes the overall expenditures of implementing a fully mature project business management methodology and reaps the management and economic benefits that such a mature process methodology can provide.

Stage 4 represents the desired end-state vision for established enterprise-wide project business management. Enterprises with more mature project business management practices and capabilities perform better in delivering projects, produce more predictable project schedule and cost performance, and can have lower direct costs in completing a project.

26.5 Components of Maturity

The major assessment categories within each maturity model stage shown in Figure 26-1 are based on the concepts discussed in the preceding four sections: Governance, Standardization, Capabilities, and Execution. Each of those sections relates process components that are applicable to the four stages. Each section also contains specific information that can affirm that each component of the four stages is in place. Table 26-2 contains examples of a few questions and desired responses relating to the four stages of the maturity model.

Appendix B contains a more extensive sample set of statements for each individual maturity stage. The questions are organized by the sections of the book with question subsets organized by chapters. Each statement is repeated for each maturity stage, but the stated maturity point is different for each of the four stages, as shown in Table 26-2. This simple four-stage

Table 26-2. Sample Stage Related Assessment Questions

		BUSINESS MANAGEMENT MATURITY MODEL		
Key Elements	*STAGE 1*	*STAGE 2*	*STAGE 3*	*STAGE 4*
Key Topics	*Standardized/Evolving*	*Defined/Emerging*	*Managed/Controlling*	*Optimized/Improving*
Capabilities	*Low Cost/Low Return*	*High Cost/Low Return*	*High Cost/High Return*	*Low Cost/High Return*
GOVERNANCE				
A formal project business management policy statement governs the use of project business management practices.	Project business management policies and procedures are ad hoc by project and business unit.	Project business management policies are developed and issued.	Project business management policies are issued and are implemented.	Project business management policies are reviewed and modified to reflect changes in the project business management operational needs.
An Enterprise Project Management Office (PMO) is chartered and is functional.	A project management office (PMO) exists in some business units.	A Business Unit PMO (BUPMO) exists in some business units.	A Division PMO (DPMO) exists in some divisions of the enterprise.	An enterprise PMO is chartered, is functional, and is supported by one or more DPMOs, one or more BUPMOs, and PMO's as required for large strategic projects.
The environment is becoming conducive to consistent application of project business management.	Business units' environment becoming conducive to consistent application of project management.	Business units' environment is conducive to consistent application of project business management methodologies.	One standard PBM methodology is recognized across business units as the enterprise's set of processes.	Business unit application of standardized project business management methodologies is institutionalized within each business unit.

STANDARDIZATION

Requirements for managing portfolios, programs, and projects are identified and documented.	Requirements for managing some programs and projects are established.	Requirements for managing each program and project are established.	Requirements for managing all portfolios, programs, and projects are established.	Requirements for managing all portfolios, programs, and projects are institutionalized.
The business and project management processes are integrated to create Project Business Management processes.	A project business management (PBM) methodology is documented and change controlled.	A PBM methodology is applied, practiced, enforced, and able to be improved.	The results of the PBM methodology are predictable because the processes within the methodology are operated within defined limits using approved procedures.	Improvements in the PBM methodology are reflected in improvements in the results from portfolios, programs, and projects.
A portfolio management processes methodology is adopted.	Enterprise's business unit environment supports development of standardized portfolio management methodologies.	Enterprise's business unit environment supports consistent application of standardized portfolio management methodologies.	Processes for managing portfolios are standardized and consistent across business units and portfolio controls methodologies are stable and repeatable.	Portfolio management methodology is focused on continuous process improvement.

CAPABILITY

Success is independent of project managers and project teams with exceptional capabilities.	Success may depend upon exceptional project managers or a seasoned project team.	Success may not depend upon exceptional project managers or a seasoned project team.	Success does not depend upon exceptional project managers or a seasoned project team, but upon a competent and capable staff.	Project success depends upon the consistent application of implemented project business management policies, practices, and procedures by a competent and capable staff.

(*continued*)

Table 26-2. (Continued)

BUSINESS MANAGEMENT MATURITY MODEL

Key Elements	STAGE 1	STAGE 2	STAGE 3	STAGE 4
Key Topics	Standardized/Evolving	Defined/Emerging	Managed/Controlling	Optimized/Improving
Capabilities	Low Cost/Low Return	High Cost/Low Return	High Cost/High Return	Low Cost/High Return
CAPABILITY (continued)				
The enterprise's staff capabilities and project business management performance of individuals are measured/assesed on a regular basis.	A process for measuring an individual's project business management performance is documented and change controlled.	A process for measuring an individual's project business management performance is applied in some business units.	A process for measuring an individual's project business management performance is consistently applied in all business units enterprise-wide.	Improvements in the process for measuring individual's project business management performance are reflected in staff performance improvements across all portfolios, programs, and projects.
Project business management performance of individuals is defined and applied on a regular basis.	Enterprise's staff capabilities in project business management (PBM) are documented and serve as a baseline for progress evaluations.	Enterprise's staff capabilities in PBM are improved through education and training, are measured, and able to be improved.	Enterprise's staff capabilities in PBM are predictable because there is a career path program in place that develops measurable improvements against the baseline.	Improvements in the staff capabilities in PBM are reflected in improvements in the results from portfolios, programs, and projects.

EXECUTION

Documented execution processes for the management of portfolios, programs, and projects exist.	PBM processes for managing the execution of portfolios, programs, and projects are documented and change controlled.	PBM processes for managing the execution of portfolios, programs, and projects are employed, practiced, enforced, and measured.	PBM processes for managing the execution of portfolios, programs, and projects are institutionalized and the processes are operated in accordance with procedures, and are able to be improved.	Improvements in the PBM processes for managing the execution of portfolios, programs, and projects are reflected in improvements in the results from portfolio programs and projects.
Strong customer-supplier relationships are established.	Business units have established strong customer-supplier relationships.	Portfolio, program, and project have established strong customer-supplier relationships.	Portfolio has established strong customer-supplier relationships on all related programs and projects.	Portfolio, program, and project customer-supplier relationships are proactive in identifying and implementing process improvements.
A documented process for strategic business planning exists.	Strategic initiatives are developed at the enterprise level.	Strategic business objectives are developed at the business unit level.	Strategic business objectives are planned down through the supporting portfolios, programs, and projects.	Strategic business planning is integrated into PBM planning and is fully implemented and undergoing continuous improvement.

MATURITY

Identification and communication of best practices and lessons learned is performed.	Identification and communication of best practices and lessons learned is performed at the individual project level.	Identification and communication of best practices and lessons learned is performed at the individual project and program levels.	Identification and communication of best practices and lessons learned is performed up through the portfolio level.	Identification and communication of best practices and lessons learned is institutionalized within the enterprise and used to improve the planning and management of current and future portfolios, programs, and projects.

(*continued*)

Table 26-2. (*Continued*)

BUSINESS MANAGEMENT MATURITY MODEL

Key Elements	STAGE 1	STAGE 2	STAGE 3	STAGE 4
Key Topics	*Standardized/Evolving*	*Defined/Emerging*	*Managed/Controlling*	*Optimized/Improving*
Capabilities	*Low Cost/Low Return*	*High Cost/Low Return*	*High Cost/High Return*	*Low Cost/High Return*
MATURITY (*continued*)				
PBM processes and procedures are in place.	PBM processes and procedures are ad hoc by project and business unit.	Portfolio-wide PBM procedures and processes are developed and issued.	Portfolio-wide PBM procedures and processes have been developed and issued and are implemented.	Enterprise-wide PBM procedures and processes have been developed, issued, and implemented and are under a continuous improvement process.
Portfolio management processes including supporting documents and templates are in place.	Portfolio management processes are well defined with respect to their inputs, procedures, and outputs and are documented and change controlled.	Portfolio management process inputs, procedures, and outputs are consistently applied in some business units.	Portfolio management process inputs, procedures, and outputs are consistently applied in all business units.	Improvements in the portfolio management processes are reflected in improvements in the results from portfolios.

capabilities maturity structure model provides the executive management team with an easy-to-use tool to perform a self-evaluation of progress toward achieving a mature project business management operation.

26.6 Evaluating Maturity

A critical success factor requirement of the enterprise-wide project management office (EPMO) is to consistently provide accurate and accessible information to the right people at the right time. This information should compare actual progress against the baseline plan of each project, program, and portfolio. Timely communication of performance measurements are required to ensure that effective corrective actions can be applied by management if the actual performance deviates from the approved work plans. The executive management team should consistently and incrementally work on improving the capabilities of applying project business management best practices across the enterprise and routinely evaluate the general maturity of the enterprise's project business management operations.

The first step in applying project management best practice principles at the enterprise level is to assess the organization's project business management competency and thereby establish a baseline against which to measure progress. The beginning baseline of most enterprises is an "ad hoc" state of managing and controlling projects. Common attributes of an "ad hoc" state include:

- Use of a PMO is nonexistent.
- Business unit environment is not conducive to a consistent application of formal or uniform project business management processes.
- Project business management practices are neither documented nor consistently applied.
- Project data is obtained from multiple nonintegrated sources.
- Project data is not compiled into and maintained within an integrated dataset.
- Work breakdown structures, if utilized for planning development, differ significantly from project to project and facility to facility.
- Project management decisions are made and actions are taken based upon minimal analysis and marginal or outdated data.
- Project success depends almost totally upon the skills of exceptional project managers and a seasoned and effective project team.
- Incurred project costs are inferred from the costs residing within the business accounting system.

The EPMO, with the support of the executive management team, should evaluate the enterprise's maturity status with respect to each of the four stages by preparing and using a customized version of the maturity assessment tool found in Appendix B. The results of previous evaluations can be color coded, thereby showing how the enterprise is progressing. Progress can also be recorded by adding a column at the end of the form for each date the evaluation is performed. Mark #1 through #4 in the column to indicate the maturity for that question on that date.

26.7 Improving Maturity

Maturity will not increase in just one discipline, practice area, or process, nor will the changes across processes and disciplines be uniform or related over time. The enterprise's project business management operations will naturally move through the four stages of maturity, as the project business management processes are defined, implemented, and matured.

The implication for managing the cost as opposed to managing only the performance for each stage is that an organization should move quickly from stage 2 (high cost and low return) through stage 3 into stage 4 (low cost and high return). This steady pace will help minimize the overall expenditures of implementing a fully mature project business management operation that reaps management and economic benefits.

Effective use of project business management practices and principles is a critical factor in achieving, maintaining, and improving an organization's PBM maturity. Improving maturity requires policies, procedures, and measures that integrate quality into the management processes. Enterprise-wide project management rests on a foundation of mature, institutionalized project business management best practices and processes that are applied consistently throughout the enterprise. A solid foundation with strong footings of integrated and standardized policies, practices, and processes is necessary to ensure that effective project business management is an integral part of the enterprise's business operations. The more uniformly and consistently a mature project business management process is applied, the greater will be the results and benefits obtained.

CHAPTER 27

PMO Case Study Results

Establishing project management offices to facilitate the adoption of project business management practices in various business units was a concept that emerged in the mid-1990s. The availability of compiled data that identifies the issues affecting the development, organization structure, and operation of project offices in organizations across multiple industries is and generally remains nonexistent.

In 1997, a two-day PMI seminar entitled "Project Support Office: A Framework for Development" was developed and led by Dennis Bolles at the PMI Symposium in Chicago. It was part of the PMI seminars program in 1998, with more than 200 participants attending sessions in Chicago and five other locations in the United States. The author began collecting case study data from the 1997/1998 participants through the use of a PMO Case Study Survey tool; that data collection is ongoing.

The details of the PMO Case Study Survey are included in this chapter. The information contained in the survey is based on 34 questions that are organized into the three phases of establishing a PMO:

- Phase One: Obtain Approval for the PMO (13 questions).
- Phase Two: Assess the Current Situation (19 questions).
- Phase Three: Document the PMO Design (2 questions).

The survey responses have been compiled into a report organized into five categories, with a number of topics in each category cross-referenced to the 34 questions.

1. General Information (8 topics).
2. Concept Approval (12 topics).
3. PM Knowledge (5 topics).
4. PM Capability, Commitment and Training (9 topics).
5. Staff Salaries (2 topics).

The following is a breakdown of the categories and topics that comprise the PMO Case Studies Summary Report:

1. General Information
   A. Product/Service
   B. Sales Volume
   C. Number of Employees
   D. Number of Concurrent Projects (Q#12)
   E. Number of Annual Total Projects (Q#12)
   F. Types of Projects (Q#13)
   G. PMO Staffing (Full Time and Part Time) (Q#33)
   H. Self Estimate of PM Maturity Level (Q#32)
2. Concept Approval Issues
   A. PMO Driving Force (Q#1)
   B. PMO Start Date (Q#2)
   C. Position In Organization (Q#3)
   D. PMO Leaders Title (Q#3)
   E. PMO Reports To (Q#3)
   F. PMO Coverage (Q#4)
   G. PMO Challenges (Q#5)
   H. Successes (Q#6)
   I. Failures (Q#7)
   J. Lessons Learned (Q#8)
   K. Resistance Level & Source (Q#9)
   L. Resistance Solutions (Q#9)
3. PM Knowledge
   A. PMO Champion (Q#10)
   B. Immediate Process Needs (Q#14)
   C. Organizational PM Knowledge (Q#16)
   D. PM Selection Criteria (Q#17)
   E. Corp. PM Policies (Q#18)
4. PM Capability, Commitment and Training
   A. PM Process Capability (Q#19)
   B. Commitment to PM (Q#20)
   C. PM Training Capability (Q#21)
   D. Commitment to PM Training (Q#22)
   E. PM Job Descriptions (Q#25)
   F. PM Tech. Infrastructure (Q#27)
   G. Information Tech. Infrastructure (Q#28)
   H. Process Audit (Q#29)
   I. Documented PM Processes (Q#31)

5. Staff Salaries
   A. Software Tools Used (Q#30)
   B. Staffing Salaries (Q334)
      1) Function Title
      2) Low Level
      3) High Level
      4) Bonus
      5) Comments

See Appendix C for a copy of the survey tool. The authors will continue collecting data as new responses to requests are received on a regular basis. Readers interested in obtaining the latest version of the report should see Appendix C for instructions. The following sections provide the authors summary of the case study results, analysis, and conclusions.

27.1 Study Results

At the time of writing this book, the PMO Case Studies Survey Report included representation from organizations providing the following products or services:

1. Telecommunications
2. Consulting Services
3. Office Automation/Dictation for Health Care Industry
4. Voice, Data, Video, Network Services
5. Space and Aviation Components and Systems
6. Information Services
7. Project Management for Integration Projects
8. Benefits Consulting and Administration
9. Project Management Business Unit
10. Retail Clothing
11. International Wholesale Banking
12. Semiconductor Development and Manufacturing
13. Fully Integrated Rail Services to railroads and rail-related industries (rail operations, engineering, training, technology, asset management)
14. National Financial Institution
15. U.S. Federal Government Agency
16. Software Development & Services
17. Biotechnology

27.2 Results Analysis

The survey summary report contains the following results that indicate a commonality among the participants:

- Self Assessed Project Management Maturity Levels:
    - 9% = 0 (information not provided)
    - 44% = 1.0
    - 22% = 2.0
    - 28% = 3.0
- PMO Coverage:
    - 50% are enterprise wide
    - 50% support a business unit (primarily IT)
- Resistance Came Primarily From:
    - 22% No Resistance
    - 44% Middle Management
    - 17% Project Managers
    - 17% Others
- Project Management Selection Criteria:
    - 72% Technical Experience
    - 33% Education Level
    - 78% Previous PM Experience
    - 33% PMP Certification
- Corporate Project Management Policies:
    - 61% Yes
    - 39% No
- Project Management Job Descriptions
    - 56% Yes
    - 44% No
- Commitment to Project Management Training:
    - 56% High
    - 17% Medium
    - 27% Low
- Management Level of Commitment to Project Management Processes and Procedures
    - 11% Nonsupportive
    - 6% Neutral
    - 22% Supportive
    - 33% Very Supportive
    - 28% Champion
- Project Management Process Audit
    - 22% Yes
    - 78% No

- Information Technology Infrastructure
  - 78% Adequate
  - 21% Inadequate
  - 1% Needs Development
- Project Management Technology Infrastructure
  - 50% Adequate
  - 1% Inadequate
  - 44% Needs Development

27.3 Study Conclusions

The following key points were drawn from the analysis of the study results and interviews with some participants: A few significant differences in the responses submitted by participants between 1997 and 2006 indicates that most organizations believe they have a Stage 2 or lower project management maturity and are still struggling with implementing enterprise-wide project management.

Project business management processes that are owned, controlled, and applied under the direction of the enterprise rather than an outside supplier can be improved and matured over time. The result is increased benefits and return on investment. This is particularly true where the enterprise has multiple projects being performed by third party suppliers over extended periods of time.

Epilogue

The discipline of project management has matured and is becoming an identifiable part of the fabric of general business management. Project business management (PBM) is the application of general business management and project management knowledge, skills, tools, and techniques in a simple top-down hierarchically integrated blend of strategic, tactical, portfolio, program, and project management and processes. PBM is an unusual approach to managing the project-related business of an enterprise. It enables enterprises to meet or exceed stakeholder needs and to derive benefits from project-related actions and activities used to accomplish the enterprise's business objectives and related strategies. The planning and execution processes used within the PBM methodology flow down from strategies to objectives, portfolios, programs, to projects and, finally, to produced deliverables and attained value/benefits. However, up to 80 percent of the value and benefit of the desired outcome can be established during the initiating and supporting planning processes, starting with identifying a single strategic initiative down through planning a project to accomplish that initiative.

The time for project management to be recognized as a business function has arrived! The enterprise needs to employ an enterprise project management office (EPMO) as the managerial vehicle to govern the integration and application of the project and business processes that comprise project business management. The EPMO governance should be a blend of several of the enterprise's governance methods, particularly those of executive, operations, portfolio, program, and project management. It must be employed at different decision-making levels and different stages within the PBM methodology to support implementation of specific business objectives and their related business strategic initiatives.

Executive management, to assure a high probability of establishing and effectively employing project business management on an enterprise-wide basis, must initiate and authorize two major strategic business objectives that need to be performed in parallel:

- Development and formal documentation of a mature, integrated set of standardized project business management processes, known as the PBM methodology, and institutionalization of those processes within the enterprise and its organizational process assets.
- Establishment of an enterprise project management office (EPMO) as an operational business unit at the executive level and staffing it with competent managers and support personnel.

Executive sponsorship is required to accomplish the two strategic business objectives. In addition, the enterprise must ensure that the necessary supporting organizational structures, systems, culture, and business practices are sufficient and available.

To achieve these two business objectives, a senior manager should be assigned to plan and manage the required development work and the resulting project business management processes should be incorporated into the enterprise's day-to-day operations. Developing, establishing, distributing, and implementing project business management on an enterprise-wide basis must not be treated as a trivial undertaking; it requires project business management to be implemented both horizontally and vertically within the enterprise's organizational structure.

The full benefits of PBM are only realized when the two business objectives are fully accomplished. The enterprise will then have a low-cost and high-performance project business management operation supported by an executive-led EPMO that can provide a consistent positive return on the investment in project, program, and portfolio management. However, the success each enterprise will have from project business management depends directly on the maturity of its project business management methodology and the associated involvement by executive and senior managements in the initiating and authorizing processes, where their decision-making will have maximum impact.

It is executive management's responsibility, with the support of portfolio management, to ensure that the correct business objectives and supporting projects are authorized at the correct time. It is the responsibility of program and project management to ensure that the selected projects are properly completed.

APPENDIX A

Forms, Tools, and Templates

The forms, tools, and templates listed below can be downloaded as PDF files or Microsoft Office 2003 files from the authors' website www.dlballc.com and as PDF files from the publisher at www.amacombooks.org/go/EnterpriseWidePM.

FORM, TOOLS, and TEMPLATE INDEX

ID	Name	Description
TMP-1	EPMO Charter	Used to define the EPMO vision, mission, goals, and objectives.
TMP-2	Project Business Management Policy Statement	Used to establish a policy that supports the enterprise-wide use of Project Business Management Methodology and the EPMO.
TMP-3	Portfolio Charter	Used to authorize a portfolio manager to start expending resources.
TMP-4	Program Charter	Used to authorize a program manager to start expending resources.
TMP-5	Program Project Charter	Used to authorize a project manager to start expending resources.
TMP-6	Enterprise Roles and Responsibilities PBMM Matrix	Table used to define the Oversight, Responsibility, Approval, Support, Informed, and Consultant for enterprise Roles for the five PBMM Process Models.
TMP-7	Objective/Project Selection Tool	Used to select programs and projects for the portfolio.
TMP-8	Program/Project Profile	Used to define program/project characteristics for the purpose of strategic planning.
TMP-9	Potential Impact Study	Used to determine the impact of a proposed project for prioritization in the portfolio.

ID	Name	Description
TMP-10	Management Team Survey	Used to assess management support for implementing changes involving the EPMO.
TMP-11	Project Evaluation Survey	Used as a checklist to determine if a project has required documentation.
TMP-12	Project Management Maturity Survey	Used to assess the business unit's use of project management practices.
TMP-13	Risk Analysis	Used to perform a risk analysis, identify a mitigation plan, response plan, and risk status reporting.
TMP-14	Project Risk Assessment	Used to identify risks, define probability and impact and contingency plan.
TMP-15	Risk Management Checklist Questionnaire	Checklist of questions used to identify potential risks.
TMP-16	Project Business Management Competency Model	Used to define project business management role competencies.
TMP-17	Project Business Management Competency Score Card	Used to score individual's competencies against the competency model.

APPENDIX B

Project Business Management Maturity Evaluation Model

The Project Business Management Maturity Evaluation Model is a tool that is intended to be modified by the using enterprise. The purpose of the model is to define capabilities the enterprise has established to meet its long-term strategic initiatives and business objectives of implementing project business management as a core competency enterprise wide. The model provides a means to complete an evaluation as discussed in Section 6 of this book to determine the current level of achievement, thereby establishing a baseline for future measurement of progress toward attaining a higher level of maturity. This basic example model with a sample set of evaluation questions can be downloaded as an Adobe PDF file or Microsoft Office 2003 file from the authors' website, www.dlballc.com or from the publisher's Website, www.amacombooks.org/go/EnterpriseWidePM.

APPENDIX C

PMO Case Study Survey

Until this book was published, no composite data providing this level of detail had been made available to the general public free of charge. The lack of information affecting the development and sustainability of PMOs was not available in 1997 when the author developed and began collecting data using the PMO Case Study Surveys.

The authors will continue to collect data with the survey as long as there are interested participants; therefore, if you are willing to participate, please download the survey and submit it to the author by email at dbolles@dlballc.com. All survey participants and their organizations are kept anonymous to protect their identity. This maturity model can be downloaded as PDF or Microsoft Office 2003 file format from the author's website www.dlballc.com. A copy of the PMO Case Study Summary Report can also be downloaded from the same website as a PDF file. Both are also available from the publisher at www.amacombooks.org/go/EnterpriseWidePM.

Index